Valentyna Romanova

DECENTRALIZATION AND MULTILEVEL ELECTIONS IN UKRAINE

Reform Dynamics and Party Politics in 2010–2021

With a foreword by Kimitaka Matsuzato

Bibliografische Information der Deutschen Nationalbibliothek
Die Deutsche Nationalbibliothek verzeichnet diese Publikation in der Deutschen Nationalbibliografie; detaillierte bibliografische Daten sind im Internet über http://dnb.d-nb.de abrufbar.

Bibliographic information published by the Deutsche Nationalbibliothek
Die Deutsche Nationalbibliothek lists this publication in the Deutsche Nationalbibliografie; detailed bibliographic data are available in the Internet at http://dnb.d-nb.de.

Cover illustration: Photo by Alina Grubnyak on Unsplash (https://unsplash.com/photos/ZiQkhI7417A)

This monograph has been published with the support of the Marie Curie Alumni Association.

ISBN-13: 978-3-8382-1700-0
© *ibidem*-Verlag, Stuttgart 2022
Alle Rechte vorbehalten

Das Werk einschließlich aller seiner Teile ist urheberrechtlich geschützt. Jede Verwertung außerhalb der engen Grenzen des Urheberrechtsgesetzes ist ohne Zustimmung des Verlages unzulässig und strafbar. Dies gilt insbesondere für Vervielfältigungen, Übersetzungen, Mikroverfilmungen und elektronische Speicherformen sowie die Einspeicherung und Verarbeitung in elektronischen Systemen.

All rights reserved. No part of this publication may be reproduced, stored in or introduced into a retrieval system, or transmitted, in any form, or by any means (electronical, mechanical, photocopying, recording or otherwise) without the prior written permission of the publisher. Any person who does any unauthorized act in relation to this publication may be liable to criminal prosecution and civil claims for damages.

Printed in the EU

Soviet and Post-Soviet Politics and Society (SPPS)   Vol. 249
ISSN 1614-3515

General Editor: Andreas Umland,   **Commissioning Editor:** Max Jakob Horstmann,
Stockholm Centre for Eastern European Studies, andreas.umland@ui.se   London, mjh@ibidem.eu

EDITORIAL COMMITTEE*

DOMESTIC & COMPARATIVE POLITICS
Prof. **Ellen Bos**, *Andrássy University of Budapest*
Dr. **Gergana Dimova**, *University of Winchester*
Dr. **Andrey Kazantsev**, *MGIMO (U) MID RF, Moscow*
Prof. **Heiko Pleines**, *University of Bremen*
Prof. **Richard Sakwa**, *University of Kent at Canterbury*
Dr. **Sarah Whitmore**, *Oxford Brookes University*
Dr. **Harald Wydra**, *University of Cambridge*

SOCIETY, CLASS & ETHNICITY
Col. **David Glantz**, *"Journal of Slavic Military Studies"*
Dr. **Marlène Laruelle**, *George Washington University*
Dr. **Stephen Shulman**, *Southern Illinois University*
Prof. **Stefan Troebst**, *University of Leipzig*

POLITICAL ECONOMY & PUBLIC POLICY
Dr. **Andreas Goldthau**, *Central European University*
Dr. **Robert Kravchuk**, *University of North Carolina*
Dr. **David Lane**, *University of Cambridge*
Dr. **Carol Leonard**, *Higher School of Economics, Moscow*
Dr. **Maria Popova**, *McGill University, Montreal*

FOREIGN POLICY & INTERNATIONAL AFFAIRS
Dr. **Peter Duncan**, *University College London*
Prof. **Andreas Heinemann-Grüder**, *University of Bonn*
Prof. **Gerhard Mangott**, *University of Innsbruck*
Dr. **Diana Schmidt-Pfister**, *University of Konstanz*
Dr. **Lisbeth Tarlow**, *Harvard University, Cambridge*
Dr. **Christian Wipperfürth**, *N-Ost Network, Berlin*
Dr. **William Zimmerman**, *University of Michigan*

HISTORY, CULTURE & THOUGHT
Dr. **Catherine Andreyev**, *University of Oxford*
Prof. **Mark Bassin**, *Södertörn University*
Prof. **Karsten Brüggemann**, *Tallinn University*
Dr. **Alexander Etkind**, *University of Cambridge*
Dr. **Gasan Gusejnov**, *Moscow State University*
Prof. **Leonid Luks**, *Catholic University of Eichstaett*
Dr. **Olga Malinova**, *Russian Academy of Sciences*
Dr. **Richard Mole**, *University College London*
Prof. **Andrei Rogatchevski**, *University of Tromsø*
Dr. **Mark Tauger**, *West Virginia University*

ADVISORY BOARD*

Prof. **Dominique Arel**, *University of Ottawa*
Prof. **Jörg Baberowski**, *Humboldt University of Berlin*
Prof. **Margarita Balmaceda**, *Seton Hall University*
Dr. **John Barber**, *University of Cambridge*
Prof. **Timm Beichelt**, *European University Viadrina*
Dr. **Katrin Boeckh**, *University of Munich*
Prof. em. **Archie Brown**, *University of Oxford*
Dr. **Vyacheslav Bryukhovetsky**, *Kyiv-Mohyla Academy*
Prof. **Timothy Colton**, *Harvard University, Cambridge*
Prof. **Paul D'Anieri**, *University of Florida*
Dr. **Heike Dörrenbächer**, *Friedrich Naumann Foundation*
Dr. **John Dunlop**, *Hoover Institution, Stanford, California*
Dr. **Sabine Fischer**, *SWP, Berlin*
Dr. **Geir Flikke**, *NUPI, Oslo*
Prof. **David Galbreath**, *University of Aberdeen*
Prof. **Alexander Galkin**, *Russian Academy of Sciences*
Prof. **Frank Golczewski**, *University of Hamburg*
Dr. **Nikolas Gvosdev**, *Naval War College, Newport, RI*
Prof. **Mark von Hagen**, *Arizona State University*
Dr. **Guido Hausmann**, *University of Munich*
Prof. **Dale Herspring**, *Kansas State University*
Dr. **Stefani Hoffman**, *Hebrew University of Jerusalem*
Prof. **Mikhail Ilyin**, *MGIMO (U) MID RF, Moscow*
Prof. **Vladimir Kantor**, *Higher School of Economics*
Dr. **Ivan Katchanovski**, *University of Ottawa*
Prof. em. **Andrzej Korbonski**, *University of California*
Dr. **Iris Kempe**, *"Caucasus Analytical Digest"*
Prof. **Herbert Küpper**, *Institut für Ostrecht Regensburg*
Dr. **Rainer Lindner**, *CEEER, Berlin*
Dr. **Vladimir Malakhov**, *Russian Academy of Sciences*

Dr. **Luke March**, *University of Edinburgh*
Prof. **Michael McFaul**, *Stanford University, Palo Alto*
Prof. **Birgit Menzel**, *University of Mainz-Germersheim*
Prof. **Valery Mikhailenko**, *The Urals State University*
Prof. **Emil Pain**, *Higher School of Economics, Moscow*
Dr. **Oleg Podvintsev**, *Russian Academy of Sciences*
Prof. **Olga Popova**, *St. Petersburg State University*
Dr. **Alex Pravda**, *University of Oxford*
Dr. **Erik van Ree**, *University of Amsterdam*
Dr. **Joachim Rogall**, *Robert Bosch Foundation Stuttgart*
Prof. **Peter Rutland**, *Wesleyan University, Middletown*
Prof. **Marat Salikov**, *The Urals State Law Academy*
Dr. **Gwendolyn Sasse**, *University of Oxford*
Prof. **Jutta Scherrer**, *EHESS, Paris*
Prof. **Robert Service**, *University of Oxford*
Mr. **James Sherr**, *RIIA Chatham House London*
Dr. **Oxana Shevel**, *Tufts University, Medford*
Prof. **Eberhard Schneider**, *University of Siegen*
Prof. **Olexander Shnyrkov**, *Shevchenko University, Kyiv*
Prof. **Hans-Henning Schröder**, *SWP, Berlin*
Prof. **Yuri Shapoval**, *Ukrainian Academy of Sciences*
Prof. **Viktor Shnirelman**, *Russian Academy of Sciences*
Dr. **Lisa Sundstrom**, *University of British Columbia*
Dr. **Philip Walters**, *"Religion, State and Society", Oxford*
Prof. **Zenon Wasyliw**, *Ithaca College, New York State*
Dr. **Lucan Way**, *University of Toronto*
Dr. **Markus Wehner**, *"Frankfurter Allgemeine Zeitung"*
Dr. **Andrew Wilson**, *University College London*
Prof. **Jan Zielonka**, *University of Oxford*
Prof. **Andrei Zorin**, *University of Oxford*

* While the Editorial Committee and Advisory Board support the General Editor in the choice and improvement of manuscripts for publication, responsibility for remaining errors and misinterpretations in the series' volumes lies with the books' authors.

Soviet and Post-Soviet Politics and Society (SPPS)
ISSN 1614-3515

Founded in 2004 and refereed since 2007, SPPS makes available affordable English-, German-, and Russian-language studies on the history of the countries of the former Soviet bloc from the late Tsarist period to today. It publishes between 5 and 20 volumes per year and focuses on issues in transitions to and from democracy such as economic crisis, identity formation, civil society development, and constitutional reform in CEE and the NIS. SPPS also aims to highlight so far understudied themes in East European studies such as right-wing radicalism, religious life, higher education, or human rights protection. The authors and titles of all previously published volumes are listed at the end of this book. For a full description of the series and reviews of its books, see www.ibidem-verlag.de/red/spps.

Editorial correspondence & manuscripts should be sent to: Dr. Andreas Umland, Department of Political Science, Kyiv-Mohyla Academy, vul. Voloska 8/5, UA-04070 Kyiv, UKRAINE; andreas.umland@cantab.net

Business correspondence & review copy requests should be sent to: *ibidem* Press, Leuschnerstr. 40, 30457 Hannover, Germany; tel.: +49 511 2622200; fax: +49 511 2622201; spps@ibidem.eu.

Authors, reviewers, referees, and editors for (as well as all other persons sympathetic to) SPPS are invited to join its networks at www.facebook.com/group.php?gid=52638198614
www.linkedin.com/groups?about=&gid=103012
www.xing.com/net/spps-ibidem-verlag/

Recent Volumes

241 Izabella Agardi
On the Verge of History
Life Stories of Rural Women from Serbia, Romania, and Hungary, 1920–2020
With a foreword by Andrea Pető
ISBN 978-3-8382-1602-7

242 Sebastian Schäffer (Ed.)
Ukraine in Central and Eastern Europe
Kyiv's Foreign Affairs and the International Relations of the Post-Communist Region
With a foreword by Pavlo Klimkin
ISBN 978-3-8382-1615-7

243 Volodymyr Dubrovskyi, Kalman Mizsei, Mychailo Wynnyckyj (Eds.)
Eight Years after the Revolution of Dignity
What Has Changed in Ukraine during 2013–2021?
With a foreword by Yaroslav Hrytsak
ISBN 978-3-8382-1560-0

244 Rumena Filipova
Constructing the Limits of Europe
Identity and Foreign Policy in Poland, Bulgaria, and Russia since 1989
With forewords by Harald Wydra and Gergana Yankova-Dimova
ISBN 978-3-8382-1649-2

245 Oleksandra Keudel
How Patronal Networks Shape Opportunities for Local Citizen Participation in a Hybrid Regime
A Comparative Analysis of Five Cities in Ukraine
With a foreword by Sabine Kropp
ISBN 978-3-8382-1671-3

246 Jan Claas Behrends, Thomas Lindenberger, Pavel Kolar (Eds.)
Violence after Stalin
Institutions, Practices, and Everyday Life in the Soviet Bloc 1953–1989
ISBN 978-3-8382-1637-9

247 Leonid Luks
Macht und Ohnmacht der Utopien
Essays zur Geschichte Russlands im 20. und 21. Jahrhundert
ISBN 978-3-8382-1677-5

248 Iuliia Barshadska
Brüssel zwischen Kyjiw und Moskau
Das auswärtige Handeln der Europäischen Union im ukrainisch-russischen Konflikt 2014-2019
Mit einem Vorwort von Olaf Leiße
ISBN 978-3-8382-1667-6

Contents

Foreword 9
Endorsements (short) 8

Introduction 15
1   The Rise of Local Authority 39
    Policy Learning 48
    Policy Change 48
2   No Rise of Regional Authority 63
    Policy Learning 63
    (Attempts at) Policy Change 69
3   The Dynamics of Regionalized Party Competition 83
4   Multilevel Elections' Incongruence and Decentralization 91
5   Multilevel Competition and Decentralization 113
6   The Aftermath of Regional Contests. The Indirect
    Elections of Regional Council Heads 135
Conclusion 151

Bibliography 161
Appendix 183

Endorsements (full)..216

Tables and Boxes

Box 1.2. Public spending on education and healthcare.
Table 4.1. Average dissimilarity indices in the three multilevel electoral cycles under investigation.
Table 4.2. Dissimilarity indices for parliamentary and municipal elections in each region in the three multilevel electoral cycles under investigation.
Table 4.3. Dissimilarity indices for parliamentary and regional elections in each region in the three multilevel electoral cycles under investigation.
Table 4.4. The number of cases of congruence between parties-frontrunners in the same *oblast*s.
Table 4.5. Average ENP at regional and municipal electoral arenas in 2010, 2015, 2020.
Table 4.6. ENP at regional and municipal electoral arenas in 2010, 2015, 2020: regional dimension.
Table 4.7. Number of cases with a dominant-party rule in regional and municipal councils elected in 2010, 2015, 2020.
Box 5.1. Major non-parliamentary parties in 2010 and 2015.
Box 6.1. Regional governors and elections in 2020.
Box 6.2. Regional governors and elections in 2010 and 2015.

Appendix

Table A1. Dissimilarity indices: the congruence of parliamentary and municipal contests in the 2010/2012 multilevel elections.

Table A2. Dissimilarity indices: the congruence of parliamentary and regional contests in the 2010/2012 multilevel elections.

Table A3. Dissimilarity indices: the congruence of parliamentary and municipal contests in the 2014/2015 multilevel elections.

Table A4. Dissimilarity indices: the congruence of parliamentary and regional contests in the 2014/2015 multilevel elections.

Table A5. Dissimilarity indices: the congruence of parliamentary and municipal contests in the 2019/2020 multilevel elections.

Table A6. Dissimilarity indices: the congruence of parliamentary and regional contests in the 2019/2020 multilevel elections.

Table A7. Parties-frontrunners in the three multilevel elections studied.

Endorsements

Valentyna Romanova provides a detailed analysis ... a valuable book for those interested in Ukrainian politics. —Paul D'Anieri

A brilliant and detailed analysis. Based on deep and empirically sound research, this book is a must-read for all students of Ukraine and post-Soviet politics. —Mikhail Minakov

Valentyna Romanova presents a rich study based on detailed understanding and years of research of local politics and elections in Ukraine. The book will be an invaluable resource for researchers of post-Soviet Ukrainian politics. — Paul Chaisty

Packed with insightful analysis and providing a longue durée *outlook,* Decentralization and Multilevel Elections in Ukraine *is an indispensable read to understand the complexity of uprooting the Soviet legacy in governance. ... profoundly interesting.* —Orysia Lutsevych

This is a very sophisticated study of decentralization and multilevel elections in Ukraine. The study is very well grounded in theory and provides a wealth of new empirical data to back up its novel conclusions. ... beautifully crafted ... The book makes an important contribution to the field of territorial politics and democratisation in Ukraine, and also to the wider field of comparative studies and local politics. —Cameron Ross

This book provides students of Ukrainian politics with amazing and surprising insights into the peculiarities of local power. —Nicolas Hayoz

Romanova's book on the most recent reforms in Ukraine is exemplary. The very careful and detailed study of current affairs in local and regional Ukraine makes this a must-read for students of Ukrainian politics.
—Ulrik Kjær

A meticulous analysis ... strongly recommended for everybody interested in Ukrainian politics. —Kataryna Wolczuk

Foreword

This monograph is a result of Dr. Valentyna Romanova's many years' research on Ukraine's subnational politics and elections. After earning a PhD degree at Kyiv-Mohyla Academy University, she spent four years at the University of Edinburgh to study and teach political science. After returning to Ukraine, she launched her career at the National Institute for Strategic Studies subordinated to the Administration of the President of Ukraine and served three presidents (Viktor Yanukovych, Petro Poroshenko, and Volodymyr Zelenskyy), with an interval when she worked at a private think-tank in Kyiv. Romanova's experience at the president's policy-making institute gave her a chance to observe Ukraine's decentralization reform from within.

As one of the editors of *Regional and Federal Studies*, Romanova gained affluent expertise in subnational politics in post-communist and even other regions of the world. This expertise allows her to exploit an institutionalist approach to analyzing Ukraine's decentralization reform and subnational elections in the light of elites' intentions and alliances. Simultaneously, this book discloses an unknown aspect of Ukraine's political history in this century.

The readers may think that Ukraine's decentralization reform after the Euromaidan Revolution, which enlarged and strengthened basic local authorities and deprived regional (*oblast*) and district (*raion*) authorities of previous competences, was a phenomenon analogous to municipal reforms performed by Visehrad countries in the 1990s. In the latter cases, the reform coalition of central and local politicians abolished meso-level governments or transformed them into state organs, regarding them as bastions of conservative forces. It might also be possible to interpret the center-local coalition in Ukraine as an attempt to weaken regional identities exploitable by separatist forces. However, Romanova's analysis based on the concept of the "advocacy coalition framework" casts doubt to these teleological interpretations. In post-Euromaidan Ukraine, policy-makers pursued both amalgamation of basic municipalities and municipalization of regions and districts, but only the former was blessed with the formation of an advocacy coalition.

Romanova traces the origin of Ukraine's decentralization reform to Roman Bezsmertnyy's project in 2005. In other words, four presidential administrations, from Viktor Yushchenko to Zelenskyy, harbored the idea of decentralization, irrespective of their geopolitical orientation. In my view, the early origin of amalgamation of municipal units is a natural result of Ukrainian reformers' institutional choice in the 1990s. The Ukrainian Constitution of 1996 defined cities, towns, and villages as municipal units, while making regions and districts units for state administration and having their chief administrators appointed by the president. Thus emerged 10,961 small municipalities with average populations of about 1,500. The small scale of municipalities put their sustainability in question.

Ukraine's bet on villages and towns as the basic unit of local self-government reminds us of Armenia's experience. Independent Armenia not only betted on village soviets as the basic unit of local self-government, but even divided them (which used to be administrative villages in the Soviet era) into spontaneous settlements. In this way, approximately eight hundred municipalities materialized often with a population of a few hundred people in this small country. Moreover, in Armenia, provinces (*marzer*) only had representatives of the central government and never enjoyed the status of an upper tier of self-government.[1]

For both Armenia and Ukraine, amalgamation of municipalities was inevitable. In both countries, this process accelerated after the revolutions (in Ukraine in 2014 and Armenia in 2018) perhaps because the post-revolutionary leaders began to adopt new tactics to win elections, in contrast to the old elites' endeavor to build a nationwide patronal hierarchy of electoral machines. In Armenia,

---

1   Kimitaka Matsuzato and Stepan Danielyan, "Faith or Tradition: The Armenian Apostolic Church and Community-Building in Armenia and Nagorny Karabakh," *Religion, State & Society* 41, 1 (2013), p. 24.

the number of municipalities slowly shrank to about five hundred by 2017, but, after the April Revolution in 2018, it decreased to 79 in 2021, with about a twenty thousand population on average.[2] As Romanova notes, the number of Ukraine's municipalities decreased from 10,961 in 2014 to 1,469 in 2020. These enlarged municipalities had an average population of about 13,000. These scales of municipalities in Ukraine and Armenia remind us of *raiony* (districts) before Nikita Khrushchev's policy of *raion* amalgamation in the early 1960s.

In contrast, Russian and Lithuanian state-builders counted on *raiony* as the basic unit of local self-government. The amended Russian Federal Law on the General Principles of Local Self-Government of 2003 made towns and villages the lower tier of local self-government, indeed with a chronical deficit of human and financial resources, while in Lithuania villages and towns were degraded to intra-municipal structures. Remarkably, when Lithuanian reformers designed the new system of local self-government in the 1990s, an option intended to divide the then existing 56 *raiony* and cities into about 90-120 smaller municipalities with average populations of twenty to thirty thousand. One of the possible criteria to demarcate these new *raiony* was the boundaries of pre-Khrushchev *raiony*.[3] In the late 1990s, the then Conservative government established five new *raiony* to reverse its falling popularity, partly responding to the former *raion* central settlements' desire to regain their previous status of which they had been deprived by Khrushchev's amalgamation policy.[4]

---

2 Interview with Daniel Ioannisyan, advisor of the Government Committee on Constitutional Reform in Armenia, January 21, 2022, Yerevan.
3 My interview with Algirdas Astrauskas, advisor of the Committee on State Administration and Local Self-Government of the Lithuanian Parliament, February 23, 2018, Vilnius.
4 Kimitaka Matsuzato, "The Last Bastion of Unitarism? Local Institutions, Party Politics and Ramifications of EU Accession in Lithuania," *Eurasian Geography and Economics* 43, 5 (2002), pp. 362-363.

Thus, we see the ghost of pre-Khrushchev *raiony* wandering in these countries despite the significant demographic changes there since the 1960s.

Another point Romanova makes is the incongruence of national, regional, and local (regional capital) elections. Conventional wisdom in political science regards significant incongruence between elections at various levels as a menace to the integrity of the state or normal functioning of federalism.[5] Subnational elections held before national elections expose potential social trends and facilitate the formation of winning coalitions for the coming national elections, as often happens in Lithuania and Poland. Honeymoon voting[6] is possible not only in parliamentary but also local elections held soon after presidential elections.

In contrast to these merits of electoral congruence for regime survival, Romanova describes inter-electoral incongruence in a positive light. A national ruling party might become the top runner at general elections in a region, but this might not be the case for the same region's regional council and/or regional capital elections.

In my view, an example of the multilevel incongruences of election results beneficial for regime survival was those observed in Russian politics during the 1990s. In 1996, influential governors and ethnic republic presidents described themselves as defenders of local interests, struggling to minimize the negative influence of the erroneous reform policy adopted by the federal government on the local population. As a result, in a series of regions, pro-communist (anti-Yeltsin) voters in the presidential elections voted for their incumbent regional leaders appointed by or coalesced with President Boris Yeltsin in the gubernatorial elections. With hindsight, the multilevel electoral incongruence facilitated the defusing

---

5 Peter Ordeshook, "Russia's Party System: Is Russian Federalism Viable?," *Post-Soviet Affairs* 12, 3 (1996), pp. 195-217.

6 Matthew S. Shugart and John M. Carey, Presidents and Assemblies: Constitutional Design and Electoral Dynamics (Cambridge University Press, 1992), Chapter 11.

of the population's social discontent and enabled consolidation of a post-communist patronal regime in Russia.

In the 2010-2012 electoral cycle in Ukraine, the vertical electoral incongruence was relatively insignificant since the Party of Regions won the presidential, subnational, and parliamentary elections in a number of regions. This means that Yanukovych had built a nationwide hierarchy of electoral machines with the exception of regions, which did not accept his regime for identity reasons.

In the 2014-2015 electoral cycle, despite the exodus of a significant portion of the pro-Russian vote from Ukraine's electoral scene, the vertical electoral incongruence increased because Poroshenko's party was forced to share the benefits of the Euromaidan Revolution with other parties. In addition, mayoral parties had already emerged in the 2015 local elections.

In the following period, Poroshenko could not build a nationwide electoral hierarchy indispensable for his reelection because there were neither national nor (statewide) subnational elections during 2016-2018. Moreover, in 2016-2018, the European Union requested Ukraine to adopt the "contest (*konkurs*) principle" in nomination of governor candidates and restricted the president's prerogative to appoint governors at his discretion.

While Poroshenko's electoral defeat in 2019 is explained by his failure in building a nationwide electoral machine, President Zelenskyy rejected it consciously in the 2019-2020 electoral cycle and soon chose to ally with growing mayoral parties. As is well known, conflicts took place between the president and mayors in coping with the pandemic of COVID-19 in the spring of 2020, but, after mayoral parties' victories in the local elections, they quickly adjusted their relations. In some regional councils, having lost their previous authority after the completion of local amalgamation, the presidential People's Servant Party and mayoral parties made deals for gubernatorial appointment.

One of the driving forces of the development of mayoral parties in regions of post-Euromaidan Ukraine was to save the lifeline for the population (daily public administration) from polarizing and ideologizing national politics. This motivation met Zelenskyy's desire. Moreover, perhaps Zelenskyy and his administration did not want to overwhelm themselves with detailed expertise for daily public administration. For the lack of desire to build a nationwide electoral machine and of expertise for providing the population with daily services, which characterizes such post-post-communist politicians as Zelenskyy and Nikol Pashinyan in Armenia, the completion of municipal amalgamation by the 2020 local elections and the alliance with pragmatist mayors after the elections would seem to be a rational choice. Yet the sustainability of this alliance over the head of weakened middle-level governments remains to be seen.

January 30, 2022

Kimitaka Matsuzato
Professor of Comparative Politics
Graduate School for Law and Politics
University of Tokyo

Introduction

When Ukraine's government announced the start of the decentralization reform in April 2014, it planned to strengthen local governance by means of local amalgamation and to increase regional authority via the introduction of the executive committees of the directly elected councils. In advance of the 2020 substate elections, the government completed amalgamation and increased local authority over public service provision and local development all over the country. However, the directly elected regional councils have not yet gained the constitutional right to establish their executive committees. The centrally appointed heads of regional state administrations continue to wield executive powers in relation to both the state and regional councils.

This book addresses two puzzles. First, it seeks to explain why the reformers consolidated and empowered local governance, but have so far failed to strengthen the directly elected regional authorities. Second, it aims at explaining the implications of the decentralization policy on multilevel elections in Ukraine.

Ukraine's official decentralization policy strategy — the Concept on Reforming Local Self-Government and the Territorial Organization of Power, approved by the government on 1 April 2014 (the 2014 Concept)[7] — outlined the ambition to strengthen local governance through the amalgamation of local communities and an increase in their financial and institutional stance. It also aimed at granting directly elected regional councils the constitutional right to establish their own executive committees. The latter task directly affects the responsibilities of the centrally appointed regional executives — the heads of regional state administration. Currently, they implement the decisions made by the respective regional councils, apart from executing the Center's decisions at the substate level. Although the 2014 Concept outlined these objectives, it was not

---

7   The 2014 Concept includes other objectives: fostering regional development, reforming the administrative-territorial system of Ukraine, etc. This book investigates only matters of local and regional authority.

unusual for policymakers to make compromises when they proceeded to the decision-making stages. The question arises as to why the local amalgamation policy was implemented, but its regional authority equivalent has yet to materialize.

The literature on public policy analysis emphasizes the core role of agenda-setting and acknowledges the agenda-setting power of crises, elections, and government change. Research on the initiation of policy changes introduces the notion of *focusing events* — unexpected events that stimulate policymakers to focus on hitherto neglected salient issues (Graeme 2013). With respect to the post-2014 decentralization policy, the major focusing event that fostered the agenda-setting stage was a change in the status of the domestic political elites after the Euromaidan Uprising. The new ruling elites who came to power in 2014 expressed their eagerness to introduce decentralization policies. On 27 February 2014, the newly established government introduced the position of vice-prime minister responsible for decentralization. Volodymyr Hroysman, an erstwhile city mayor, was awarded the portfolios of Vice Prime Minister and Minister of Regional Development, Building, and Communal Service of Ukraine. During 2002-2006, he served in the Vinnytsia city council, and was subsequently mayor of Vinnytsia during 2006-2014. On 5 March 2014 Prime Minister Arseniy Yatsenyuk stated that decentralization would be a priority for the newly formed government: "[r]ights should be granted to regions" (Yatsenyuk 2014). On 1 April 2014, the government adopted a decentralization reform agenda (the 2014 Concept) followed by an action plan with a precise implementation schedule. On 13 April 2014 the acting president Oleksandr Turchynov issued a decree and instructed the Cabinet of Ministers to draft laws on decentralization, with an emphasis on empowering territorial communities and introducing regional council executive committees. President Petro Poroshenko, elected in May 2014, expressed enthusiasm for the decentralization reform outlined in the 2014 Concept. The parliamentary coalition, established soon after the October 2014 elections, voiced similar support in its coalition agreement.

The violation of Ukraine's territorial integrity in Crimea and Donbas did not stop central policymakers from initiating the decentralization reform. Maryna Rabinovych argues that "Ukraine's [territorial integrity] crisis response strategy has been comprised by three key axes: security operations ...; diplomatic efforts ...; and domestic reforms, including inter alia the decentralization reform" (Rabinovych 2020: 5). The launch of the decentralization reform increased expectations that the "implementation of reforms may help to facilitate a de-escalation and peaceful settlement of the violent conflict in the Donbas region. Even if the reform is first implemented elsewhere in the country prior to a full cessation of the conflict in Donbas, Kyiv will be able to demonstrate to the people of Donbas that it is serious about reducing national state authorities and enhancing local authority. This would likely make the region's acceptance of reintegration with the rest of the country easier as local people realize that being a part of Ukraine brings local empowerment and potentially more effective governance" (USAID 2014: 20). Anatoliy Tkachuk (2015) highlighted that the government approved the decentralization agenda before the outbreak of the armed conflict in Donbas; he warned that introducing the regional council executive committees before strengthening local governance and during Russia's hybrid war against Ukraine could be dangerous. Largely in agreement with this statement, Madoian has recently argued that "[s]uccessful conflict settlement is possible if Ukraine proceeds with a decentralisation process that shifts power from a regional to a community level" (Madoian 2020: 1).

Scholarship on local governance suggests three major reasons why policymakers introduce local amalgamation: (i) to improve the quality of public service delivery; (ii) to improve the efficiency of local self-government; (iii) to promote participatory democracy (Swianiewicz 2010; Ebinger et al 2019). Arguably, the core objective of local amalgamation in Ukraine has been to improve the ability of local self-governance to provide basic public services: to take responsibility for primary and secondary education, primary healthcare, the provision of administrative services, etc. Prior to the reform, Ukraine's local governance was fragmented; the capacity of local self-government to manage allocated functions was limited

(Hanushchak 2013; OECD 2014; Tkachuk 2017; OECD 2018; Zhalilo et al 2019; Shevchenko et al 2020). The quality of public services was deteriorating for decades. Under Soviet rule, the delivery of public services at the local level was often managed and funded by big state-owned enterprises (Leitch 2017: 1144). After the Soviet Union collapsed, many of these enterprises were either privatized or experienced financial hardship. In either case they took less care in the provision of public service at the local level. In these circumstances, local self-government was asked to take over social services previously provided by state companies, without any increase in resources (O'Connell and Wetzel 2003). "Local governments [were] supposed to provide basic social and administrative services: preschool, primary, secondary, and technical-vocational education; preventive medicine and primary and secondary healthcare; keeping the public peace; the organization of residential service delivery, public transit, and so on" (Chumak and Shevliakov 2009: 6).

Despite the lack of funding, the number of local authorities — directly elected local councils — increased (Tkachuk 2017). That increase became possible in accord with the law on local governance (the Law "On Local Councils and Local & Regional Self-governance") introduced on 7 December 1990, on the eve of Ukraine's independence. In 1991 there were 9,211 local councils in Ukraine. By 2014, that number increased to 10,961 (*Monitorynh protsesu detsentralizatsiyi vlady ta reformuvannya mistsevoho samovryaduvannya stanom na 10 veresnya 2020 roku* 2020). With an average population of approximately 1,500 inhabitants, many local councils were afflicted with a low capacity to provide basic public services and to promote local development. In these circumstances, regional and subregional authorities assumed responsibility for public service delivery and received subsidies and transfers from the central budget for the purpose. The majority of the transfers were conditional (Ladner et al 2016); the centrally appointed regional executives administered the transfers to municipalities from the central budget, and "the regional budget would act as an intermediary between the state and the city budget when allocating subventions" (Martinez-Vazquez and Wayne 2011: 21, cited in Platonova 2020:

149). "Most health and social protection expenditures [took] place at [the *oblast* and *rayon*] levels" (O'Connell and Wetzel 2003: 358).

Even though the quality of public services in most localities deteriorated, there was one notable exception—the cities of *oblast* significance (Chumak and Shevliakov 2009: 6; OECD 2018). Their ability to perform their duties with respect to public service delivery largely resulted from the allocation of a considerable share of Personal Income Tax to their local budgets. In Ukraine, Personal Income Tax is often paid not on the basis of where taxpayers live, but where they are employed (Levitas and Djikic 2017: 52). Because major enterprises generating legal income are registered in the cities of *oblast* significance (Levitas and Djikic 2017: fn 9), the capacity of local governance in these cities was often sufficient to deliver basic public services to their inhabitants.

When Ukraine's system of multilevel governance is considered as a whole, it becomes clear that "real problems have been caused by the fact that as local (self) governments the character of *oblasts* and *rayons* has always been compromised by the national government appointment of their governors" (Levitas and Djikic 2017: 4). This highlights the division of power between the elected authorities and the appointed governors—the matter that has been at the core of center-periphery relations in Ukraine since independence. As Kimitaka Matsuzato puts it: "[a] specific feature of the local reforms in Ukraine [has been] the status of regional and district authorities, which have been repeatedly municipalized in times of decentralization and stratified in times of centralization" (Matsuzato 2000: 45).

In the days of the Ukrainian SSR there were executive committees of the directly elected regional councils. In 1992, soon after gaining independence, Ukraine abolished these committees and introduced regional executives—presidential representatives. Presidential representatives were in charge of implementing the decisions of the president at the substate scales and for ensuring state oversight of decision-making in the directly elected councils. After two years, the national parliament abolished the regional executives and transferred their responsibilities to the elected regional and sub-regional councils, which had the right to establish executive committees. These shifts in regional authority were the outcome of attempts by the president and the parliament to advance their own authority in the Center (Matsuzato 2000).

A major policy change occurred in 1995-1996. The Constitutional Treaty and the Constitution made the executive committees of the directly elected regional councils into regional state administrations—regional executives—appointed and dismissed by the president (Wolczuk 2002). Since then, the directly elected regional councils have served as regional self-government bodies, while the appointed heads of the regional state administrations have acted as regional executives.[8] Regional councils had power to declare no confidence in the head of the relevant state administration, on the basis of which the President of Ukraine had to make a decision. The state could take on the responsibility of the tasks assigned to local and (sub)regional self-government, and which were delegated to (sub)regional state administrations.[9]

Despite Ukraine having signed and ratified the European Charter of Local Self-government (1996 and 1997, respectively) and passed new domestic legislation on self-government (Law "On Local Self-government in Ukraine," 1997), in practice, regional executives often concentrated substate power in their hands, often to the benefit of the ruling party in the Center (Matsuzato 2001). "These state-appointed heads [of regional and subregional state

---

8 Since then, the heads of regional councils have been elected in their respective councils and not by popular vote, as in 1994.
9 Broadly speaking, matters of public service provision refer to substate authorities' delegated tasks. 'The central government is formally responsible for those functions and provides subordinate governments with targeted funds to carry out these tasks. They "transit" through local budgets but subnational government authorities have limited authority over them. Subnational governments also have limited autonomy in the management of their functions. Legal obligations, service organisation, financing, human resources, performance standards, etc., are all defined and monitored by the central government, leaving little or no discretion for subnational governments in the performance of delegated functions' (OECD 2018: 179). 'By contrast, "exclusive functions" mainly concern local public goods such as utilities, housing and social protection for which subnational governments have more autonomy and which are financed from general transfers but also own resources. They are vaguely defined and represent a minor portion of subnational expenditure' (OECD 2018: 180).

administrations], in turn, exert considerable influence over the hiring and firing of the directors of most local departments (e.g. Health, Education, Social Welfare). And both the heads of *oblasts* and *rayons*, and the departmental directors whose careers they control are subject to a dual subordination, at once responsible to higher level state (e.g. line ministries) and their democratically-elected councils. As a result, there is a profound confusion of local and national authority at the *oblast* and *rayon* levels" (Levitas and Djikic 2017: 14).

The 2004 constitutional reform, which introduced a parliamentary-presidential regime into Ukraine (Matsuzato 2005; Herron 2007; Kudelia 2007), considered center–periphery relations only in the context of power distribution in Kyiv (Romanova 2011a). In line with the reform, the heads of regional state administrations became responsible to the president and to the government (prior to 2004, they were responsible to the president alone), both accountable to and under the control of higher-level bodies of the executive branch (Article 118). The president was now granted the right to appoint the heads of (sub)regional state administrations in negotiation with the central government, a similar procedure existing for their dismissal. As early as 2010, the 2004 constitutional reform was annulled, only to be re-introduced again in 2014. These shifts of the provisions of the 2004 constitutional reform reflected changes in the division of power between central policymakers and did not affect regional councils' powers.

In this book, I assess policymaking relating to the increase in local and regional authority with the help of the Advocacy Coalition Framework (ACF) of public policy analysis. The ACF interprets policymaking as a competition between two or more advocacy coalitions operating within a policy subsystem (Sabatier 1998). Advocacy coalitions comprise actors who share similar policy beliefs and coordinate their political actions "to achieve similar policy objectives" (Sabatier & Weible 2007: 196). Although some policy beliefs can change over time, core policy beliefs change very slowly and are associated with normative values. The ACF assumes that actors who seek to translate their beliefs into policy actions join coalitions of allies and confront opponents in order to succeed.

Sharing beliefs is a minimal condition for actors to qualify as a coalition, whereas true advocacy coalitions also coordinate their actions (Graeme 2013). Simply put, policy changes often result from the success of a more powerful advocacy coalition. The ACF is particularly useful for analyzing policymaking in times of uncertainty and when there are numerous actors. In addition, it emphasizes the role of expert inputs in policymaking without necessarily prioritizing party politics. Finally, the ACF is crucial for public policy analysis over an extended period. This framework helps me to explain why the pro-reform advocacy coalition was able to implement the policy of local amalgamation, despite internal divisions and inconsistent coordination efforts, while the alternate advocacy coalition succeeded in postponing decision-making regarding the introduction of executive committees into regional councils.

There are two approaches to understanding the legacy of the 2014 decentralization reform in Ukraine. On the one hand, Anatoliy Tkachuk, a senior advisor to the government that approved the 2014 Concept, repeatedly stressed that the Concept "was prepared in 2008-2009 and was first approved in July 2009, when Yulia Tymoshenko served as prime minister" (Tkachuk 2015) and that the post-2014 decentralization reform was implemented according to the outlines drawn up in "2008-2009 ... [when] the main law drafts were prepared: on the right of territorial communities to amalgamate, on the administrative-territorial structure [of Ukraine] ... If we compare the approved [amalgamated territorial] communities and districts as of 2020, they do not differ much from the ones that were drafted in 2008-2009" (Tkachuk 2020). On the other hand, international experts, familiar with the government's policy documents on decentralization, drafted in 2005-2006 and in 2008-2009, claim that the post-2014 decentralization reform is based on the policy recommendations first drafted in 2005 (e.g. USAID 2014).

I reconstruct the Concept of Administrative-Territorial Reform, drafted by the government in 2005, using the detailed feedback report of the Council of Europe, prepared for the Ukrainian government. The Concept of Local Government Reform, prepared by the government in 2009, is available in a valuable secondary source (Aleksandrova and Koliushko 2011). Apart from these two policy documents, I examine the draft of the Concept of Reforming Local Self-government and the Territorial Organization of Power prepared by the government in 2012-2013. When analyzing and comparing these and some other policy documents, I refer to the corresponding Council of Europe feedback reports.[10]

When comparing the government's policy documents on decentralization drafted before and after the launch of the 2014 decentralization reform, I identify the extent to which policymakers specified the policy objectives of local amalgamation and the increase of regional authority, how policymakers aimed at achieving those goals, and the extent to which they proceeded towards decision-making and implementation. The comparative analysis of subsequent government policy recommendations on decentralization helps to clarify the input of various actors into the aggregation of the pro-reform advocacy coalition and its opponents since 2005.

I find an unexpected continuity in efforts at domestic policy learning throughout 2005-2014, with little — if any — interruption. This continuity had little to do with party politics as manifested in elections. The policy learning efforts consisted in collecting and analyzing the data necessary to design potential local amalgamation scenarios, as well as for drafting laws, i.e. on local amalgamation, and receiving feedback on those drafts from domestic and international experts, including Council of Europe experts. When the core data-driven policy documents were drafted by the government, policymakers interacted with substate authorities (at the stage of data collection) and domestic think tanks (at the stage of data analysis). Such efforts did not compare with the scope of more recent, post-2014 public consultations or with the new scope of expert engagement, but they helped to generate policy recommendations for local amalgamation based on data collected by substate authorities all over Ukraine, which were passed on to government policy analysts for further data analysis. Those policy learning efforts helped

---

10 In a PhD thesis that evaluates international influence on Ukraine's "stateness," Podolian (2020) regards the input of the Council of Europe among the most substantial.

to engage actors into the emerging advocacy coalition in favor of decentralization policies. I suggest that this long and drawn out policy learning made it possible for the ruling elites—those who came to power in 2014 and possessed the political will to bring about policy change—to finally launch decentralization reform.

When it comes to local amalgamation, the pro-reform advocacy coalition incorporated actors with extensive experience of policy learning in previous governments. The policymakers possessed the political will to take on board their policy recommendations, enhanced by professional feedback from the Council of Europe. The pro-reform advocacy coalition's activities were facilitated by well-coordinated and increased international support. It is difficult to overvalue the input of enhanced international support for the post-2014 decentralization reform, namely in identifying the shortcomings of policy implementation at the local level and in engaging the government and diverse stakeholders in policy discussions in order to make the necessary adjustments. This input limited the ability of the opponents of local amalgamation to present the government's policy as harmful.

It is doubtless challenging to introduce policy changes that require constitutional amendments and it was dangerous to introduce executive committees into regional councils in the midst of Russia's hybrid war against Ukraine. In this book, I highlight other factors that account for the delay in increasing regional authority in Ukraine.

In contrast to local amalgamation policy, the policy learning experience relating to the growth of regional authority was less specific. Domestic policymakers have mostly disputed either (i) increasing vs. limiting regional authority, or (ii) regional authorities' subordination to the president, the parliament, or the government. Prior to 2014, domestic policymakers drafted many laws regarding constitutional amendments containing brief clauses about regional council executive committees, but there was no consensus on how to ensure the lack of overlap between the potential executive duties of regional self-governance and the executive duties of the state. This gap in policy learning had severe implications, because the "blurred" division of responsibilities between substate authorities and the input of regional governors into the system of multilevel governance constituted the major crux of center-periphery relations in Ukraine. In Summer 2014, Summer 2015, and Winter 2019-2020, central policymakers attempted to foster constitutional changes related to increasing regional authority, but there was no consensus on the division of responsibilities between the Center, regional governors, and substate councils.

Moreover, in advance of the 2020 substate elections, the pro-reform advocacy coalition failed to address the criticisms of the alternate advocacy coalition. The latter's members were to be found not only in parliament. The alternative coalition was strengthened after incorporating local authorities who effectively opposed the policy recommendation to introduce state supervision over both delegated and own responsibilities of local self-government. The capacity of local authorities to engage in debates on matters of regional authority is striking. For their part, regional councils did not actively call for an increase of their powers.

As with the policy of local amalgamation, the post-2014 policy recommendations related to increasing regional authority had little to do with party politics. The strongest party, whose manifesto declared its commitment to increasing regional authority via introducing executive committees into the directly elected councils, was a loser in the Euromaidan Uprising. The political parties that opposed president Viktor Yanukovych during the Euromaidan Uprising did not present decentralization as a major demand. Although their manifestos contained declarations of their commitment to strengthening local self-governance, those declarations lacked concrete policy recommendations, apart from generic references to the European Charter of Local Self-Government.

The second puzzle that this book addresses relates to the implications of decentralization on multilevel elections in Ukraine.

Mierzejewski-Voznyak (forthcoming) warns that Ukraine's party politics could get "localized" during the implementation of the decentralization policy. Before the 2015 substate contests, it was clear that "the newly elected regional and local councils won't necessarily follow the lines of party competition in the current national parliament" (Romanova 2015a). As soon as the electoral outcomes were known, Andrew Wilson questioned the validity of interpreting them according to "the classic trope of a Ukraine-still-divided-between-west-and-east … The Brownian motion of Ukrainian politics means there are too many new forces in Ukraine." (Wilson 2015). The decline of parliamentary parties' representation in the substate councils elected in 2015 made Rozumnyi and Pavlenko conclude that a "crisis of parliamentary parties" (Rozumnyi and Pavlenko 2015: 5) had occurred. In contrast, the Razumkov Centre finds a "sufficient stability of [electoral] support of parties that belong to the [parliamentary] coalition in all regions [of Ukraine]" (Razumkov Centre 2016: 15).

In advance of the 2020 contests, Neljas argued that "it is probable, that in many big cities parties led by popular Mayors prevail. Potentially this approach could also reduce tensions between the central and local governments. However, if in elections opposition parties achieve a strong foothold and form coalitions in the Eastern (Opposition Platform—For Life) and Western (European Solidarity, Batkivschyna) parts of the country, the tensions between local and central government and also between different regions of the country could also grow more serious" (Neljas 2020: 15). Once the 2020 elections were held, Lutsevych highlighted the electoral losses of the ruling party and other parliamentary parties and "victories in large cities by political parties with no affiliation to national parties … With more tax revenue staying in the communities where it is collected, mayors are able to invest more in local infrastructure and public service upgrades, leading to increased satisfaction with and trust in local authorities, at exactly the same time that trust in Zelenskyy and the national government is declining. Mayors have been unwilling to share the trust they have gained with the president's party by running on a Servant of the People ticket" (Lutsevych 2020). As Hunashchak puts it, "the all-Ukrainian political projects were defeated by local ones" (Hunashchak 2021) largely because local authorities benefited from the decentralization reform. In contrast, Pavlenko (2020: 2) and Frosiniak (2021: 90) stress that representatives of parliamentary parties in all substate councils elected at the 2015 substate contests accounted for 18.65% of the total; however, their share increased to 54.65% in the 2020 substate elections. Both Pavlenko (2020) and Frosiniak (2021) interpret this change as evidence of the increased representation of parliamentary parties in substate councils; they stress that this dynamic resulted from changes to the electoral rules that disadvantaged independent candidates.

However, numerous factors could account for the observed incongruence of electoral outcomes in multilevel electoral arenas in Ukraine. Based on the comparative analysis of the outcomes of mayoral elections in 2010, 2015, and 2020, Masatomo Torikai argues that the collapse of the Party of the Regions gave rise to a power vacuum, and, in turn, the incumbent mayors' authority at sub-state scales stimulated the growth of local parties (Torikai 2021). Research results related to Ukraine's multilevel elections, which were held prior to the introduction of the post-2014 decentralization policy, identified the incongruence in the parties' vote share in parliamentary and regional council elections in the same regions, even when the multilevel contests were held simultaneously and according to the same electoral rules, as in 2006 (Henderson and Romanova 2016; Romanova 2013). The 2006 parliamentary elections demonstrated "greater nationalization and lower fragmentation" compared to the 2006 regional council elections (Henderson and Romanova 2016: 220). Indeed, as early as 2006, parties that contested regional council elections only in one or in several regions undermined the performance of strong parliamentary frontrunners, which contested regional elections in each region (Henderson and Romanova 2016). Multivariate analysis of multilevel electoral competition has profiled voters who were not likely to split their ticket but, instead, vote for the same political party at both parliamentary and regional elections: their native language was Ukrainian, they spoke Ukrainian at home, they supported Ukrainian as the single state language, and they wanted the *oblast*s to gain more competencies from the Center (Henderson and Romanova 2016: 221). A comparative analysis of Ukraine's regional council elections held in 2006 and 2010 showed that during the authoritarian turn the outcomes of multilevel contests become more congruent, compared to contests that allowed free and fair political competition (Romanova 2013). This is probably not unique to Ukraine: under authoritarian rule, the party of power tends to ensure its overwhelming electoral success in regional contests across the country (Ross 2011a, b), although its vote share can still differ across the country (Ross and Panov 2019).

In order to understand whether and how the post-2014 decentralization reform made a difference, this book compares the electoral outcomes in the parliamentary, regional, and municipal electoral arenas (i) before and (ii) after the implementation of the decentralization policy.[11]

I employ a comparative method, more specifically, the most similar system design, which explains differences or similarities using similar cases that differ from each other only in terms of a key variable. The most similar system design operates with causal arguments that are usually correlational in nature (Garaz 2012).The key limitation is the so-called Galton's Problem: identifying a relationship between two phenomena does not necessarily mean that relationship is causal, since the observed outcome might have been caused by some intervening variable(s). This is relevant for the probabilistic approach in the social sciences, which implies that "explanatory factors increase or decrease the likelihood of an outcome, rather than determine it" (Garaz 2012: 17). The advantages (and limitations) of the subnational comparative method have been explained in detail in Snyder (2001).

Research on the interplay between the increase of substate authority and regional elections is rich (e.g. Palares and Keating 2003; Jeffery and Hough 2003; Chhibber and Kollmann 2004; Wyn Jones and Scully 2006; Thorlakson 2007, 2009; Bardi and Mair 2008; Hough and Jeffery 2006; Henderson and McEwen 2010; Schakel

---

11 I gratefully acknowledge that I finalized this research design after the discussion of my conference paper "Voting Rules, Voting Rights, and Electoral Outcomes of Ukraine's Municipal Elections" by Professor Mizoguchi Shuhei (Hosei University) who acted as a panel discussant at the Convention of the Japan Association of Russian and East European Studies held on 17 October 2020.

2013 a, b; Schakel and Jeffery 2013; Schakel 2015; Baumann et al 2020; Schakel and Romanova 2018, 2019, 2020, 2021, 2022). Scholarship offers several major explanatory angles as to why the increase of regional authority often decreases the congruence of multilevel elections. Chhibber and Kollmann (2004) prove that decentralization generates incentives for political actors to choose under what parties they contest elections: when substate authorities gain more decision-making power, political actors get motivated to contest elections under their own party labels. Thorlakson (2007) proves that decentralization policies provide incentives for both political actors and electors to prioritize substate agendas and seek representation in substate rather than national authorities. Jeffery and Hough (2003), Pallarés and Keating (2003), and Wyn Jones and Scully (2006) specify that the distinct voting preferences in constituencies with distinct territorial identities and interests go hand in hand with the enhanced electoral performance of regional parties. The literature in the field of territorial politics often labels regional parties as non-statewide parties and, in turn, refers to national parties as statewide parties (e.g. Hepburn and Detterbeck 2013). Unlike statewide parties, which contest both general and substate elections across the country (Fabre 2008), regional, or non-statewide, parties tend to prioritize elections in a limited number of constituencies (Swenden and Maddens 2009: 9). Decentralization modifies party competition: it not only generates favorable conditions for establishing and promoting non-statewide parties, but can also affect the electoral strategies that both statewide and non-statewide parties employ when contesting elections in multiple arenas (Schakel 2013b: 218).

A literature review of studies that consider local elections when investigating multilevel voting (Gendźwiłł and Steyvers 2021: 1-3) demonstrates that the gap in knowledge is still vast, but research accomplishments are growing fast (e.g. Kjaer and Elklit 2010a; Kjaer and Elklit 2010b; Kjaer 2013; Kjaer and Klemmensen 2014). The extent of the growth is evidenced by *The Routledge Handbook of Local Elections and Voting in Europe* (Gendzwill et al 2022). Comparative research on local elections in forty European countries finds that only "[i]n about one-third of all country cases, the predominance of national political parties [at local elections] is high" (Gendzwill et al 2022: 521). In practice, "not all national political parties field candidates in all municipalities at the local elections" (Kjaer and Elklit 2010b: 427). The ruling parties are often eager to broaden their representation at the substate scales in order to maximize the chances of gaining support across the country for centrally imposed policies. "By taking part in elections at different levels, national parties become important links between various electoral arenas. Similar patterns of national parties' competition reproduced in various municipalities homogenize local elections" (Gendzwill et al 2022: 505). Opposition parties at the national level can be motivated to improve their performance at the local scales (Kjaer 2012, cited in Gendzwill et al 2022: 505) in order to improve their chances of political survival. Local parties can be motivated to gain power in local councils in order to then proceed to contest national elections (Kjaer 2012, cited in Gendzwill et al 2022: 505). The research results so far indicate that "the polarization of local electorates is not necessarily organized along the national issues" (Gendzwill et al 2022: 508).

There is fruitful research that compares the electoral performance of parties in the national, regional and local arenas (e.g. Golder et al 2017). Using the analytical framework of Ordeshook (1996), Matsuzato (2002a) investigated the emerging multilevel party system in Ukraine in the late 1990s and early 2000s. The analytical framework comprised (a) three horizontal axes: the Center, the regions, and the sub-regions (cities and districts), and (b) three vertical axes: intergovernmental relations, the relations among the levels of the party system, and non-institutionalized relations among elites. Matsuzato (2002a) tailored this analytical framework to the Zakarpatska *oblast* in Ukraine in order to explain how the interactions between central policymakers, regional governors, and city mayors both contributed to and prevented the institutionalization of the ruling party. Notably, studies of national, regional, and local elections can be "autonomous" from each other. The evidence is that scholars have measured (a) party system nationalization at the national level (Bochsler 2010), (b) multilevel party system nationalization based on parties' performance in the national and regional arenas (Schakel 2015), and (c) local party system nationalization (Kjaer and Elklit 2010 a, b) using different methodologies.

As already mentioned, Ukraine's decentralization reform has increased the powers and finances of local authorities. Prior to the 2020 regional and municipal elections, the Ukrainian government completed local amalgamation across the country. In the 2020 municipal elections, voters elected newly more powerful local authorities, while the responsibilities of regional authorities remained largely unchanged. Based on the theoretical assumptions in the literature on multilevel elections, my expectation is to find an increased incongruence between parliamentary and municipal elections held in the same regions since the implementation of the reform. At the same time, I do not expect to find any meaningful change with respect to the incongruence between parliamentary and regional elections held in the same regions. Finally, I expect to find an improved electoral performance by non-parliamentary parties in the municipal elections after the completion of the local amalgamation policy, but I do not expect to observe a similar phenomenon in the regional council elections.

The policy of local amalgamation was completed on the eve of the 2020 substate contests; therefore, I categorize only these as contests held after the implementation of the decentralization reform. The Central Electoral Commission of Ukraine only provides official records on substate elections held in 2010, 2015, and 2020. As a consequence, in order to compare multilevel elections before and after the implementation of the decentralization policy, I compare the 2019/2020 elections with two previous multilevel cycles. My comparative analysis thus comprises three multilevel electoral cycles: (1) the 2020 substate elections held on 25 October compared to the 2019 parliamentary elections held on 21 July; (2) the 2015 substate contests held on 25 October compared to the 2014 parliamentary elections held on 26 October; (3) the 2010 substate elections held on 28 October compared to the 2012 parliamentary elections held on 31 October.

In the case of the 2014/2015 and the 2019/2020 electoral cycles, the substate contests were held one year after parliamentary elections. In the case of the 2010/2012 electoral cycle, substate elections were held two years prior to parliamentary contests. I recognize that this plays a role and deserves special attention when interpreting the research results. At the same time, even simultaneous parliamentary and regional elections, held in 2006, when Ukraine's democratic performance was recognized as exceptionally high, produced highly incongruent electoral outcomes in the same regions (Henderson and Romanova 2016). The elections under investigation were mostly recognized as free and fair; however, the 2010 regional contests (Romanova 2013) and the 2012 parliamentary elections (Herron 2014) were held during the authoritarian turn.

In the Ukrainian language, the term for "local elections" refers to all substate elections. For the sake of clarity, I use the terms "regional elections" and "regional council elections" interchangeably when referring to direct elections of regional councils. Similarly, "municipal elections" and "municipal council elections" are both used when considering the same phenomenon—direct elections of municipal councils. When the reference is to both regional and municipal elections, I employ the term "substate elections."

I compare the electoral outcomes of parliamentary, regional, and municipal elections in the same *oblasts*. The parliament—the *Verkhovna Rada*—is made up of one house, elected by popular vote. Regional councils are directly elected, while the heads of those councils are elected by a simple majority of councillors. Apart from *oblasts*, the capital city of Kyiv and the city of Sevastopol are regarded as regions. Exceptionally, Kyiv is the only city where a directly elected city mayor simultaneously serves as the head of the municipal state administration (the regional executive). In other regions, except for regional councils that represent regional self-government, the heads of regional state administrations are centrally appointed. In municipalities, voters elect municipal councils and mayors. In this book I am interested primarily in municipal council elections. The local amalgamation policy changed the geographical boundaries of most localities in Ukraine; however, the boundaries of cities having the status of *oblast* centers [*oblasni centry* in Ukrainian, or *oblast* capitals] did not change much. Thus, when investigating municipal council elections, I examine the electoral outcomes only in *oblast* capitals.

As a consequence of Russia's hybrid war against Ukraine, "[t]he regions now occupied by Russia or Russian proxies contained roughly 12 percent of the voters in the 2012 parliamentary elections" (D'Anieri 2019: 89). Since 2014, it has been impossible to hold any domestic elections in the Autonomous Republic of Crimea or the city of Sevastopol (due to annexation by Russia), and in the non-government-controlled territories in Donetska and Luhanska *oblasts* (due to the armed conflict in Donbas). Since 2014, Ukraine has not held regional council elections in Donetska and Luhanska *oblasts*. Internally displaced persons were not able to vote in the 2015 substate elections (Shapovalova and Romanova 2020: 210-212), but were able to cast their ballots in the 2020 substate contests.

Based on an analysis of the 2014 general contests, Chaisty and Whitefield (2018) conclude that the general terms of electoral competition in Ukraine did not change after 2014, despite crucial shifts in party politics. Based on an analysis of the Ukrainian presidential and parliamentary elections held in Donetska and Luhanska *oblasts* in 2019, Paul D'Anieri (2021) concludes that voter alignments that were identified before 2014 still persist. These research findings signal that it is possible to conduct a comparative analysis of elections held before and after 2014.

Officially, parties in Ukraine are all-Ukrainian. The 2001 Law "On Political Parties in Ukraine" prohibits regional parties (or non-statewide parties, if we apply the terminology used in the literature in the field of territorial politics). To be registered, a party must collect 10 thousand voter signatures in no less than two-thirds of the districts [*rayons*] in two-thirds of Ukraine's regions; that is, in 24 *oblasts*, the Autonomous Republic of Crimea, Kyiv, and Sevastopol. In practice, most parties, including the big winners of general contests, have had regionalized electorates since the early years of independence (e.g. Birch 1995, 1998; Melvin et al 1999; Melvin et al 2002; Katchanovski 2006; Melvin et al 2008; Clem and Craumer 2008). Strictly speaking, this undermines the distinction between statewide and non-statewide parties in Ukraine. In this book, I use "parliamentary party" when referring to a party that has an officially registered parliamentary faction in the corresponding multilevel electoral cycle. I categorize parliamentary parties into parties in office and parties in opposition. Conversely, I use "non-parliamentary party" to refer to a party that does not have an officially registered parliamentary faction in the corresponding multilevel electoral cycle.

In the three electoral cycles under consideration, parliament was elected according to a parallel system with a 50:50 split: 50% of the members (MPs) were elected according to first past the post (FPTP) in single-member electoral districts, while another 50% were elected according to closed-list proportional representation rules (CLPR) in multi-member electoral districts. The threshold was five percent. In 2020, regional and municipal council elections followed open-list proportional representation rules (OLPR) with a five percent threshold.[12] In 2015, another type of proportional representation rule obtained for regional and municipal council elections: CLPR, with a five percent threshold. In 2010, regional and municipal councils, local councils in towns/cities, were elected according to the parallel system with a 50:50 split: 50% of councillors were elected according to FPTP in single-member electoral districts, while another 50% were elected according to CLPR in multi-member electoral districts, with a three percent threshold. Every city/town was considered a multi-member district.

When exploring the incongruence of multilevel elections, for each *oblast* I examine (a) the dissimilarity between parties' parliamentary and municipal vote shares and (b) the dissimilarity between parties' parliamentary and regional vote shares. To measure these two types of dissimilarity, I calculate the dissimilarity index (Palares and Keating 2003; Jeffery and Hough 2009; Schakel 2015). I add the differences between parliamentary parties' vote shares gained in the parliamentary and either the regional or municipal elections in each *oblast* and then divide the sum by two. This helps me calculate the dissimilarity index for a given *oblast* in each

---

12 Local elections in rural and urban localities with less than 10,000 voters were held according to the multi-mandate majoritarian system.

multilevel electoral cycle and compute an average—the dissimilarity index for the whole country in each multilevel electoral cycle. In my calculations, I use parties' vote shares scored according to proportional representation rules. I obtain (a) the dissimilarity index referring to the parliamentary and municipal arenas and (b) the dissimilarity index referring to parliamentary and regional arenas in each multilevel electoral cycle. This enables me to compare how dissimilarity changes (i) before and (ii) after implementation of the decentralization reform.

Further, I compare the parties that gain the largest vote shares in the parliamentary, regional, and municipal elections in the same *oblast*s in each multilevel cycle under investigation. When exploring the fragmentation of the party system in the regional and municipal electoral arenas, I calculate the effective number of parties (ENP) for each regional and municipal contest and compute the average ENP for regional and municipal elections in each electoral cycle. I calculate the effective number of parties by taking the inverse of the sum of the fractional vote share of each party (Laakso and Taagepera 1979). Henderson and Romanova (2016) used these methods to investigate the incongruence between parliamentary and regional elections in 2006. In this book I adjust the methods for the comparative analysis of the incongruence of multilevel elections in the parliamentary, regional, and municipal arenas in Ukraine. Additionally, I identify instances of dominant-party rule, when parties-frontrunners in regional and municipal elections score more than 50% in the contests.

Finally, I examine the indirect elections of the heads of regional councils in 2010, 2015, and 2020. In line with Matsuzato (2002b), I compare the party affiliation of the heads of elected regional councils with the parties-frontrunners in the corresponding regional elections, identifying parties' alliances and strategies in the indirect elections. I interpret the outcomes as illustrating the scope of political competition in the regions.

I collected data on the electoral outcomes from primary sources. Also, data for the analysis of the indirect elections of regional councils' heads in 2010 and 2015 was obtained from the Dataset "Political elites in Ukrainian regions" hosted by the University of Tokyo. The corresponding data on the most recent electoral cycle was collected from the official websites of regional councils. When identifying what accounts for parties' electoral success or failure in the 2020 substate elections and whether or not parties were responsive to the incentives provided by the decentralization reform, and also when assessing parties' interactions during the indirect elections of the heads of regional councils, I complement primary sources with secondary ones.

I find that the dissimilarity between the outcomes of parliamentary and municipal elections in the 2019/2020 multilevel electoral cycle doubled compared to the 2014/2015 electoral cycle. Moreover, the 2019/2020 electoral cycle witnesses the most striking extent of vertical incongruence between the frontrunners in the parliamentary and municipal contests. However, I find that the extent of vertical congruence between parties-frontrunners in the regional and municipal arenas in the corresponding units did not change much in the three multilevel electoral cycles studied. Notably, after the 2020 substate contests, the extent of vertical congruence between parties-frontrunners in the simultaneous regional and municipal council elections was higher than in the parliamentary and substate electoral arenas.

Importantly, comparative research demonstrates the decline of the fragmentation of Ukraine's party system in the municipal electoral arena after the decentralization reform was implemented. Simply put, the municipal councils elected in 2020 are less fragmented compared to the ones in the 2015 elections.

It was reasonable to expect that the ruling party and the opposition parties would seek to increase their representation at the substate scales. However, the scope of the decentralization introduced in advance of the 2020 contests was probably not significant enough to generate feasible incentives for the domestic parliamentary parties. They did not make enough of an effort to improve their institutionalization, leading to a loss in competitiveness. As a result, the electoral performance of the non-parliamentary parties improved. This reflected the enhanced capacities of ambitious local incumbents to contest the 2020 elections separately from parliamentary parties and to distance themselves from those (central) actors on whose support they used to rely in previous substate contests.

Because the fragmentation of the regional councils remained high in 2020, it stimulated compromises in the election of heads of regional councils; in many instances, these benefited the ruling party in Kyiv. In 2020, there were ten instances of the heads of regional councils whose affiliations did not align with the parties that came first in the regional elections. In eight out of ten of these, the Center's ruling Servant of the People party was the beneficiary. In the overwhelming number of instances, in 2020, the parliamentary parties that opposed the Center's ruling party failed to secure their leadership positions in regional councils. Comparative research shows that regional governors' engagement in the indirect elections of the heads of regional councils declined in 2020. Even without the regional governors' input, the new ruling party was able to obtain the leading positions in the elected regional councils in nearly one half of the country despite not leading the race in most instances in the 2020 regional council elections.

The structure of the book is as follows.

- **Chapter 1** investigates the major policy learning efforts that contributed to establishing the pro-reform advocacy coalition capable of implementing the local amalgamation policy in 2014-2020. ACF is then used to explain the outcomes of post-2014 decision-making regarding the increase in local authority.
- **Chapter 2** explains why policymakers generally agreed on granting regional councils constitutional rights to establish their own executive committees, but did not handle the task in advance of the 2020 contests. It argues that the long period of policy learning was not accompanied by a consensus regarding the division of responsibilities between the core central, regional, and local authorities after the anticipated augmentation of regional authority.
- **Chapter 3** reviews the ongoing research on the shifts in the geographical contours of the party system since 2014 and shows the added value of applying a multilevel perspective to elections.

- **Chapter 4** investigates in detail how parties' electoral performance changed in the parliamentary, regional, and municipal electoral arenas both before and after the implementation of the decentralization reform. It assesses the congruence of parties' vote shares in multilevel arenas, compares parties-frontrunners in the *oblasts*, evaluates the degree of fragmentation of the party system at the regional and municipal levels, and identifies cases where dominant-party rule was established in the regional and municipal councils in the three electoral cycles under investigation.
- **Chapter 5** investigates how party competition changed after the local amalgamation policy was implemented. It seeks to understand what accounts for parties' electoral success or failure in the 2020 substate elections, and examines whether Ukraine's parliamentary and non-parliamentary parties were responsive to the incentives provided by the decentralization reform.
- **Chapter 6** studies instances when the party affiliations of the heads of regional councils did not align with the party affiliation of the frontrunners in the corresponding regional elections. Also, it explores how the strategies that parties employ to enable such shifts signal the prevalence of either confrontation or cooperation at the critical moment of decision-making in regional councils.

1 The Rise of Local Authority

This chapter seeks to explain why the reformers succeeded in consolidating and empowering local authorities in advance of the 2020 substate contests. It analyzes the government's decentralization policy documents drafted before the Euromaidan Uprising and submitted to the Council of Europe for feedback. These policy documents represent the major policy learning component that enabled the policymakers who came to power in 2014, and possessed the political will for policy change, to initiate the reform. The chapter further assesses post-2014 decision-making related to the increase of local authority and explains its outcomes using ACF.

Policy Learning

Arguably, the very first policy document to mention the objective of local amalgamation was the Concept on Administrative Reform in Ukraine approved by Presidential Decree № 810/98 in 1998 (the 1998 Concept). President Leonid Kuchma approved the 1998 Concept the year after Ukraine ratified the European Charter of Local Self-Government (1997) and introduced the law "On Local Self-government" (1997). The 1998 Concept contained a policy measure "to integrate territorial communities." The document's concluding section included the task "to outline the measures related to implementing the policy of integrating territorial communities" [*nakreslyty zahody shchodo zdiisnennya polityky integracii terytorialnyh hromad*]. According to Malynovskyi (2013: 19), the associated working group did not hold any meetings or produce any relevant policy outputs. Thus, the 1998 Concept policy measure ("to integrate territorial communities") was not carried out by policymakers. At the same time, the responsibilities of regional executives were strengthened. In exchange for providing administrative support to the president and pro-presidential political parties during the presidential elections of 1999 and the parliamentary elections of 1998 and 2002, regional executives acquired the predominance of power on the substate levels (Matsuzato 2001: 422).

The second attempt took place in 2005. The Concept on Administrative-Territorial Reform (the 2005 Concept) was drafted by

The second attempt took place in 2005. The Concept on Administrative-Territorial Reform (the 2005 Concept) was drafted by the working group chaired by Roman Bezsmertnyi, the First Deputy Prime Minister in the government led by Prime Minister Yulia Tymoshenko.[13] The 2005 Concept proposed the objective of improving the capacities of the state and self-government to provide services to citizens and to boost regional development. According to Tkachuk (2007: 6), the working group drafted three policy proposals. The first proposal envisioned establishing eight regions in Ukraine; 250–500 subregions (*rayons*), and 4,000 territorial communities (*hromadas*). The second proposal recommended establishing no more than two levels in the administrative-territorial system comprising approximately 70 regions and 5,000 communities. The third proposal was the basis of the draft law "On the Territorial Structure of Ukraine." It recommended introducing a three-level administrative-territorial system: regions, including all *oblasts*, Crimea and Sevastopol, and the so-called "cities-regions" (cities with at least 750,000 residents); subregions (*rayons*) with no fewer than 70,000 residents, including the so-called "cities-*rayons*" (cities with more than 70,000 residents); and territorial communities (*hromadas*) with no fewer than 5,000 residents. Notably, the reform was meant to start in territorial communities. Small localities were expected to merge in order to improve their ability to provide basic services to residents; the number of subregions (*rayons*) was expected to shrink. The 2005 Concept recommended introducing the principle of subsidiarity. The proposal recommended transferring some competences from the subregional level to territorial communities. The working group collected the relevant data and made the data-

---

[13] Previously Bezsmertnyi was the parliamentary representative of President Kuchma (1997-2002) and served on the parliament's Committee on State Building and Local Governance (1998-2002). Afterwards he joined Our Ukraine [*Nasha Ukraina*] — the party that opposed President Kuchma. After the victory of the Orange Revolution, he joined the central government. In November 2005 — soon after Prime Minister Tymoshenko was dismissed in September 2005 — Bezsmertnyi left his position. In 2006, he became an MP and joined the Committee on State Building, Regional Policy, and Local Governance.

driven calculations related to amending local and subregional units in Vinnytska, Luhanska, Ivano-Frankivska, and Odeska *oblasts* (Tkachuk 2007: 6).

Those familiar with the original policy recommendations of the Bezsmertnyi-chaired working group conclude that his "reform package … served as the main model for the decentralization reforms … being proposed in the country [in 2014]" (USAID 2014: 13), and "a new decentralization plan [proposed in 2014] is being drawn up that draws heavily from the plan originally spearheaded by Bezsmertnyi in 2006-08" (USAID 2014: 14).

The 2005 Concept and the supporting law drafts were officially submitted to the Council of Europe, as evidenced by the Council's Appraisal of the Concept Paper and Draft Law on the Administrative-Territorial Reform of Ukraine issued on 16 February 2009 (Council of Europe 2009). The Appraisal states that "[a] comprehensive administrative territorial reform (ATR) of local government and local state administration has been on the agenda of Ukraine for many years. In autumn 2005, a detailed reform programme, with a strategic document and five draft laws, had already been submitted to the Council of Europe for an opinion. However, this reform project never reached the parliamentary discussion stage." Based on interviews with local stakeholders and experts, USAID (2014: 14) suggests that the major constraint was "resistance from local populations. Many communities did not want to abandon their present village councils for larger units in the form of *hromadas*. In discussing this history with interviewees, numerous people outside of Kyiv noted that the failure to convince local populations of the structure was due to the fact that it was a decision being imposed from Kyiv, and they did not understand its purpose." Maynzyuk and Dzhygyr (2010: 270) state that the 2005 Concept "was widely criticized for weak argumentation and understanding of [the] fiscal and political consequences of creating an additional local tier, as well as its costs." Although Tkachuk (2007) claims that the draft law "On the Territorial Structure of Ukraine" was widely discussed throughout Ukraine, Maynzyuk and Dzhygyr (2010: 270) maintain that the 2005 Concept was "developed by an isolated group of experts and presented as a ready-made piece of draft legislation, lacking consideration of alternative opinions, and lacking statistical evidence in the argument."

The third attempt to move forward the policy agenda of local amalgamation was made in 2008-2009. In October 2008, the newly established Ministry of Regional Development and Construction approved guidelines for data collection and data analysis to study the possibility of designing capable and sustainable territorial communities. The guidelines outlined the modelling stages and specified the supporting documents (data) required. The regional authorities were in charge of their implementation. The Deputy Minister of Regional Development and Construction, Anatoliy Tkachuk, supervised the regional authorities that drafted the design of the territorial communities.

On 29 July 2009, the Cabinet of Ministers, led by Prime Minister Yulia Tymoshenko, approved the Concept on Local Government Reform (the 2009 Concept) that was presented to the government by the Ministry of Regional Development and Construction (Order № 900-p). The 2009 Concept was crafted following the conclusion of data collection and analysis. On 2 December 2009, the government approved its Action Plan (Decree № 1456-r). The Action Plan outlined the laws that were to be drafted by the government in 2010, including those on the amalgamation of territorial communities and the revision of Ukraine's administrative and territorial divisions in line with service provision needs.

According to the text cited in Aleksandrova and Koliushko (2011), the 2009 Concept stated that localities' self-governing bodies would operate within new territorial boundaries, the distance between the administrative center and the most remote periphery being no greater than 11 km. These territorial communities were meant to have direct inter-budgetary relations with the central budget (Aleksandrova and Koliushko 2011: 426). The 2009 Concept stressed the principle of subsidiarity in public service delivery. It called for transferring power to the lowest level at which it was feasible and appropriate to exercise power. It also emphasized the necessity to provide funding for carrying out duties by assigning additional tax shares to local budgets and sharing funds from the central budget, applying a formula-based approach in order to minimize bargaining. However, the complete set of principles for identifying the territorial boundaries of all administrative and territorial units was outlined in another policy document, the Concept on Reforming the Administrative-Territorial Structure of Ukraine, drafted in 2009, which aimed at "providing accessibility and quality in the delivery of public and administrative services to people" (Aleksandrova and Koliushko 2011: 425).

Aleksandrova and Koliushko (2011: 422) state that the working group that drafted this Concept carefully studied the policy drafts produced "during the first attempt to introduce the [administrative-territorial] reform [i.e., presumably, in 2005]" and similar reforms in other countries, such as Poland. They further maintain that the draft of the 2009 Concept was submitted to the regional state administration, regional councils, and local self-government associations, some of which provided feedback. The Ministry submitted a draft of the 2009 Concept to the Council of Europe for feedback.

The Council presented its Appraisal of the Concept Paper and Draft Law on the Administrative-Territorial Reform of Ukraine on 16 February 2009 (Council of Europe 2009). Notably, the Appraisal acknowledged the ongoing policy learning trajectory. It stated: "The 2008 ATR project builds on the 2005 project. The documents prepared by the Ukrainian Ministry for Regional Development and Construction are clearer and better developed than the previous drafts, from the viewpoint of both their political scope and implementation strategy" (Council of Europe 2009: 2). While welcoming the 2009 Concept paper and highlighting its progress compared with the 2005 Concept, the Appraisal recommended further revisions before proceeding with local amalgamation. Notably, the Appraisal paid special attention to maintaining a balance between bottom-up and top-down incentives for local amalgamation, as suggested in the Concept. "The draft Law provides for a bottom-up consolidation process, as the establishment of the new *hromadas* builds on voluntary merging (compulsory decisions being taken only after the one-year deadline for voluntary merging)" (Council of Europe 2009: 5). "While the time limit of one year ... may be taken as providing strong encouragement to existing communities to merge into viable hromadas, it is understood that if they do not do this voluntarily, new hromadas will be created by working groups set up by the Cabinet of Ministers. If the working groups are to deliver their proposals within one year, the current Concept paper and draft Law do not provide an adequate basis" (Council of Europe 2009: 18).

The 2010 presidential elections changed the ruling elites in Ukraine. Somewhat unexpectedly, in 2010, the Ministry of Regional Development and Construction prepared the draft law "On Stimulation and State Support of Unification of Rural Territorial Communities." It proposed that new territorial communities would have at least 4,000 residents, and the distance between the administrative center of every Amalgamated Territorial Community (ATC) and its most remote village should not exceed 20 km. The Ministry submitted this law to the Council of Europe for feedback, receiving an Appraisal from the Council on 22 February 2011. The Appraisal opens with the statement: "The draft law on '*Stimulation and State Support of Unification of Rural Territorial Communities*' should become a part of the legal basis for implementing an ambitious local self-government reform [outlined in the Concept for which the Council of Europe had previously provided feedback], together with the draft laws 'On Local Self-Government' and 'On Local State Administration'. An introductory sentence of the draft law explains that '*this Law establishes the procedure for the resolution of issues related to the unification of rural territorial communities*.' The draft law provides for a legal framework for amalgamating rural communities (*hromadas*) in order to improve service provision and save administrative costs ... It is ... submitted before the general Strategy for local self-government in Ukraine is adopted, although the need for the Strategy has been discussed for more than ten years and has given rise to many reform projects under all governments" (Council of Europe 2011: 2). This suggests that the draft law "On Stimulation and State Support of Unification of Rural Territorial Communities" looked like an attempt to further the policy procedures that were initially designed under the previous government(s). The notable difference was the exclusive focus on rural communities (villages, settlements). This indicates that the central policymakers who came to power in 2010 considered the option of excluding urban communities (cities, including the cities of *oblast* significance) from local amalgamation.

One of the core concerns of the Council of Europe regarded the incentives for local amalgamation. The Appraisal questioned the feasibility of the policy claim that either a village council/initiative group consisting of at least ten inhabitants or subregional authorities — the sub-regional (*rayon*) state administration and sub-regional councils — would be capable of initiating and organizing local amalgamation. The Appraisal suggested that the input of regional authorities should be considered, too (Council of Europe 2011: 10-11). Additionally, the Appraisal doubted whether the financial incentives envisioned in the draft law for the newly amalgamated communities would be enough to motivate the merger of local communities and ensure their ability to deliver public services of reasonable quality (Council of Europe 2011: 13-15).

On 14 December 2011, the Ukrainian government's draft of the law "On Amalgamation of Territorial Communities" № 9590 was registered in parliament. It looked like an upgraded version of the previous policy document on local amalgamation in Ukraine. The draft law envisioned the guiding role of the central government, which was meant to approve a perspective plan for establishing amalgamated territorial communities in each *oblast*. In turn, local authorities were expected to agree to amalgamation, in line with the government's suggestions. Then local referenda or conferences in localities were envisioned as a means to ensure approval for amalgamation and give local authorities the grounds to approve it. Afterwards regional councils would give their approval, and regional executives would inform the government and apply for funding from the central budget via the central government. The parliamentary committee on state building and local self-government submitted the draft of the law "On Amalgamation of Territorial Communities" to the Council of Europe for feedback. On 13 March 2012, the Council of Europe presented its Appraisal. Anatoliy Tkachuk was one of the experts who prepared the Appraisal on behalf of the Council of Europe. The Appraisal acknowledged that this new draft extended the principles of the Draft Law of Ukraine "On Stimulation and State Support of Unification of Rural Territorial Communities," but removed several previous inconsistencies (Council of Europe 2012a: 4). While the Appraisal welcomed the idea of "perspective plans" of new territorial communities, it drew attention to the lack of guidelines on (i) the drafting of the "perspective plans" by the regional state administration according to the methodology outlined by the government; (ii) approval of the plans by the respective regional council; and (iii) the submission of the plans for the government's final approval (Council of Europe 2012a: 6-9). As a matter of fact, the draft of the law "On Amalgamation of Territorial Communities" № 9590 did not pass the first reading stage in parliament on 17 May 2012, and this illustrated central policymakers' lack of political will to introduce the policy change.

In 2012, the policymakers annulled the 2009 Concept; simultaneously, they proceeded to including the local amalgamation policy in their decentralization reform plans. This is evident from three drafts of the Concept of Reforming Local Self-government and the Territorial Organization of Power to which the Council of Europe refers in its three feedback reports in 2012 and 2013. In all three cases, the Council of Europe was explicit about its approval, pending some minor revisions.

The first draft of the Concept prepared by the Ukrainian government in 2012 was accompanied by a policy document that presented the government's risk assessment and placed the policy recommendations in relation to some alternative scenarios and an overview of feedback that the government received from various domestic stakeholders (*Dopovidna Zapyska* 2012). According to the Appraisal prepared by the Council of Europe (at the request of the government) on 12 June 2012, the 2012 draft of the Concept presented a substantial basis for launching the decentralization reform in Ukraine, once some revisions were introduced into it. The Appraisal stressed the need to provide incentives to territorial communities to motivate them to join the voluntary amalgamation process.

Also, it highlighted that the policy document did not specify how local governance was expected to achieve and sustain financial autonomy and did not touch upon the transferring and training of personnel once amalgamation was completed (Council of Europe 2012b).

The Report of the Centre of Expertise for Local Governance Reform of the Council of Europe, prepared on 12 September 2012, was in response to the second draft of the Concept prepared by the Ukrainian government in 2012. The Report highlighted that it represented feedback on the sixth draft of Ukraine's concept of decentralization and reasserted that the policy document represented a substantial basis for launching the reform, once the domestic government introduced some revisions into it. In particular, the Council of Europe welcomed the intention of the draft Concept to identify financial incentives for local amalgamation, but recommended greater specificity, especially in outlining personal income tax shares that would benefit the budgets of the new territorial communities (Council of Europe 2012c).

The Appraisal of the Council of Europe delivered on 1 October 2013 (Council of Europe 2013) referred to the 2013 draft of the Concept. Again, Anatoliy Tkachuk was one of the experts who prepared the Appraisal on behalf of the Council of Europe. The Appraisal emphasized that "[t]he draft of the Concept prepared in August 2013 does not substantially differ from the drafts prepared in March and September 2012" (Council of Europe 2013: 3). The Appraisal welcomed (without question) the fact that the draft Concept was discussed with substate authorities, including municipalities across the country. However, it stressed that the 2013 draft of the Concept still did not cover the matter of the transferring and training of personnel. Most importantly, the Appraisal stated that "all Concepts [on Reforming Local Self-government and the Territorial Organization of Power] submitted to the Council of Europe for feedback represent the adequate basis for the comprehensive reform of local self-government; the CoE continues recommending the approval of the Concept on the highest political level without further discussions and delays. Later on, when implementing the reform and drafting the corresponding legal acts, it would be possible to introduce further improvements and amendments. Nevertheless, the authorities decided to take one more year and prepare a new edition of the Concept's draft, which does not differ much from the previous versions. In addition, the majority of recommendations of the CoE was not considered; the 2013 draft is not the improved version of the Concept. The major change is that the action plan covers a longer period of time. Nevertheless, the CoE advises to approve this version of the Concept" (Council of Europe 2013: 2-3).

Having compared the content of the policy documents under study, I observe an unexpected continuity in the policy learning efforts undertaken by different domestic governments in 2005-2013. Prior to 2014, policymakers had enough political will to draft the Concepts regarding decentralization reforms and laws on local amalgamation. But the failure of parliament to approve the law on local amalgamation in May 2012 illustrates a limited capacity to introduce policy change in practice. Still, domestic authorities' largely uninterrupted policy learning efforts contributed to shaping core policy beliefs with respect to local amalgamation and provided fertile ground for introducing policy change, as happened when the focusing event occurred (i.e. the post-Euromaidan change of elites) and when the 2014 Concept on Reforming Local Self-government and the Territorial Organization of Power was adopted.

Policy Change

In 2014, the policy opportunity structure allowed civil society influence in policymaking (Shapovalova and Burlyuk 2018). Core civil society actors with key policy learnings were able to promote policy change. The civil society actors who had contributed to the initial policy design of decentralization in 2008-2009 shared their policy learning experiences with the policymakers who assumed office in 2014. "Many of the same experts who had worked on Yushchenko and Bezsmertnyi's failed decentralization reforms previously [prior to the Euromaidan Uprising] are working with the government on new constitutional amendments now [i.e. since 2014]" (USAID

2014: 7). Probably the most revealing examples of such experts were Anatoliy Tkachuk (Civil Society Institute), Yuri Hanushchak (Institute for Regional Development) and Ihor Koliushko (Centre for Political and Legal Reforms), all of whom had acquired extensive policy experience drafting policy documents on decentralization in 2008-2009. In 2014, Tkachuk was appointed as an advisor to Minister Hroysman. In Spring 2015, Tkachuk, Hanushchak, and Koliushko joined the Constitutional Commission established by President Poroshenko.

In Spring-Summer 2014, domestic policymakers intended to launch the local amalgamation policy by amending the Constitution. USAID (2014) presents a comprehensive overview of this scenario and discusses its rationale and constraints. Due to lack of political will in parliament, the introduction of constitutional amendments necessary for local amalgamation did not proceed further than the drafting stage.

The policy change began with the introduction of financial incentives to promote local amalgamation. In December 2014, parliament amended the budget and tax codes and introduced fiscal decentralization, aimed at enabling ATCs to assume responsibility for public service delivery (primary and secondary education, primary healthcare [up to 2018], administrative services, local development, etc.).

ATCs obtained "independent budgets, made of tax grants and non-tax revenues, and have direct fiscal relations with the central government via their oblast administrations" (OECD 2018: 178). ATCs were granted direct inter-budgetary relations with the Center. This was meant to make inter-budgetary relations transparent, as well as to make local authorities less dependent on substate executives whose decisions often involved bargaining (Tkachuk 2017). In fact, ATCs were granted budgetary benefits similar to those of the cities of *oblast* significance, with greater taxation powers and an increased tax share, including a 60% share of Personal Income Tax.

ATCs also received donations and subventions (including a subvention for establishing institutional and social infrastructure in newly established ATCs until 2020) and special equalization grants for ameliorating disparities in local development in different territorial communities. As highlighted by the OECD, "[p]rior to 2015, the grant system was comprised of one equalisation grant and one social grant, together representing 90% of all transfers ... After the 2014 reform, there are still two main categories of grants, but their composition is very different than before. There is the equalisation grant and several formula-based central government transfers earmarked to fund sectoral expenditures, particularly in the education and health sectors" (OECD 2018: 189).

Also, local authorities in ATCs were granted the right to apply to the State Fund for Regional Development in order to get co-funding for local development projects. Previously only regional authorities were eligible to apply (Zhalilo et al 2019: 67).[14]

Still, it was not always easy for local communities to gauge the extent of financial resources that they could count on in the future. "Delegated expenditure (i.e. in healthcare, education, social protection) amount[ed] to almost 80% of subnational expenditure ... Many local authorities lack[ed] the resources to support their exclusive competences, in particular those necessary for the economic and social development of their territories" (OECD 2018: 207). Financial support especially designed to help infrastructure development in the newly established ATCs was available between 2015-2020, but that incentive was more beneficial for the communities that amalgamated early. In 2017, "the level of financial incentives offered by the central government for *hromadas* to amalgamate began to recede; in 2017, the 207 new ATCs that were formed received only 465 hryvnia per capita of investment from the central budget, compared to 785 hryvnia in 2016" (Dudley 2019: 19). This decline partially resulted from the fact that the amount of money annually allocated for the subsidy of social and economic territorial development and the subsidy of infrastructure development did not automatically increase as more ATCs were established. Although "[t]he new system of local taxes and fees comprises four main local taxes:

---

14 The State Fund for Regional Development was established in 2013, before the decentralization reform was introduced.

the single tax (also called the unified tax), the property tax, the parking fee and the tourist tax...[,] local taxes and fees still represent a small share of subnational tax revenues and total revenues, respectively 29% and 12%" (OECD 2018: 198).

With this in mind, Levitas and Djikic stress that the increased finances available to ATCs went hand in hand with increased responsibilities, not to mention that those increased financial gains were generated by and large at the expense of regional and subregional budgets' income. "[D]ecentralisation has resulted in a reallocation of spending responsibilities across subnational levels (particularly from the rayon to cities and the UTCs [ATCs]) instead of a reallocation of charges between the central (ministry) and subnational levels" (OECD 2018: 181). While fiscal decentralization benefited ATCs and the cities of *oblast* significance in 2015-2016 (Levitas and Djikic 2017), "2017 saw a slowdown in their momentum and a significant boost to the budgets of oblasts in particular, which has caused concern that the expected shift of resources from oblasts and rayons to ATCs might be stalling ... Oblast revenues, meanwhile, grew by 44% in 2017 compared to the previous year, and rayon revenues by 15%" (Dudley 2019: 19). Notably, "[p]rior to the reform, PIT [Personal Income Tax] receipts were fully redistributed to the subnational governments (except for Kiev). With this reform, the central government now receives 25% of the PIT as a general rule" (OECD 2018: 195).

Local amalgamation procedures deserve special attention. Soon after introducing financial incentives for local amalgamation in December 2014, the parliament adopted the Law "On Voluntary Amalgamation of Territorial Communities" in February 2015. In April 2015, the government approved "The Methodology for Establishing Sustainable Territorial Communities" that outlined the criteria for ATCs and specified the procedure for local amalgamation.[15] The government's guidelines for local amalgamation

---

15 For example, it was possible to amalgamate local self-government units within territories that were contiguous, which were located within the same region, and which possessed historical, natural, ethnic, cultural or other unifying characteristics. Potential amalgamation partners could be no more than 25–30 km

emphasized identification of the administrative centers of potential ATCs—the locality where most public services were expected to be delivered to the residents of an ATC. This approach to local amalgamation implied that those localities that did not fit the corresponding criteria had little chance of becoming the administrative centers of ATCs.

The procedures of local amalgamation comprised bottom-up and top-down dimensions as follows.

On the one hand, local mayors, local councillors (numbering no less than one-third of the local council's strength), and local residents could initiate the voluntary amalgamation of territorial communities. According to the government-imposed rules, the initiators would then invite their local partners to join public discussions regarding their potential amalgamation (in line with the government's methodology on the choice of the prospective ATC's location, the development of the prospective ATC's infrastructure, etc.). On reaching a consensus, they drafted the decisions of the local council and passed them on to the relevant regional state administration in order to double-check compliance with the constitution and domestic laws. Given a positive response, the local council could decide to establish the ATC. However, this did not mark the end of the process. They then returned to the same regional state administration so that the latter would officially address the Central Electoral Committee and request it to schedule the first local authority election in the newly established ATC.[16] Only after the first local elections were held did the ATC officially receive the rights and responsibilities to which it was entitled.

---

away from the ATC center, while the ATC center was required to be a relatively large local government unit with administrative and social infrastructure.

16 The elected local authorities in the newly established ATC included a directly elected head of the ATC and a directly elected local council (once elected, the council appointed its own executive committee). A proportional representation electoral system was applied. In addition, residents of those villages and towns situated outside the settlement where the administrative center of the ATC was located directly elected their representative, who then joined the executive committee of the local council of the ATC. A majoritarian electoral system was applied in this case.

On the other hand, regional authorities in each *oblast* prepared a "perspective plan" for its ATC. Along with the bottom-up processes of voluntary amalgamation, the government requested each regional state and regional council administration to prepare and consider approving an ATC "perspective plan," respectively (in line with the methodological guidelines). The "perspective plans" were then approved by the government to ensure that potential ATCs would have enough resources to assume responsibility for public service delivery at the local level (Romanova 2020a: 191).

Although the policy of local amalgamation had been drafted and re-drafted by the central government for quite a while, its implementation in 2014-2020 faced some challenges. I assume that the Center expected both regional governors and regional councils to join the pro-reform advocacy coalition. Presumably, the Ministry of Regional Development, Construction, Housing and Utilities fostered both top-down and bottom-up coordination between the ministry and the regional executives (who underwent rotation after the 2014 change in the ruling elites in Kyiv) when verifying the data previously collected from the regional state administration. The regional councils operative until the 2015 substate elections were elected in 2010; they possessed information about the upcoming local amalgamation policy and should have been prepared for its eventual implementation. After the 2015 substate elections, the one half of the country's heads of regional councils were affiliated with the president's ruling party. Still, there is little evidence that this helped mobilize regional councils into joining the pro-reform advocacy coalition.

There was the political will on the local level to engage in local amalgamation. After holding 149 interviews in 2017-2018 with representatives of the newly formed amalgamated territorial communities in the Kharkiv and Odesa regions, Bader (2021) found that in most cases mayors initiated local amalgamation. The most active initiators were local authorities in territorial communities with the potential to become the administrative centers of prospective ATCs, since such administrative centers would host not only the local council and the mayor, but also better schools (*oporna shkola*), better healthcare facilities, the center providing administrative services, etc.

Policy changes with respect to public services, over which ATCs gained additional responsibilities, required additional coordination in the government, because the decentralization reform and other reforms such as those involving healthcare, education, etc. were implemented simultaneously (Zhalilo et al 2019: 59). However, ministries in the same government could hold different views on public service provision at the substate level and on fiscal decentralization. Initially, the reformers planned to decentralize healthcare; however, they switched to introducing the centralized funding system as early as in 2017. "[N]umerous tasks [were] being transferred to the UTCs [ATCs] without a clear understanding of the impact in terms of charges and constraints. Apart from the fact that many small and/or under capacitated communities [were] ill-equipped to take on new responsibilities, the transfer of several functions to the local level is not always appropriate" (OECD 2018: 207).

Despite a number of challenges and a tight schedule, the local amalgamation policy completed the decision-making and decision-implementation stage in advance of the 2020 substate contests. In order to reach this goal, administrative means for local amalgamation were introduced. On 5 December 2019 regional councils lost their right to approve "perspective plans"; this augmented the role of the regional state administration in the process and gave the Center greater means to regulate the pace of local amalgamation (Zhalilo et al 2019: 14). While such administrative means to speed up local amalgamation signaled Kyiv's inconsistent decision-making, which first promoted the voluntary character of local amalgamation and then enforced it through government decree, switching to administrative amalgamation was critical to policy execution ahead of the substate elections scheduled for October 2020. By May 2019, 61.8% of the "old" territorial communities—around 6,774 villages and towns—had not voluntarily amalgamated. Approximately 30.13% of the Ukrainian population lived in non-amalgamated communities. 38.2% of the "old" communities (4,187 communities) had been amalgamated into 899 ATCs. They comprised

38.9% of Ukraine's territory and 27.2% of its population. In addition, 42.85% of Ukraine's population lived in cities of *oblast* significance, which enjoyed strong local self-governance even prior to amalgamation (*Monitorynh protsesu detsentralizatsiyi vlady ta reformuvannya mistsevoho samovryaduvannya stanom na 10 travnia 2019 roku* 2019: 4-9).

I suggest that the local amalgamation policy was finalized in a timely way, despite its numerous inconsistencies, largely because during agenda-setting, the government already possessed the major policy documents required: preliminary data analysis on local amalgamation, law drafts, and feedback generated by the Council of Europe's international and domestic experts. In addition, the Ministry of Regional Development, Construction, Housing and Utilities[17] combined its efforts with domestic experts (civil society actors) who had contributed to producing and revising those policy documents in 2008-2009. The core of the pro-reform advocacy coalition comprised policymakers and experts with similar policy beliefs and equipped with previously designed policy solutions based on data analysis and feedback from the Council of Europe's experts. I believe that these domestic experts were able to easily communicate their core beliefs to the Minister of Regional Development, Volodymyr Hroysman, because he had previously served as a city mayor and was familiar with the salient policy problem that the local amalgamation policy was intended to address.

Importantly, the political will existed to foster local amalgamation despite the subsequent changes in the ruling elites after the 2019 presidential and parliamentary elections. In September 2019, the newly elected President Zelenskyy announced his intention to foster decentralization. Subsequently, the president, the parliament and the government made decisions that largely followed (a) the 2014 Concept and (b) the Action Plan for completing the decentralization reform that the government of Volodymyr Hroysman had introduced in January 2019. Zelenskyy promoted the draft laws on the decentralization policy prepared under President Poroshenko,

---

17 On 29 August 2019, it changed its name into the Ministry for Communities and Territories Development of Ukraine.

which had the benefit of domestic and international experts but suffered from a lack of political will in parliament to proceed with policymaking. Largely due to the decisions made by the president, the government and the parliament in 2020, local amalgamation was fully completed in July 2020 by the use of administrative stimuli.

Finally, the government made efforts to address issues and problems during policy implementation in a timely manner. It relied on both domestic and international expertise (Rabinovych et al. 2018). Ukraine benefited from legal expertise provided through the Council of Europe program, including the "Decentralisation and Local Government Reform in Ukraine" project. Notably, an EU-led multi-donor Ukraine—Local Empowerment, Accountability and Development Programme (U–LEAD) (2016-2023) established its offices in each region to collect and analyze the data necessary for the assessment of reform proceedings in order to understand the errors made and recommend evidence-based policies to the Ukrainian government (DIIS 2018: 26). In addition, domestic think tanks such as the National Institute for Strategic Studies served a similar purpose by providing policy advice on decentralization to domestic policymakers. Moreover, since 2017, Germany's special envoy, Professor Georg Milbradt, has taken the initiative to reach out to central and substate policymakers involved in local amalgamation (Romanova and Umland 2019: 7).

Despite the numerous divisions within the pro-reform advocacy coalition and despite the challenges that it faced, its opponents, although not less numerous, suffered from far poorer organization.

Some local authorities resisted voluntary amalgamation when it became clear that their communities would not become administrative centers of the prospective ATCs. In such cases, the corresponding localities often faced the challenge of closing down their schools and hospitals after local amalgamation, although these difficult measures were balanced by the benefits of better schools and healthcare in the ATC's administrative centers. Additional measures regarding transportation were required, and people in remote localities had no expectation that such changes would occur.

As William Dudley puts it, "[o]ne of the consequences of the amalgamation process is that local facilities in many of the amalgamating villages will have to be closed and consolidated into single facilities for the entire hromada, a step necessitated not only by logistics but by Ukraine's dramatic demographic decline; there are many villages with very low-quality primary school and healthcare facilities, for example, that simply don't have the number of users to justify their presence. Despite this, hromada councils are often reluctant to agree to giving up facilities on their own ground, fearing that they will be unfairly treated in the redistribution of the new ATC's assets; the relocation of important schools and healthcare facilities to villages miles away can be quite a serious blow, especially given the generally abysmal state of roads in rural areas" (2019: 28).

Box 1.2. Public spending on education and healthcare.

In 2008, the World Bank calculated that "Ukraine has a greater number of health system inputs than EU countries. Ukraine has a large number of hospitals: 5.6 per 100,000 people in 2005. This is in contrast to averages of 2.6 per 100,000 for EU-10 countries and 3.2 per 100,000 for other EU members. In addition, in Ukraine there were 868 hospital beds per 100,000 people in 2005, compared to 644 for EU-10 countries and 571 for other EU countries. Regarding health personnel, there were more doctors in Ukraine (302 per 100,000 in 2005) than in EU-10 countries (261). And Ukraine had more nurses per 100,000 (782) than did EU-10 countries (548) or other EU members (750)" (World Bank 2008: xiii). With respect to schooling, "[p]ublic spending on education (mostly undertaken through local governments) is high (and is increasing) … Student/teacher ratios have been falling dramatically recent years, reaching 9.4 (average for 2005) for basic and secondary education. This ratio is one of the lowest in the world (almost half of the ratio for OECD countries)" (World Bank 2008: xvi).

Ten years later, the situation had not changed much: "Ukraine still has about 40 percent more hospital beds per capita than the EU average. This infrastructure consumes most of the available funding while often providing only very basic services … In recent years public spending on education has declined, however, despite falling enrolment rates Ukraine maintains an extensive network of education institutions" (World Bank 2017: 8; 10). "Ukraine has significantly more doctors, nurses and hospital beds per 100,000 inhabitants than the vast majority of EU countries and one of the lowest pupil/teacher ratios in the world" (Levitas and Djikic 2017: 15).

Poor territorial communities did not want to amalgamate if they lacked taxable enterprises and were not keen on managing social infrastructure even with the Center's financial support (Samoorg 2018: 2). Although they "often do not have the capacity to maintain and repair their medical and education facilities, as all their resources are dedicated to operating expenditure" (OECD 2018: 193), their inhabitants would still prefer to make use of the available facilities rather than gain access to better ones located in the ATCs' administrative centers. Additionally, rich territorial communities, such as the cities of *oblast* significance, did not want to amalgamate and share their resources with their poorer neighbors. In order to address the latter issue, parliament passed a law, signed by the president in May 2018, which required the cities of *oblast* significance to participate in local amalgamation when invited by suitable partners.

Based on data obtained from focus groups and interviews, the Ukrainian Center for Independent Political Research (UCIPR) argued that "[t]the lack of trust among members of financially weak communities regarding the fulfilment of existing social obligations by newly formed local self-government bodies posed a risk to decentralisation. In some regions, this challenge was met through the signing of memorandums between the territorial communities and local self-government bodies that set out detailed obligations in the area of social development (street lighting, roads, school repairs, etc.). In particular, communities of the Dnipropetrovsk region signed a memorandum setting out a clear action plan and obligations for all sides. As a rule, such memorandum items have been implemented after the amalgamations" (UCIPR 2017: 11).

Finally, after local amalgamation, mayors and councillors elected in the territorial communities that merged into ATCs lost their mandates and had to contest afresh in the first local elections within the newly established ATCs. This prospect discouraged some local policymakers, although it encouraged others who were ready to compete for votes and hoped to gain more opportunities once elected.

In addition to the local level, the reform faced resistance at the regional level. The limited progress of voluntary local amalgamation during 2015-2019 was largely due to regional councils' resistance to the regional ATC "perspective plans." The principal reason was their unwillingness to give up the responsibilities and resources associated with public service delivery. I also suggest that the new norms of fiscal decentralization, which disadvantaged the budgets of regional councils, could have demotivated regional councils from supporting the local amalgamation policy, because "virtually all types of Oblast revenue declined sharply after the 2015 reforms" (Levitas and Djikic 2017: 26). Most importantly, regional councils were often comprised of representatives of local interest groups, and their decision-making regarding local amalgamation reflected the corresponding business interests (USAID 2014: 17). "For example, in some places a dominant local powerbroker has seen in decentralization an opportunity to strengthen and extend his (it is almost invariably his) influence over a wider area through the creation of a new amalgamated community. By contrast, in other areas competing local powerbrokers have been wary of promoting a new amalgamated community in case their interests might be threatened if their rivals were to prosper from the change. Such rivalries between competing interests have sometimes been a factor in determining the boundaries between new communities" (UNDP 2019: 15). In most cases, regional governors' resistance was latent, that is, they delayed the drafting of the ATC "perspective plans."

Finally, there were constraints at the central level. Parliament's input was crucial; at times the resistance it demonstrated to the government's local amalgamation policy recommendations led to inconsistent policy implementation. Prior to the reform, "[t]he funding for exercising the powers delegated to local governments [were] allocated by the Verkhovna Rada [parliament] during the adoption of the state budget for every following year. However, in determining the ultimate volume of transfers to local budgets, VR deputies [MPs] [did] not take into account the financial state of local governments or the range of powers delegated to them. Consequently, the transfers [were] not always sufficient to fully finance the delegated powers" (Chumak and Shevliakov 2009: 8). The procedures did not change after 2014, and every year the representatives of the pro-reform advocacy coalition had to ask parliament to allocate the necessary funding to ATCs, etc. (e.g. Tkachuk 2017).

In addition, there was no political will in parliament to annul the subvention for the socio-economic development of the territories, which benefited MPs elected in single-member districts and who used the subvention to improve their electoral prospects. "The extent of such subventions, introduced originally in 2005 and widely used under the pre-Maidan government, has burgeoned in recent years … while the subventions are allocated for specific projects, the criteria for approving them are opaque. No objective, formula-based and transparent criteria have been officially stated or are detectable in practice … In practice, MPs themselves play a key role in selecting them ... Since these subvention-funded projects may respond to immediate community needs they are often popular with local constituents. However, the practice reinforces the quasi-feudal nature of local politics by reaffirming the classic role of local communities as recipients of 'gifts' from their political masters in exchange for electoral backing ..." (UNDP 2019: 9).

While MPs' voting behavior indirectly affected the speed of local amalgamation, the Central Electoral Commission repeatedly postponed its decision-making regarding the announcement of the first local elections in the newly merged ATCs and greatly contributed to delaying the implementation of the local amalgamation policy (Bevz 2020).

Nevertheless, the opponents of local amalgamation demonstrated a lower capacity for coordination than the pro-reform advocacy coalition. Moreover, political parties did not effectively guide their efforts. The political leaders of Fatherland and Opposition Bloc, the parties that opposed local amalgamation most strongly, contributed to the preparation of the major policy documents on local amalgamation in 2008-2009 and 2012-2013. This may explain why these parties criticized local amalgamation during electoral campaigns and in parliament, but did not promote alternative research-based policies that would address the same policy issues.

The comparative analysis of the major policy recommendations related to local amalgamation prepared by the government, in 2014 and earlier, reveals striking similarities. The texts of the two drafts of the Concept on Reforming Local Self-government and the Territorial Organization of Power prepared by the government in 2012 and 2013 contain numerous similarities to the 2009 Concept and, moreover, resemble the 2014 Concept approved by the government on 1 April 2014. There are some stylistic differences between the 2013 draft of the Concept and the 2014 Concept, but their content and structure are so remarkably alike that, at times, the two policy documents look nearly identical.

This chapter has pointed out that the pro-reform advocacy coalition succeeded in introducing and finalizing the local amalgamation policy thanks to its extensive policy learnings and because it included policymakers with the political will to make decisions and implement them with the assistance of advanced international institutional and financial support, which helped the government solve problems on the ground and prevented the opponents of local amalgamation from portraying the government's policy in a negative light. All of this helped to eliminate institutional opportunities to undermine policy implementation efforts on the substate level. The pro-reform advocacy coalition largely consolidated its decision-making and -implementing capacities after including the newly elected President Zelenskyy, who had no alternative decentralization agenda, along with the pro-presidential parliamentary majority and the pro-presidential government. As a result, the local amalgamation policy switched from encouraging voluntary adoption to exercising administrative tools, which helped finalize the policy ahead of the 2020 local elections, but which revealed a predominantly top-down policy.

The alternate advocacy coalition, which provided direct or indirect resistance, managed to slow down local amalgamation and posed a threat to its completion before the local elections scheduled for October 2020. In some instances, regional governors and regional councils tried to slow down local amalgamation to avoid undermining their power. Cities of *oblast* significance did not want to join the amalgamation process, as this would mean sharing resources with poorer neighbors. For their part, poor localities did not want to amalgamate with rich ones because they risked losing their small local councils and budgets and becoming deprived peripheries of large, wealthy amalgamated communities in which their interests were underrepresented. However, the alternate advocacy coalition lacked any alternative policy agenda backed by research-based insights and draft laws. I propose that, because the leadership of the parties that contributed to challenging local amalgamation in 2015-2020 had previously contributed to designing local amalgamation in 2005-2013, their resistance to the post-2014 decentralization policy was neither systematic nor continuous. The role of the alternate advocacy coalition was limited to blocking the existing policy proceedings and delaying implementation. This was successful on those occasions when the pro-reform advocacy coalition lacked the political will to overcome such resistance.

2 No Rise of Regional Authority

As evidenced by the 2014 Concept, policymakers agreed on granting regional councils constitutional rights to establish their own executive committees. Still, the reformers did not approve the required constitutional amendments in advance of the 2020 contests. In this chapter, I propose my explanation of why this happened. In contrast to the case of local amalgamation, the long experience of policy learning was not accompanied by policymakers' consensus regarding the division of duties between regional executives and substate councils. This was evidenced by the policymakers' lack of agreement on the draft laws to divide responsibilities between the core central, regional, and local authorities after the planned increase of regional authority.

Policy Learning

As stated in the Introduction, the early years of Ukraine's independence witnessed substantial policy changes related to regional authority. In line with the 1995 Constitutional Agreement between the president and the parliament, and with the 1996 Constitution, regional councils lost the constitutional right to appoint their executive committees (Wolczuk 2002). There followed an increase in the actual powers of the centrally appointed heads of *oblast* state administrations (Matsuzato 1999), who executed both the Center's decisions on the substate level and the decisions made by the corresponding regional councils. The dual subordination of regional executives led to a diffusion of responsibility (OECD 2014; OECD 2018). As Chumak and Shevliakov state, '[u]p to 80% of the powers of local governments are duplicated by the powers of local state administrations' (Chumak and Shevliakov 2009: 7).

Policymakers have mostly argued about increasing vs. limiting regional authority, or else about regional authorities' subordination to the president, the parliament, or the government. Their disputes lacked detailed data-driven policy recommendations on how to divide responsibilities between the core central, regional, and local authorities after the planned increase of regional authority.

and local authorities after the planned increase of regional authority.

The first attempt to change the "status quo" with respect to regional authority dates back to 2003. During Leonid Kuchma's second presidential term, the president and the parliamentary opposition, confronting each other, prepared a few constitutional drafts aimed at changing the responsibilities of central policymakers. One of those constitutional drafts explicitly referred to regional authority: the draft of the law on constitutional amendments № 3207-1, registered in the parliament on 1 July 2003. The draft law was produced by the temporary parliamentary constitutional commission; its co-authors represented numerous factions that opposed President Kuchma: the Yulia Tymoshenko Bloc (Anatolyi Matvienko), Viktor Yushchenko's Bloc "Our Ukraine" (Viktor Musiyaka), the Communist Party of Ukraine (Adam Martynyuk), and the Socialist Party of Ukraine (Oleksandr Moroz). Among other objectives, which included the distribution of power in the Center (Razumkov Centre 2007: 13),[18] the draft law recommended establishing executive committees in regional and subregional councils (Article 140). In Autumn 2003, the parliamentary opposition accepted the major policy recommendations related to the division of power between the president, the parliament, and the government in Draft Law № 4105, registered in parliament on 4 September 2003. The question of substate authorities and the administrative-territorial system became the priority objective of draft law № 3207-1. On 12 December 2003, this draft law passed the first reading stage in parliament and proceeded to the Constitutional Court of Ukraine, as procedurally required for constitutional amendments. When policymakers negotiated the 2004 constitutional reform during the Orange revolution, draft law № 3207-1 was included in the parliament's agenda, as a

---

18   The draft of the law № 3207-1 contained a recommendation to reorganize the administrative-territorial system of Ukraine by introducing the basic unit of the *hromada* (along with the corresponding basic unit of local governance) that would consist of one or several localities. This suggests that the initiators of the draft law may have (briefly) considered a local amalgamation policy.

part of a political compromise between the major contending parties. On 8 December 2004, it (again) passed the first reading stage and proceeded to the Constitutional Court of Ukraine. On this occasion,[19] it took the Constitutional Court of Ukraine more time to make its decision with respect to the law draft. On 7 September 2005 it decided that draft law 3207-1 largely satisfied the requirements of Articles 157 and 158 of the Constitution of Ukraine, and made a few minor suggestions to introduce further improvements.

By that time, the political regime in Ukraine had already shifted to parliamentary-presidentialism as a result of the 2004 constitutional reform; the responsibilities of the parliament had strengthened, whereas the power of the president had been weakened (Matsuzato 2005). The 2004 constitutional reform did not affect the authority of regional councils; it considered center–periphery relations only in the context of power distribution in the Center (Romanova 2011a). According to the 2004 constitutional reform, the heads of regional state administration became responsible to the president and the government. This was in contrast to their primary subordination to the president, according to the 1996 Constitution. In line with the 2004 constitutional reform, the president was granted the right to appoint the heads of (sub)regional state administrations only through negotiations with the central government, with a similar procedure being in place for their dismissal.

Having achieved the core goal of changing the division of power in the Center, domestic policymakers were hesitant about introducing any further changes regarding regional authority. During the parliamentary hearings on "Decentralization of Power in Ukraine: To Broaden the Rights of Local Self-Government" held on 12 October 2005, Roman Bezsmertnyi—the First Deputy Prime Minister in the government led by Prime Minister Yulia Tymoshenko—attempted to foster draft law № 3207-1, along with the Concept on the Administrative-Territorial Reform that envisioned establishing subregional (rather than regional) councils' executive

---

19   On 30 October 2003, the Constitutional Court of Ukraine decided that draft law № 3207-1 largely satisfied the requirements of the Constitution of Ukraine, namely Articles 157-158.

committees. During the parliamentary hearings, he explicitly highlighted the need to establish executive committees in subregional (*rayon*) councils: "The responsibilities of regional state administrations (executive functions) should be delegated to the corresponding self-governing bodies" (*Parlamentski Sluhannia* 2005). MPs and substate authorities demonstrated their common lack of understanding of this matter (*Parlamentski Sluhannia* 2005). On 23 December 2005, Draft Law № 3207-1 was (once again) passed by MPs and directed to the Constitutional Court of Ukraine. However, policymakers' lack of eagerness to jointly promote the policy change meant that the draft law proceeded no further.

The next attempt began on 29 July 2009, when the government approved the Concept on Reforming Local Self-government (the 2009 Concept), presented by the newly established Ministry of Regional Development and Construction of Ukraine. Among other objectives, the policy document recommended the introduction of executive committees in regional councils. The 2009 Concept anticipated that the requisite changes would be implemented at the fourth (and last) stage of the decentralization reform. The 2009 Concept was followed by an Action Plan that outlined the laws that the government would draft in 2010, including amendments to the 1997 Law "On Local Self-government in Ukraine" and the 1999 Law "On Regional State Administration." The Council of Europe, in its Appraisal of the Concept Paper and Draft Law on the Administrative-Territorial Reform of Ukraine, presented on 16 February 2009, stated: "This is the first time since discussions in Ukraine on local government reform started that such a major change has been considered by the Government" (Council of Europe 2009: 5).

The 2010 presidential elections led to a change in the ruling elites. The new authoritarian turn soon became evident. On 30 September 2010, the newly elected President Yanukovych restored the 1996 Constitution, in line with a controversial decision by the Constitutional Court.[20] This led to strengthening the role of regional

---

20   One of the first decisions taken after the triumph of the Euromaidan Uprising on 21 February 2014 was to restore the 2004 constitutional reform.

governors at the substate scales, directly subordinated to the president. Ukraine under President Yanukovych represented the case of a ruling party in the Centre, which took office with a regionalist manifesto, promoting centralization (Romanova 2010). The ruling party's "pre-electoral and post-electoral positions on the centre-periphery relations significantly differ ... When in national office, [it] promote[s] centralisation, which is beneficial for [the] territorial interest groups they represent—territorially bounded heavy industries that require central investment" (Romanova 2011b).

Simultaneously, a few signs indicated that there was the political will to introduce executive committees into regional councils and to empower the directly elected regional councils—and to amend the Constitution for these purposes.

In 2011, the Constitutional Assembly—an advisory body subordinated to the President of Ukraine—was established. Its agenda was broad and included the increase of regional authority. In 2012 and 2013, the government prepared drafts of the Concept on Reforming Local Self-government, which recommended introducing executive committees into regional councils. To a very considerable extent, both resembled the 2009 Concept on Reforming Local Self-government, and I have no doubt that they were based on the 2009 Concept.

As stated in chapter 1, in 2012-2013 the domestic authorities repeatedly requested the Council of Europe's feedback on the decentralization reform agenda. The Council of Europe's feedback report, delivered on 12 June 2012 (Council of Europe 2012a), confirmed its opinion that the draft of the Concept presented in 2012 was relatively ready for approval by the domestic authorities after including a few revisions. One of the major recommendations was that the division of responsibilities between regional councils and the regional state administration be clarified, because the 2012 draft of the Concept was not accompanied by any corresponding draft laws. According to the Council of Europe's next report, delivered on 12 September 2012 (Council of Europe 2012b), domestic policymakers introduced minor changes to the decentralization reform agenda. For example, they recommended introducing executive committees into regional councils at the second stage (not the fourth) of reform implementation. However, the policy document still did not propose any solutions regarding the division of responsibilities between the elected and the appointed regional authorities. Anatoliy Tkachuk was one of the experts who prepared the next feedback report—the Council's Centre of Expertise for Local Governance Reform Appraisal—on the subsequent edition of Ukraine's decentralization reform agenda, which was delivered on 1 October 2013 (Council of Europe 2013a). The Council of Europe's Appraisal reiterated that the draft of the Concept was adequate for approval and implementation by domestic authorities. Also, it clearly stated that the 2013 draft of the Concept did not incorporate the revisions previously recommended by the Council of Europe.

The Constitutional Assembly requested and obtained the Council of Europe's policy advice on reforming regional authority in Ukraine. On 9 October 2013, the Council of Europe's "On the Revision of the Constitution of Ukraine: Provisions on the Territorial Organisation of State and Local Self-Government" (Council of Europe 2013b) was delivered by the Centre of Expertise for Local Government Reform. This Policy Advice welcomed the policy recommendation to introduce executive committees into regional councils and specified that "[t]his does not mean that the State administration should disappear from the local level. Indeed, in all countries with decentralised local government there is a local State administration with supervisory functions (over local authorities) and own responsibilities (with regard to State functions and administration) … There are two issues for the local State administration: the relationship with local self-government and the relationship with local branches of central executive bodies. The issues at stake are ensuring the implementation of central government (State) policies, their coordination at local level and compliance with the law. The decentralisation will shift most of operational tasks to the local self-government bodies, and the local State administration will keep only a supervisory function. According to the ECLSG [European Charter of Local Self-Government], this supervisory function should be limited to the legality of the decisions (art.8)" (Council of Europe 2013: 9). This lengthy explanation indicates that the

Constitutional Assembly did not share any specific policy document outlining the functions of regional executives after the expected policy change: the introduction of executive committees into regional councils. The Policy Advice further explicitly highlighted that it approved the draft of the Concept on Reforming Local Self-government prepared in 2012 and 2013, subject to some minor revisions.

Thus, the political documents mentioned the objective of introducing executive committees into regional councils, but did not demonstrate any consensus regarding the division of duties of the regional executives in relation to the Center, the regional councils, or the local authorities. In turn, the Council of Europe's feedback reports repeatedly highlighted the need to address this matter. Notably, they provided explanatory notes regarding the supervisory functions of regional executives.

(Attempts at) Policy Change

Subsequent attempts at policy change refer to the implementation of the post-2014 decentralization reform, in line with the 2014 Concept approved by the government on 1 April 2014. The central policymakers who came to power in 2014 could rely on extensive policy learning: there were many draft laws relating to constitutional amendments that briefly mentioned the objective of introducing executive committees into regional councils. However, there was no consensus on how to prevent overlap between the executive duties of regional self-governance (exercised by the executive committees of the regional councils) and the executive duties of the state (exercised by the regional executives). I suggest that this was the major shortcoming of the pro-reform advocacy coalition.

Parliament's inability to produce a constitutional draft on decentralization became evident in Spring 2014. On 4 March 2014 parliament established its temporary special commission for preparing a draft law on amending the Constitution of Ukraine with respect to decentralization. It was expected to submit its constitutional draft on 15 April 2014. On 2 April 2014 the deadline was postponed till 15 May 2014; however, no constitutional draft was finally presented to parliament. According to Ruslan Knyazevych, Fatherland MP and head of the temporary special commission, the commission received numerous proposals from various MPs and summarized them in a comparative table.[21] On 16 May 2014 and 19 May 2014, the leading domestic media outlets *Dzerkalo Tyzhnia* (Rakhmanin 2014) and *Ukrainska Pravda* leaked the proceedings of the temporary special commission, comprising the three columns of the comparative table: (1) existing constitutional norms; (2) proposed constitutional norms; (3) alternative recommendations. According to this table, the commission proposed introducing executive committees into regional councils, annulling regional state administrations and, in their place, introducing state agencies (*derzhavni predstavnytstva*) whose heads would be appointed by the president on the recommendation of the government. The state agencies would coordinate substate executive bodies and supervise the compliance of local self-government acts with the laws and the constitution. Only the government could dismiss the heads of the state agencies and cancel the decisions of the executive branch at the substate scales. No MPs denied the authenticity of the leaked information. No further outputs of the temporary special commission have been made available.

On 26 June 2014 the newly elected President Petro Poroshenko registered his constitutional amendment draft № 4178a in parliament (a revised version was submitted on 2 July 2014). Notably, the president's representative to the parliament was the Fatherland MP Ruslan Knyazevych, who served as head of the temporary special commission in March-May 2014. The constitutional draft contained the objective of introducing executive committees into regional councils and recommended doing away with the positions of the heads of regional state administration in favor of the president's representatives, who could be appointed and dismissed by the president. They were responsible for, accountable to, and under the control of the president; their decisions could be cancelled by the

---

21 Apart from decentralization, the proposals concerned the judicial branch and the division of responsibilities between the president and parliament.

president alone. Thus, the government would no longer engage in either appointing or dismissing regional executives. Such an attempt was not unusual: in the early 1990s, presidents and parliaments competed with each other for the right to subordinate regional authorities (Matsuzato 2000), whereas in the 2000s, such competition took place between the president and the prime minister (Romanova 2011a).

The constitutional draft law suggested by President Poroshenko in 2014 had a major issue. According to his constitutional draft law, the president's representatives, appointed and dismissed by the president, were entitled to supervise local self-government authorities to ensure compliance with the Constitution and the laws of Ukraine; they could inform the president about their concerns regarding the decisions of the local governance bodies or the parliament of the Autonomous Republic of Crimea, and, in turn, the president had the power to suspend such decisions and simultaneously ask the Constitutional Court to evaluate the extent to which their decisions conformed to the Constitution. If the Court confirmed that the local authority's decisions did not align with the Constitution, the president could dissolve that local authority (Article 106 par 1.8). Also, the president's representatives could suspend a decision of a body of local self-government, if they considered such a decision not to comply with the laws of Ukraine, and simultaneously refer it to an administrative court (Art. 144).

In order to strengthen both the international and domestic legitimacy of his constitutional draft, President Poroshenko requested the Venice Commission to prepare its recommendations on his draft amendments. The preliminary opinion of the Venice Commission was sent to the Ukrainian authorities on 24 July 2014. It was subsequently endorsed by the Venice Commission on 10–11 October 2014. Although the Venice Commission welcomed the recommendation to establish executive committees in regional councils, it was cautious about the proposed role of the president's representatives and the president's functions with respect to local governance: "It would seem more appropriate to provide for referral of decisions, both in case of suspected unconstitutionality and of suspected illegality—by the President's representatives to the administrative courts, which may then, if need be, raise a question of constitutionality before the Constitutional Court" (Venice Commission 2014: 11). Notwithstanding its warning that the president would gain considerable power over local self-government authorities, its assessment was largely positive. Because President Poroshenko registered his first constitutional draft less than a month after he became president on 7 June 2014, it was next to impossible to hold meaningful public discussions. Still, the Venice Commission included the following statement in its official feedback: "[t]he draft amendments under consideration will therefore have to be submitted to public discussion in the course of the subsequent procedure and before their final adoption" (Venice Commission 2014: 12).

Many domestic policymakers interpreted the 2014 constitutional draft as the president's bold attempt to increase his power by subordinating regional executives (e.g. Tkachuk 2014). "[A] variety of experts and political actors in the country have expressed concern with the initial constitutional amendments proposed by President Poroshenko due to what they perceive as their potential to lead the country back to a 'patronal presidential' model ... Additionally, political elites at the local level are suspicious that the 'president's representative' on the local level will serve to unduly exert Kyiv's will on local governments" (USAID 2014: 10; 17). Due to such criticisms, President Poroshenko withdrew this constitutional draft for further revisions on 11 November 2014 – soon after the 2014 parliamentary elections.

He made more effort to prepare his next constitutional proposal that proposed introducing executive committees into regional councils. On 3 March 2015, President Poroshenko established the Constitutional Commission – in charge of drafting the constitutional amendments to be submitted to parliament – in order to enhance public engagement. It comprised both policymakers and experts, including Anatoliy Tkachuk, Yuri Hanushchak, and Ihor Koliushko. The Constitutional Commission was expected to deliver a constitutional proposal to President Poroshenko (Razumkov Centre 2016). The Deputy Speaker of the Parliament, Oksana Syroyid

(Self-Reliance [*Samopomich*]), severely criticized the functioning of the Constitutional Commission. According to Syroyid, the text of the constitutional proposal was written by the Commission's Secretariat, which had no authorization to do so, and the members of the Commission did not know who belonged to the Secretariat (Syroyid 2015). According to Kozlov and Meyer-Resende who closely observed the operation of the Constitutional Commission, the working group on decentralization initially considered two constitutional drafts: (a) the 2014 draft of the constitutional amendments by President Poroshenko; (b) the drafts of the constitutional amendments proposed by domestic experts, i.e. Yuri Hanushchak. As Kozlov and Meyer-Resende state, "[t]he Presidential draft also suggested that local officials [regional executives], whose principal duty would be to monitor the observance of the Constitution and laws at the local level should be appointed by the President (and be called "presidential" representatives according to the draft) while the proposal by Mr. Hanushchak reserved the power of appointment for the government" (Kozlov and Meyer-Resende 2015: 2). At some point, the stakeholders involved found a way to merge the two drafts into one; later on, the merged constitutional draft was proposed to President Poroshenko, who then submitted it to parliament.[22]

The constitutional draft delivered by the Constitutional Commission's working group abandoned the notion of the president's representatives, recommending instead the use of prefects. According to the constitutional draft, prefects were expected to become public servants, appointed and dismissed by the president upon the recommendation of the Cabinet of Ministers. The notion of the state's supervision of local authorities, assigned to prefects, resembled the 2014 constitutional draft. However, there were notable differences: the 2015 constitutional draft allowed the president to suspend the powers of substate councils and mayors if their decisions posed a threat to the sovereignty of the state, to territorial integrity

---

22 According to the Constitution of Ukraine, the president or a body of 150 MPs has the right to initiate constitutional amendments.

or to national security, and then to appoint temporary state commissioners. Additionally, prefects were allowed to issue acts which shall be mandatory at the respective territory, in line with the law (Art. 119). The Opinion of the Venice Commission (Venice Commission 2015) questioned the extent to which the latter policy recommendations were justified, but endorsed the 2015 constitutional draft, subject to minor revisions.

Like in 2014, there was a sharp contrast between the Venice Commission's feedback, which stated that the constitutional draft could be considered for approval after introducing specified revisions, and that provided by domestic actors. Notably, the 2015 draft included a clause intended to grant the special status of local self-government to the temporarily non-government-controlled territories of Donetsk and Luhansk *oblasts* as required by the Minsk Agreements. That controversial policy recommendation raised multiple concerns in Ukraine (Marlin 2016: 285-286; Niland 2016; Dudley 2019: 15-16; Palermo 2020). But partners within the pro-presidential coalition, like Self-Reliance, opposed Poroshenko's draft not only because it was linked to the controversial Minsk Agreements, but also because they suspected that the president would further strengthen his power and suppress local authorities. They did not give their approval to the full extent of responsibilities granted to regional executives with respect to supervising local authorities' decisions, and suspected that the constitutional draft represented an attempt to increase the powers of the president. Although the 2015 constitutional draft managed to pass first reading on 31 August 2015, tensions were rife, and the pro-presidential coalition in parliament soon fragmented. Moreover, civil discontent, fomented by opponents of the Minsk Agreements, grew too rapidly to control. As a result, the president did not attempt to proceed with his constitutional draft.

The exercise of supervision over both delegated and own responsibilities of the strengthened local authorities was one of the decisive factors in the constitutional amendment. On 26 April 2018, representatives of the central and substate authorities participated in a "'Strasbourg format' meeting (in camera moderated negotiation) of the Ukrainian stakeholders, organised by the Council of Europe, where the key features of the administrative oversight model in Ukraine were agreed upon by all major stakeholders, in line with the Article 8 of the Charter [the European Charter of Local Self-Government]" (Council of Europe 2020a: 1-2). Among other matters, the detailed conclusions of the meeting specified that "a distinction should be made between supervision over own and delegated competences" and "the new law on legality supervision should aim at … making legal advice available to local self-government authorities" (Council of Europe 2020a: Appendix II, 1-2). In sum, "the consensus reached at the Strasbourg format meeting proposed the creation of a very light system of supervision, which would be one of the most flexible and protective of local self-government in Europe" (Council of Europe 2020a: 2). However, in the coming years, as Söller-Winkler puts it, "there is still no detailed legal framework for the implementation of supervision. For this reason, supervision is often carried out ad hoc by many different central agencies in an inconsistent manner, without making the necessary distinction between self-governing tasks and delegated ones" (Söller-Winkler 2021).

The next attempt to increase regional authority via introducing executive committees into regional councils was made by President Zelenskyy in December 2019.[23] Like many other of the policy provisions on decentralization under his presidency, his constitutional draft was based on President Poroshenko's 2015 constitutional draft. This legacy was also highlighted in the Council of Europe's feedback report on Zelenskyy's draft of the constitutional amendments (Council of Europe 2020a: Appendix I). Similarly to Poroshenko's second constitutional proposal, Zelenskyy's constitutional draft recommended making regional executives public servants. However, there were notable differences. First, the latter draft recommended appointing and dismissing them according to a

---

23　The draft law "On Amendments to the Constitution of Ukraine (On the Decentralization of Power)" № 2598 was registered in parliament on 13 December 2019, withdrawn on 27 December 2019, registered again on 27 December 2019, and withdrawn on 17 January 2020 for further consultations.

special procedure. Second, prefects would serve for a maximum of three years after their appointment. These policy measures were aimed at reducing bargaining between political actors in the Center and at the substate scales when selecting candidacies for regional executives. Some domestic experts criticized the policy provision which entailed prefects' dual subordination to the president and to the Cabinet of Ministers (Solougub 2019). Koliushko (2019) explicitly highlighted the need to subordinate prefects to the government. However, the most critical feedback referred (a) to the policy suggestion that allowed the president to temporarily suspend the responsibilities of mayors, as well as those of local, subregional, and regional councils on the advice of prefects, and (b) to the policy recommendation regarding state oversight of local governance exercised by prefects. At the same time, some welcomed the policy provision regarding state supervision of local authorities proposed in the 2019 constitutional draft (Hanushchak 2019 a, b).

Although President Zelenskyy had enough political support in parliament to expect that MPs from the pro-presidential single-party majority would support his constitutional initiative, he decided to withdraw his constitutional drafts for one major reason: numerous local authorities declared their opposition. Their criticisms were shared by experts. As with the domestic concerns regarding Poroshenko's constitutional drafts, Zelenskyy's were criticized for introducing state supervision of both delegated and own responsibilities of the strengthened local authorities, the intention being to increase the responsibilities granted to regional executives with respect to supervising local authorities' decisions and to increase the corresponding powers of the president over local authorities. Moreover, in addition to criticizing the content of these proposals, local authorities accused the pro-reform advocacy coalition of preventing them from expressing their position and concerns. They called for genuine public discussions and opportunities to share feedback for consideration by central authorities.

Because the importance of public engagement in constitutional reforms regarding decentralization increased dramatically, in February 2020 President Zelenskyy initiated broad public discussions on constitutional changes that included central policymakers, substate authorities, and the general public. The public discussions looked like an attempt of the pro-reform advocacy coalition to build trust with their opponents at local scales. Such public discussions were not confined to a particular constitutional draft. Instead, they represented a facilitated and structured discussion of the issues that the participants consider necessary to be covered within the constitutional reform on decentralization (such as state supervision of the decisions of local authorities with respect to both delegated and own responsibilities), the scope of potential solutions, and their expected impact. Some pointed out that local authorities were only represented by mayors during public discussions (Tkachuk 2022). That said, I suggest that the initiators of the public discussions on the constitutional amendments prioritized the engagement of mayors, because mayors had fiercely opposed the previous constitutional drafts and the representatives of the Center's pro-reform advocacy coalition sought to minimize any further confrontation with them.

In Spring 2020, during the COVID-19 pandemic, the divisions between the president, the central government, and the centrally appointed regional executives, on the one hand, and local authorities, on the other hand, greatly increased: the two cohorts of actors had diametrically opposed views on fighting the COVID-19 pandemic. In advance of the 2020 regional and local elections, tensions between them peaked.

However, once the 2020 elections were held and brought little gains to the president's party, the pro-reform advocacy coalition stopped confronting city mayors. In October 2020, the draft laws aimed at dividing responsibilities between regional governors and substate self-governing bodies were prepared in parliament. The reformers intended to produce a draft law on regional executives that would be approved by parliament before introducing the constitutional amendments regarding the executive committees of regional councils. The draft law "On Amendments to the Law of Ukraine 'On Local State Administrations' and Other Legislative Acts of Ukraine on Reforming Territorial Organization of Executive Power in Ukraine" № 4298 (30 October 2020) was meant as such a policy document. The draft law recommended amending the previously proposed subordination of regional executives and their duties with respect to supervising local authorities. As Hanushchak (2021a) puts it, "the draft law shift[ed] the center that guided regional executives from the president to the government." Regional executives (prefects) were meant to become civil servants, with a maximum three-year tenure. They were meant to be appointed in line with the procedures envisioned for civil servants. Only the court could suspend the acts of local authorities. Both international (Council of Europe 2020a: 6) and domestic (Hanushchak 2021a) experts welcomed the fact that the draft law proposed that local authorities would consult with regional executives regarding the application of the legislation, which meant that regional executives were likely to advise beforehand rather than discipline local authorities after they made decisions that did not comply with the laws or the Constitution. As Hanushchak (2021a) stressed, this provision would be especially helpful to small localities with limited personnel. Thus, some provisions related to the supervision of local authorities looked more favorable to the latter than the ones then in place.

Importantly, the content of the draft law was significantly changed after it passed first reading in parliament on 4 March 2021.

On 18 December 2021, the draft Law № 4298 was revised in such a way that the president would benefit the most from subordinating regional executives: it proposed appointing regional executives for the tenure of the president and simplified the procedure for dismissing regional executives by the president. However, these significant changes largely considered prefects' subordination to the Center and did not touch upon prefects' interactions with local authorities. That is probably why the latter did not actively oppose the revised draft Law № 4298 (Vedernikova 2021). Still, the lack of their opposition did not indicate that local authorities joined the pro-reform advocacy coalition at that stage.

Simultaneously, the Parliamentary Committee on the Organization of State Power, Local Self-Government, Regional Development and Urban Planning presented the output of the public discussions on the constitutional amendments, with their detailed proceedings (Amendments to the Constitution of Ukraine 2021). City mayors took part in the public discussions for more than a year. In contrast to the amended draft Law № 4298, the newly introduced policy document states that regional executives (prefects) "shall be selected on a competitive basis. The tenure of a prefect office in ... *oblast*, in the cities of Kyiv and Sevastopol may not exceed three years. The prefect is a civil servant." (2021: 7). This provision reminds of Zelenskyy's constitutional draft and indicates its approval by those who joined the public discussions.

This design of a policy document highlighted the priority preferences of those stakeholders who participated in the public discussions and paved a way for further bargaining in the parliament. The policy document outlined two alternatives regarding the subordination of regional executives: "The prefect shall be appointed and dismissed from office by [Option 1: the President of Ukraine upon the advice of the Cabinet of Ministers of Ukraine; Option 2: the Cabinet of Ministers of Ukraine] in the manner prescribed by law" (Amendments to the Constitution of Ukraine 2021). In addition, '[w]hen executing his/her powers, the prefect shall report and be subordinate to [Option 1: the President of Ukraine and the Cabinet of Ministers of Ukraine within the scope of their powers; Option 2: the Cabinet of Ministers of Ukraine]' (Amendments to the Constitution of Ukraine 2021).

The matter of state oversight of local authorities, exercised by regional executives, was presented in a form that favored the local authorities. According to the amendments, '[t]he prefect of a given territory shall: ... ensure preliminary consultations of public authorities with local self-governments in the process of planning and decision-making on all issues related to local self-governance; execute other supervisory and coordination powers specified by the law of Ukraine" (Amendments to the Constitution of Ukraine 2021). Moreover, there is evidence of an increase of mayoral authority vis-à-vis local councils. The 2021 policy document proposes the following: "Community local self-governments include a council and a community head. The community head shall form and manage an executive body and preside over a council session" (Amendments to the Constitution of Ukraine 2021. This contrasts with the existing situation: "[a] local council establishes its executive committee, and a mayor is in charge of suggesting the list of candidacies for the respective executive committee. The councillors cannot suggest any alternatives; however, they can decline the mayor's list of candidacies, and this legal mechanism helps to balance power relations between a mayor and a majority of councillors in a local council. The mayor chairs the executive committee and can veto its decisions, as well as the decisions of the respective local council" (Romanova 2022: 348). The 2021 policy document makes it clear that mayors had convinced central policymakers to provide additional institutional means to establish their dominant role at the local scales. This indicates that mayors could join the pro-reform advocacy coalition at this point.

On 16 December 2021, a working group for constitutional amendments was established in parliament. It was in charge of producing a draft of the constitutional amendments on decentralization in March 2022. As of January 2022, constitutional amendments on the introduction of executive committees into regional councils were still in progress. It was still unclear whether the constitutional draft on decentralization was going to grant regional councils the right to establish their executive committees and transform regional governors into prefects, who would have the status of civil servants, with the power to supervise local authorities' decision-making regarding both own and delegated responsibilities.

In 2014-2021, regional councils were not actively aggregated into the pro-reform advocacy coalition as regards increasing regional authority. I find no evidence that regional councils attempted to collectively bargain with the Center to obtain additional responsibilities — the constitutional right to establish their own executive committees. I maintain that the reason is that regional councils were reluctant to join a pro-reform reform coalition aimed at promoting local amalgamation.

This was in contrast to the exceptionally active engagement of local authorities in the alternate advocacy coalition. Local authorities made considerable attempts to block constitutional amendments that would strengthen regional authority at their expense. Their active engagement was provoked by the fact that all draft laws on the constitutional amendments related to decentralization included clauses on state supervision of both delegated and own responsibilities of the strengthened local authorities.

Arguably, the harshest opponents of increasing regional authority were found at the local scales, and their opposition to the 2019 constitutional draft was the major reason for the president's decision to withdraw his initiative from parliament in advance of the 2020 substate contests. However, it looks like both their attitude to and their input into the constitutional reform radically changed soon after the 2020 substate elections. The interests of the local authorities — mainly mayors — were taken into account in the output of the public consultations regarding the constitutional amendments presented on 29 November 2021. The 2021 policy document proposed establishing the dominant role of mayors at the local scales, where the institutional relations between mayors and local councils were concerned. Presumably, this is why mayors did not actively criticize the model of state oversight of local authorities, proposed by the draft Law "On Amendments to the Law of Ukraine 'On Local State Administrations' and Other Legislative Acts of Ukraine on Reforming Territorial Organization of Executive Power in Ukraine" № 4298.

The policy documents drafted by the central government in 2005-2013, and the Council of Europe's feedback reports, indicate that policymakers during the presidencies of Yushchenko and Yanukovych had repeatedly drafted policy recommendations aimed at introducing executive committees into regional councils. This lengthy policy learning experience contributed to shaping numerous policymakers' and experts' core policy beliefs and made it possible to include the notion of increasing regional authority into the 2014 Concept when the focusing event occurred (i.e. the post-Euromaidan change of elites). However, this policy learning experience did not lead to a consensus among policymakers about how to prevent overlap between the duties of self-governance and those of the state. Simply put, the reformers declared their commitment at the stage of agenda-setting, but could not agree on how to achieve their goal in practice. I propose that this was the first major constraint on the pro-reform advocacy coalition preventing increasing regional authority in advance of the 2020 elections.

The second major shortcoming involved the alternate advocacy coalition. At the stage of decision-making, this coalition managed to redirect attention from the core policy issue at stake: the increase of regional authority. Instead, it prioritized other salient issues: (a) the attempt to grant the special status of local self-government to the temporarily non-government-controlled territories of the Donetsk and Luhansk *oblasts*; and (b) the attempt to increase regional authority at the expense of local authorities. Because of the sensitivity of these issues, even the core members of the pro-reform advocacy coalition adopted different approaches to increasing regional authority (Hanushchak 2019 a, b; Vedernikova 2019).

The most active participants of the pro-reform advocacy coalition were in the Center: President Poroshenko and President Zelenskyy. Parliament's engagement was ambiguous. Regional councils' input into the pro-reform advocacy coalition was limited, and local authorities were most often aggregated into the alternate advocacy coalition. Local authorities' ability to affect the pace of the constitutional reform on decentralization greatly increased, along with their bargaining power. Before 2020, the pro-reform advocacy coalition failed to address the criticisms of the alternate advocacy coalition, which recruited local authorities whose responsibilities had been strengthened; as a result, it proved impossible to promote the increase of regional authority in advance of the 2020 substate contests.

3 The Dynamics of Regionalized Party Competition

The academic literature has generated rich research results regarding the regionalized electoral performance of parties in Ukraine. This chapter reviews ongoing research on the shifts in the geographical contours of the party system since 2014.

Ukraine is regionally diverse (Sasse 2001; Hrytsak 2019; Podolian and Romanova 2018). The core division that has structured party competition in Ukraine since independence has been "the ethnolinguistic/geo-political cleavage" (Chaisty and Whitefield 2018). This cleavage was identified in the 1990s. Arel and Khmelko (1996) explained Ukraine's regionalized voting behavior: "the status of the Russian language and Ukraine's geopolitical orientation toward the Russian state." Barrington and Faranda (2009) found that ethnicity also affected voting behavior in Ukraine. Due to these factors, public attitudes regarding center-periphery relations, including language policies (Arel 1995; Kulyk 2011), and geopolitics have been highly regionalized. In the 1990s and the 2000s, the electoral geography of presidential elections often divided the country into two halves, along the Dnipro River, while parliamentary elections generated a "third" Ukraine in the geographical center (Kuzio 1995; Birch 1995, 1998, 2000; Hesli 2007; Hesli et al 1998; Clem and Craumer 2008; Kuzio 2014).

The first major deviation from this pattern occurred during the general contests held in 2014. The victory of the Euromaidan Uprising and Russia's hybrid war against Ukraine paved the way for the electoral success of those parties that manifested pro-Western attitudes (Herron 2014; Shevel 2015; D'Anieri 2019). Simultaneously, the number of constituencies in which Ukrainian citizens were able to cast their votes and where domestic parties were able to run shrank. In the constituencies that were "temporarily lost," voters' preferences have been broadly regarded as pro-Russian (D'Anieri 2019).

On 25 May 2014—at the first general contests held after the Euromaidan Uprising—Petro Poroshenko won the first round of the early presidential elections; Yulia Tymoshenko obtained the second largest vote share. Vitaliy Klitchko won the mayoral election in the capital. All three were the leaders of the Euromaidan Uprising. After the early parliamentary elections, held on 26 October 2014,[24] six parties established parliamentary factions, five[25] of whom formed a coalition with a pro-Western agreement. Opposition Bloc underperformed in the 2014 parliamentary elections as it had lost its electoral strongholds in Crimea and Donbas as a result of Russia's hybrid war.

The second major electoral swing became evident in the 2019 general elections. Volodymyr Zelenskyy, with no party, won the 2019 presidential race with 73% of votes in the second round. Previously, "each of Ukraine's four turnovers (1994, 2004, 2010, 2014) came about because the opposition was able to mobilize strong regional support—alternatively Russophile and Ukrainephile—to overcome incumbent advantages" (Way 2015: 45). Instead, in the 2019 presidential elections, Zelenskyy won sizable vote shares across the whole country. As Minakov puts it, "Zelensky's victory mainly rode on three expectations of Ukraine's frustrated voters: (1) peace in the Donbas, (2) good governance and an end to corruption, and (3) the improved well-being of ordinary Ukrainians" (Minakov 2021a). In the early parliamentary elections later in the year, the newly established president's party repeated Zelenskyy's own electoral victory. The electoral map of the 2019 parliamentary contests showed no regional divide: the newly established ruling party

---

24 The electoral results, according to proportional representations rules, were as follows: People's Front (*Narodnyi Front*), led by the prime minister, 22.14%; the Petro Poroshenko Bloc "Solidarnist" (*Bloc Petra Poroshenko "Solidarnist"*), established by the president, 21.82%; Self-Reliance (*Samopomich*), 10.97%; Opposition Bloc (*Opozytsiinyi Bloc*), 9.43%; the Radical Party of Oleh Lyashko (*Radykalna Partiya Oleha Lyashka*), 7.44%; and Fatherland (*Batkivshchyna*), 5.68%.

25 These were the president's party, the Petro Poroshenko Bloc; the prime minister's party, People's Front, Self-Reliance (*Samopomich*), the Radical Party of Oleh Lyashko, Fatherland.

obtained the largest vote shares in every constituency of Ukraine, except for the Donetska, Luhanska, and Lvivska *oblasts*.

The outcomes of the 2019 parliamentary elections allowed the frontrunner to form a single-party majority in the *Verkhovna Rada*.[26] Apart from Servant of the People, there were four other parliamentary fractions (the Opposition Platform—For Life; Fatherland; European Solidarity; Voice) and two deputy groups (For the Future; Trust). Servant of the People and Voice were new parties, but other parliamentary parties were well-established. The Petro Poroshenko Bloc "Solidarity" changed its name to European Solidarity. In 2018 the Opposition Platform—For Life was established based on the Opposition Bloc. Fatherland had already contested a number of previous elections under the same name. As Odarchenko highlighted, '[t]he Servant of the People faction has 247 seats in the Rada, which gives it the formal ability to pass any draft laws. Only for constitutional amendments does the faction need to form a coalition with opposition parties. Thus, formally, the Rada [parliament] has a so-called 'mono-majority.' … Voting patterns in parliament show that the mono-majority has fragmented into informal groups influenced by competing politicians or oligarchs … Since spring, the presidential faction has consistently needed the support of other factions" (Odarchenko 2020).

These electoral outcomes bore no similarity to preceding contests and recalled nothing of the political alignment associated with the Euromaidan Uprising. This was unusual for Ukraine and drove academics to double check whether the core cleavage that used to structure political competition in Ukraine was still in force.

On the one hand, there are research findings that suggest that the drop in electoral support for pro-Russian parties and the overwhelming electoral dominance of pro-Western parties after the Euromaidan Uprising signal a major change in Ukraine's party

---

26 The electoral results of the 2019 parliamentary elections, according to proportional representation rules, were as follows: Servant of the People (*Sluha Narodu*) scored 43.16%; Opposition Platform—For Life (*Opozytsiina Platforma "Za Zhyttya"*)—13.05%; Fatherland—8.18%; European Solidarity (*Yevropeiska Solidarnist*)—8.10%; Voice (*Holos*)—5.82%.

system. On the other hand, other research results indicate that the cleavage that has underlain Ukraine's party system remains the same, but that party realignment has drastically changed.

Let us begin by examining the arguments of the first cohort of scholars. Mykola Riabchuk, the author of the "myth of two Ukraines" points out that in the aftermath of the Euromaidan Uprising "the Ukrainian nation is much more united than many experts and policymakers expected" (Riabchuk 2015: 138). The special issue "Identity Politics in Times of Crisis: Ukraine as a Critical Case," published in *Post-Soviet Affairs* in 2018, presents evidence that "Ukraine is becoming more Ukrainian, while identity boundaries are hardening" (Arel 2018: 188). However, Arel is cautious about extrapolating from findings on elections and party politics: "it is too early to know if political parties will reconstruct themselves along a geopolitical/language of preference axis" (2018: 188). For their part, Fedorenko et al. argue that "the increase, before the 2014 parliamentary elections, of pro-Western attitudes across the Ukrainian electorate resulted in a sea-change in Ukraine's electoral landscape. The broadly pro-Western stance of the active electorate reduced the salience of one of Ukrainian politics' most enduring and prevalent challenges—the sharp and seemingly irreconcilable regional cleavages in the electoral support for different parties prior to 2014 ... The marked decline of this cleavage's salience is not only consequential for the future of Ukraine's party system, but can, more broadly, be seen as a sign of the emergence of a consolidated political nation in Ukraine" (Fedorenko et al. 2016: 624). Furthermore, Fedorenko et al. acknowledge that the consolidation they observe "leaves out Crimea and the occupied territories of the Donets Basin, [as well as] ... large numbers of Ukraine's current internally displaced persons," and the electorate of the banned Communist Party of Ukraine (ibid).

Now let us turn to the research results of the second cohort of scholars, the ones who find the major cleavage in political competition in Ukraine to be still operative.

To determine whether any new salient issues guided party competition and voting behavior after the victory of the

Euromaidan Uprising, Chaisty and Whitefield tested the theoretical assumptions regarding "frozen cleavages" and "critical elections" theory against the case of the 2014 parliamentary elections. They found that the parliamentary elections held in October 2014 did not change the parameters of electoral competition, despite high electoral volatility, and that the principal cleavage remained the same. The findings of Chaisty and Whitefield (2018) correlate with the results of the experiment performed by Timothy Frye. In June 2014, Frye surveyed 1,000 residents and assessed their support for fictional candidates in parliamentary elections, who differed from each other in their ethnicity (Russian or Ukrainian), native language (Russian or Ukrainian), and support for closer economic ties with Russia or the EU. Frye (2014) confirms that three elements constitute the principal cleavage in Ukraine — language, ethnicity, and geopolitical orientation, the latter affecting voting preferences the most. The comparative analysis of public attitudes before and after the Euromaidan Uprising conducted by Pop-Eleches and Robertson (2018) prove that the significance of ethnic identity changes a little bit, but still accounts for political attitudes. Research in the 2019 general contests conducted by Chaisty and Whitefield confirms that the cleavage in Ukraine's party system remains frozen: "the main line of division in how voters chose parties remained over identity and system-level issues relating to the fundamental orientation of the country" (Chaisty and Whitefield 2020). D'Anieri conducted research on voting preferences in Donbas in 2019 and found that "voter alignments identified before 2014 persist" (D'Anieri 2021). His research results confirm that most electors continue to support pro-Russian political parties, and, if given the right to cast their ballot, would support policymakers associated with the political parties overthrown by the Euromaidan Uprising in 2014.

If the core cleavage that structures party competition has not changed, unlike party realignment, then what accounts for the observed changes in Ukraine's electoral geography in 2019?

The academic literature has found an answer. Research on the 2019 parliamentary elections indicates that "SN [Service of the People] voters were significantly more likely than the supporters of other parties to 'agree' or 'fully agree' that all parties offer the same programmes ... Given the high level of cynicism about political parties in Ukraine, and the political class more generally, these marginal effects are striking ... This highlights the extent of the anti-establishment mood that SN was able to capture across the entire society" (Chaisty and Whitefield 2020: 8). Simply put, the majority of votes in favor of Zelenskyy in nearly every region of Ukraine in the 2019 general contests reflected the protest of the majority of voters against parties' strategies. "In Ukraine big business and politics remain closely fused, because (as in other post-Soviet countries) in the absence of a functioning rule of law, one of the best ways to protect and advance one's business interests is by entering politics, either directly, or via proxies embedded in (sometimes several) political parties" (Whitmore 2014: 3). As Herron and Sjoberg argue, "[o]ver the last two and a half decades, the participation of business elites in elections has given rise to localised political machines (D'Anieri 2007), where smaller-scale economic and political actors ... attempt to use patronage to benefit themselves and their close compatriots" (Herron and Sjoberg 2016: 985). Arguably, stark ideological polarization of Ukraine's party system, evident before 2014, brought to the fore parties' programmatic linkages and, as a result, masked the dominance of parties' clientelist linkage strategies. Instead, soon after the Euromaidan Uprising, voters got disillusioned and manifested their protest against the dominance of clientelist linkage strategies by voting for the challenger party, as Chaisty and Whitefield (2020) categorize Zelenskyy's Servant of the People.

In the next chapters, I will apply a multilevel perspective on elections and pay special attention to the regional and local contests that followed the 2019 general elections. The analysis will demonstrate that electors did not necessarily stop voting for parties that exploited clientelistic linkages, or that parties started prioritizing programmatic linkages . The 2020 substate elections did not display particularly strong programmatic substance in the parties. There is little evidence that the well-established parliamentary parties switched to a greater reliance on programmatic linkages. The new party of power largely neglected to get ready for the 2020 substate elections. The well-established parliamentary parties that opposed the newly elected president found it difficult to sustain their clientelistic linkage mechanisms. When a clientelistic party loses power in the Center, it may then suffer electoral losses in substate elections even in its electoral strongholds, especially if heavily targeted by the ruling party (Ogushi 2020).

In such circumstances, the non-parliamentary parties that prioritized substate contests, and which recruited substate incumbents and relied on substate interest groups, enhanced their competitiveness. On the one hand, they effectively exploited clientelistic linkages. "Regional and local authorities are closely connected with business in all regions of Ukraine, without exception ... By attaching themselves to political power in this way, business elites protect and further their interests ... Frequently, important business figures are themselves members of elected government bodies. In some places several managers from a significant local company are members of a city or town council" (UNDP 2019: 5, 6).

On the other hand, such parties had the chance to establish programmatic linkages with voters, but not necessarily via party manifestos. I suggest that substate authorities' official strategies of regional and local development, financially supported and actively implemented at the substate scales since 2015, in line with the decentralization reform,[27] could present the incumbents' policy priorities and policy positions with respect to issues that were important to voters. Their past performance would provide evidence of their capacity to deliver their promises. According to public polls, the performance of substate authorities was often perceived positively, especially when compared to the performance of central institutions (Council of Europe 2020b).

---

27 The State Strategy for Regional Development of Ukraine was approved in August 2014 and continued until 2020. In line with this all-Ukrainian strategy, *oblasts* and municipalities approved and then implemented their development strategies, which specified their priority objectives, the means of achieving them, and their finances, in line with the post-2014 decentralization reform.

4 Multilevel Elections' Incongruence and Decentralization

This chapter explores how parties' electoral performance changes across the parliamentary, regional, and municipal electoral arenas (i) before and (ii) after the implementation of the decentralization reform. It assesses the congruence of parties' vote shares across multilevel arenas, compares parties-frontrunners in oblasts, evaluates the fragmentation of the party system at the regional and municipal levels, and identifies the instances when dominant-party rule was established in regional and municipal councils in the three electoral cycles under investigation.

As stated in the Introduction, I expected to find that the incongruence between parliamentary and municipal elections would increase in the 2019/2020 electoral cycle, as a result of the increase of local authority advance of the 2020 substate contests. I did not expect to observe any meaningful changes in the incongruence between parliamentary and regional contests in the 2019/2020 electoral cycle, as regional authority had not changed much.

I measured the extent of congruence of parties' vote shares in the parliamentary and regional elections in the same regions, as well as in the parliamentary contests and municipal council elections in the corresponding *oblast*s and *oblast* capitals. For each multilevel electoral cycle, I calculated two types of dissimilarity indices for each region where multilevel contests were held. Then, I computed two average dissimilarity indices for the whole country for each multilevel electoral cycle: (a) the dissimilarity index that categorizes the dissimilarity of parliamentary contests and municipal council elections in Ukraine and (b) the dissimilarity index that characterizes the dissimilarity of parliamentary elections and regional council contests in Ukraine. Importantly, I calculated the differences in the vote shares obtained according to the proportional representation rules.

The 2012 parliamentary elections were held in 27 regions (including the Autonomous Republic of Crimea, the city of Sevastopol, and the Donetska and Luhanska *oblast*s). On 31 October 2010,

Sevastopol, and the Donetska and Luhanska *oblasts*). On 31 October 2010, no regular regional elections were held in the city of Kyiv or the Ternopilska *oblast*; thus, I investigate the regional council elections in 25 out of 27 regions. In the municipal arena, no regular elections were held in the city of Ternopil in 2010, and the results of municipal council elections in the city of Cherkasy were annulled; thus, I investigate municipal council elections in 21 out of the 23 *oblast* capitals. While exploring multilevel elections in the two subsequent cycles, I investigated regional council elections held in 23 regions (excluding the Autonomous Republic of Crimea, the city of Sevastopol, and the Donetska and Luhanska *oblasts*) and municipal council elections held in 21 *oblast* capitals (excluding the cities of Donetsk and Luhansk).

I found that the dissimilarity between the outcomes of the parliamentary and municipal elections in the 2019/2020 multilevel electoral cycle doubled that of the 2014/2015 electoral cycle. It increased from 13.37 to 27.33. This finding corresponds to theory-driven expectations and proves that the increase of substate authority at the local level in Ukraine is associated with an increase of incongruence between parliamentary and municipal contests.

Also, I observe that prior to the completion of the local amalgamation policy, the extent of the incongruence of parliamentary and municipal elections was lower than that of parliamentary and regional elections: 18.42 vs 23.61 in the 2010/2012 multilevel elections cycle; 13.37 vs 14.55 in the 2014/2015 multilevel electoral cycle. In contrast, in the 2019/2020 multilevel electoral cycle the extent of the incongruence of parliamentary and municipal elections was higher than that of parliamentary and regional elections: 27.33 vs 23.72 (Table 4.1; Table 4.2; Table 4.3).

At the same time, I acknowledge that decentralization is not the only factor that accounts for the incongruence of multilevel elections in Ukraine. Previous research on the regional elections held in 2006 and 2010 identified the role of the political regime (Romanova 2013). My study confirms that the quality of the political regime makes a difference in relation to municipal elections, too. In the 2010/2012 multilevel electoral cycle, the dissimilarity between the outcomes of parliamentary and municipal elections was 18.42. It was lower than that found in the 2019/2020 multilevel electoral cycle, but higher than the one in the 2014/2015 cycle. Aside from the quality of the political regime, the temporal difference between the general and substate elections played a role. The 2010 substate elections were held on 31 October 2010, and the 2012 parliamentary elections were held on 28 October 2012. Thus, there was a temporal difference of two years. In contrast, the temporal difference in the two other multilevel elections under study was one year.

Notably, I found that the incongruence between the outcomes of parliamentary and regional elections also increased; however, I did not expect this to happen. The increase is significant: from 14.55 (2014/2015 multilevel elections) to 23.72 (2019/2020 multilevel elections). The incongruence of the 2019/2020 multilevel elections increased to nearly the same extent as that in the 2010/2012 multilevel electoral cycle. We need to proceed further to understand why this was the case.

Table 4.1. Average dissimilarity indices in the three multilevel electoral cycles under investigation.

	Average dissimilarity index referring to parliamentary and municipal contests	Average dissimilarity index referring to parliamentary and regional contests
the 2010/2012 multilevel electoral cycle	18.42	23.61
the 2014/2015 multilevel electoral cycle	13.37	14.55
the 2019/2020 multilevel electoral cycle	27.33	23.72

Note: Following academic literatures in the field of territorial politics (Palares and Keating 2003; Jeffery and Hough 2009; Schakel 2015), I calculate the dissimilarity index by adding the differences between parties' vote shares gained at in the parliamentary and the substate elections in each oblast and then divide the sum by two. I use parties' vote shares scored according to proportional representation rules.

Table 4.2. Dissimilarity indices for parliamentary and municipal elections in each region in the three multilevel electoral cycles under investigation.

	The 2010/2012 multilevel electoral cycle	The 2014/2015 multilevel electoral cycle	The 2019/2020 multilevel electoral cycle
Vinnytska	21.64	20.52	26.2
Volynska	17.99	3.38	28.79
Dnipropetrovska	19.73	16.24	30.5
Donetska	9.05	-	-
Zhytomyrska	19.76	16.73	25.14
Zakarpatska	29.25	12.1	32.91
Zaporizka	12.04	14.4	24.1
Ivano-Frankivska	12.29	3.26	32.73
Kirovohradska	27.42	7.84	24.15
Lvivska	23.8	5.07	32.27
Luhanska	2.85	-	-
Mykolaivska	14.26	22.01	29.62
Odeska	23.99	4.47	27.29
Poltavska	22.43	13.16	27.0
Rivnenska	12.44	9.96	24.43
Sumska	24.05	30.35	40.76
Ternopilska	-	7.9	30.10
Kharkivska	13.26	26.69	23.97
Khersonska	16.67	11.64	24.69
Khmelnytska	29.08	17.66	25.23

Cherkaska	-	10.52	28.15
Chernivetska	24.06	11.99	35.02
Chernihivska	10.88	14.98	28.33
Average	18.42	13.37	27.33

Note: I calculate the dissimilarity index by adding the differences between parties' vote shares gained at in the parliamentary and the substate elections in each oblast and then divide the sum by two. I use parties' vote shares scored according to proportional representation rules.

Source: Author's calculations on the basis of official data from the Central Electoral Commission.

Table 4.3. Dissimilarity indices for parliamentary and regional elections in each region in the three multilevel electoral cycles under investigation.

	The 2010/2012 multilevel electoral cycle	The 2014/2015 multilevel electoral cycle	The 2019/2020 multilevel electoral cycle
Crimea	31.17	-	-
Vinnytska	29.64	15.13	20.19
Volynska	24.24	9.33	21.3
Dnipropetrovska	21.93	16.11	23.51
Donetska	10.2	-	-
Zhytomyrska	23.21	14.89	24.71
Zakarpatska	32.6	16.57	21.97
Zaporizka	15.79	12.4	22.84
Ivano-Frankivska	24.19	14.18	22.12
Kyivska	33.36	13.29	24.01
Kirovohradska	27.57	15.47	28.08
Lvivska	28.2	8.41	29.63

Luhanska	10.75	-	-
Mykolaivska	15.06	19.96	21.18
Odeska	25.14	20.82	25.4
Poltavska	21.53	13.5	23.55
Rivnenska	22.24	21.32	25.62
Sumska	24.1	17.16	24.73
Kharkivska	18.32	24.61	24.01
Khersonska	19.37	12.61	20.69
Khmelnytska	32.28	5.63	22.44
Cherkaska	27.61	10.9	25.83
Chernivetska	30.6	10.79	26.98
Chernihivska	18.88	14.35	20.86
Kyiv	-	15.7	20.91
Sevastopol	22.34	-	-
Average	23.61	14.55	23.72

Note: I calculate the dissimilarity index by adding the differences between parties' vote shares gained at in the parliamentary and the substate elections in each oblast and then divide the sum by two. I use parties' vote shares scored according to proportional representation rules.

Source: *Author's calculations on the basis of official data from the Central Electoral Commission.*

In order to obtain a more nuanced picture, I identified the parties that obtained the largest vote shares in multilevel arenas in each multilevel electoral cycle and then compared them across the three cycles under investigation (Table 4.4.).

Table 4.4. The number of cases of congruence between parties-frontrunners in the same *oblast*s.

	The 2010/2012 electoral cycle	The 2014/2015 electoral cycle	The 2019/2020 electoral cycle
The number of cases of congruence between the parties that obtained the largest vote shares in the same *oblast*s **in the parliamentary, regional, and municipal elections**	10 out of 21	3 out of 21	0
The number of cases of congruence between the parties that obtained the largest vote shares in the same *oblast*s **in the parliamentary and regional elections**	14 out of 25	7 out of 23	4 out of 23

The number of cases of congruence between the parties that obtained the largest vote shares in the same *oblast*s **in the parliamentary and municipal elections**	12 out of 21	3 out of 21	0
The number of cases of congruence between the parties that obtained the largest vote shares in the same *oblast*s **in the regional and municipal elections**	13 out of 21	10 out of 21	9 out of 21

Source: Author's calculations on the basis of official data from the Central Electoral Commission.

In the 2019/2020 multilevel electoral cycle, there are no cases of vertical congruence between parties-frontrunners in the parliamentary elections, regional council elections, and municipal council elections in the same *oblast*s.

There are only 4 instances out of 23 in which the same party won the largest vote shares in the parliamentary and regional council elections in the same regions. In all four regions, the ruling party, Servant of the People, came first in both the parliamentary and regional elections.

In other words, in 19 out of 23 regions, different parties won the largest vote shares in the 2020 regional council elections and in the 2019 parliamentary contests. Both parliamentary and non-parliamentary parties contributed to the vertical incongruence between the frontrunners in the parliamentary and regional elections in the same *oblasts*. In as many as 9 out of 19 regions, non-parliamentary parties obtained the largest vote shares in the 2020 regional elections. A closer look at these nine cases identifies as many as three instances in which the non-parliamentary parties were led by incumbent city mayors and contested regional and municipal elections only in one corresponding *oblast*.[28] Arguably, those three parties put a priority at the municipal level, because the incumbent city mayors, who led those parties, personally contested the mayoral elections in the corresponding *oblast* capitals. While the regional council elections were not a priority for them, they still scored more votes than both their parliamentary and non-parliamentary competitors. Thus, non-parliamentary parties contributed to the increased incongruence of multilevel elections on both the regional and municipal levels. I will give an interpretation of this phenomenon in the next chapter.

The comparative analysis of the parliamentary and municipal electoral arenas indicates that in no instance did the same parties come first in both the parliamentary and municipal contests in the 2019/2020 electoral cycle.

Only in 5 out of 21 *oblast* capitals did parliamentary parties gain the largest vote shares in the 2020 municipal council elections.[29] Their electoral scores in the municipal council elections in these five cities outperformed the ruling party, but this means that

---

28 Kharkiv Bloc—Successful Kharkiv in the Kharkivska *oblast* in Eastern Ukraine; The Team of Symchyshyn in the Khmelnytska *oblast* in Western Ukraine; Native Home in the Chernihivska *oblast* in Central Ukraine.
29 Fatherland came first in the municipal council elections in the city of Uzhorod in Western Ukraine and in the city of Sumy in Central Ukraine. European Solidarity got the most votes in the municipal council elections in the cities of Lviv and Rivne in Western Ukraine. Opposition Platform gained the most votes in the municipal council elections in the city of Mykolaiv in Southern Ukraine.

in 16 *oblast* capitals, the parliamentary parties were less competitive than the non-parliamentary parties.

Finally, I compared the regional and municipal electoral arenas. In as many as 9 out of 21 corresponding *oblast*s and *oblast* capitals,[30] the same parties won the largest vote shares in both the regional and municipal council elections. In only three out of nine cases that the same party obtained the largest vote shares in the simultaneous regional and municipal council elections was the frontrunner a parliamentary party. In as many as six out of nine cases, non-parliamentary parties came first in both the regional and municipal council elections in 2020. In three out of six cases, three non-parliamentary parties— often, but not always led by incumbent city mayors— prioritized contests in one or several municipalities, and obtained the largest vote shares in both municipal and regional elections in the corresponding *oblast*s.[31]

In the 2020 municipal council elections, six non-parliamentary parties that prioritized municipal council elections obtained the largest vote shares in eight *oblast* capitals.

Prior to 2014, non-parliamentary parties, which prioritized the municipal electoral arenas and performed better than parliamentary parties, were not very numerous, and their electoral strength was often limited. In 2010, one such party obtained the largest note shares in the municipal council elections in two *oblast* capitals. In the 2010 substate elections, the Conscience of Ukraine [*Sovist Ukrainy*], led by Vinnytsia's incumbent city mayor Volodymyr Hroysman, contested municipal council elections in several cities. Its electoral performance was the best in two of the *oblast* capitals in Central Ukraine: Poltava and Vinnytsia. In both instances, it was

---

30 For the sake of consistency, I categorized the city of Kyiv as a region, but I acknowledge that it is possible to perceive it as the center of the Kyivska *oblast*.
31 Kharkiv Bloc—Successful Kharkiv in the Kharkivska *oblast* in Eastern Ukraine; The Team of Symchyshyn in the Khmelnytska *oblast* in Western Ukraine; Native Home in the Chernihivska *oblast* in Central Ukraine.

the frontrunner in the mayoral contests and municipal council elections.[32]

The 2015 contests also presented one non-parliamentary party that prioritized the municipal contests and performed better than parliamentary parties: Trust in Actions (*Doviryai Dilam*). It was co-chaired by Hennadiy Trukhanov, the mayor of the City of Odesa.[33] In 2015, Trust Actions gained 42% (27 out of 64 mandates) in the Odesa City Council elections and, arguably, attracted voters who would have otherwise supported the Opposition Bloc. In the 2020 municipal council elections, Trust Action secured its largest vote shares; however, its electoral performance declined when compared to the previous elections: 23% in 2020 vs 42% in 2015.

In 2020, six parties obtained the largest vote shares in the substate elections in four *oblast*s (the Vinnytska, Kharkivska, Khmelnytska, and Chernihivska *oblast*s) and eight *oblast* capitals, including five *oblast* capitals (Vinnitsia, Zaporizzha, Kharkiv, Odesa, and Chernihiv) in which the frontrunner was led by the incumbent city mayor, and three *oblast* capitals (Dnipro, Zhytomyr, and Kirovohrad) with one frontrunner, Proposition, established by a few incumbent city mayors. As in 2010 and 2015, these parties prioritized

---

32 In the subsequent electoral cycles, the party benefited from its connections with Prime Minister Hroysman. For this reason, it would be incorrect to classify it as a non-parliamentary party in the 2015 municipal council elections. In the 2015 elections, *Sovist Ukrainy* was rebranded as Vinnytska European Strategy (*Vinnytska Yevropeiska Stratehiya*) and greatly benefited from its connections with Prime Minister Hroysman. In 2015, Vinnytska European Strategy gained the most votes in the Vinnytsia City Council: 20 out of 54 seats. Prior to the 2020 substate contests, it was rebranded as the Ukrainian Strategy of Hroysman. Its electoral performance in the Vinnytsia *oblast* sharply increased: the party obtained the largest vote shares in the regional council contests and municipal council elections; the incumbent city mayor, a party affiliate, was re-elected.

33 In 2012–2014, the incumbent city mayor Hennadiy Trukhanov was an MP affiliated with the Party of Regions, elected in single-member district No. 136 in Odesa. In February 2014, Trukhanov left the parliamentary faction of the Party of Regions. While contesting the early municipal elections in Odesa held in May 2014, he collaborated with the winners of the Euromaidan Uprising. In the 2015 mayoral elections, he decided to stay away from the rivalry between the government and the opposition, and established Trust Actions, co-chaired with the mayor of Kharkiv. In the 2020 mayoral elections, which Trukhanov won, his major competitor was a representative of the parliamentary party Opposition Platform.

mayoral elections and, subsequently, municipal council contests, but their electoral performance in the regional council elections proved outstanding.

Now, I turn to the 2014-2015 electoral cycle and apply the same algorithm of investigation.

In three instances, the same party gained the largest vote share in the parliamentary, regional, and municipal elections. This was evident in the Dnipropetrovska, Zaporizka, and Khersonska *oblast*s. In the first two instances, the frontrunner was the Opposition Bloc, and in the latter it was the ruling party, the Petro Poroshenko Bloc.

In the 2014/2015 electoral cycle, there were seven instances when the frontrunners in the parliamentary and regional elections in the same regions were the same political parties; that number dropped to four in the 2019/2020 multilevel electoral cycle.

In only four regions did non-parliamentary parties obtain the largest vote shares in the 2015 regional council elections. In all other instances, parliamentary parties took the lead in the 2015 regional contests. People's Front—the parliamentary party that obtained the largest vote shares in the 2014 parliamentary elections and formed a sizable faction within the parliamentary coalition—decided not to contest the 2015 substate elections. The major reason was its poor institutionalization at the substate scales. This decision greatly affected the extent of vertical incongruence in multilevel elections. In most instances, voters in the regions where People's Front obtained the largest vote shares in the 2014 parliamentary elections (according to proportional representation) switched to supporting the core ruling party, the president's party, the Petro Poroshenko Bloc. However, there were two exceptions. In the Volynska and Khmelnytska *oblast*s, non-parliamentary parties took the lead in the 2015 regional council elections (UKROP [Ukrainian Association of Patriots] in the Volynska *oblast* and For Concrete Actions in the Khmelnytska *oblast* in Western Ukraine).

When I compared the parliamentary and municipal electoral arenas, I found three *oblast*s where the same party was the frontrunner in the 2014 parliamentary elections and the 2015 municipal council elections: the Dnipropetrovska, Zaporizka, and Khersonska *oblast*s.

There were ten instances in which the parties that came first in the 2015 regional council elections were also the frontrunners in the municipal elections in the *oblast* capitals.

Finally, turning to the 2010/2012 electoral cycle, I observe the highest extent of congruence between the frontrunners that contested multilevel elections in the same regions.

In ten instances, the same parties obtained the largest vote shares in the parliamentary, regional, and municipal elections in the 2010/2012 electoral cycle. In the subsequent (2014/2015) electoral cycle, the number dropped to three. In the most recent (2019/2020) electoral cycle, there were no instances at all.

Also, I compared the outcomes of the parliamentary and regional elections held according to proportional representation rules. In 14 out of 25 cases, the same parties were the frontrunners in the regional and parliamentary contests in the same regions. This number halved in the 2014/2015 electoral cycle and then dropped to four in the 2019/2020 electoral cycle.

Among these 14 cases, there were ten regions in which the ruling Party of Regions won the most votes in the same regions in the 2010 regional elections and the 2012 parliamentary contests.[34] Fatherland, the major opposition parliamentary party, was suppressed by the regime during both the 2010 regional elections and the 2012 parliamentary contests.[35] However, if we compare the electoral scores exclusively according to the proportional representation rules, we find that in the 2012 parliamentary elections,

---

[34] These regions were found in the south and east of the country (Crimea, the Dnipropetrovska, Donetska, Zaporizka, Luhanska, Mykolaivska, Odeska, Kharkivska, Khersonska *oblast*s, and the City of Sevastopol). In three instances, Fatherland was the frontrunner in the same regions in the 2010 regional elections and the 2012 parliamentary contests (the Volynska, Ivano-Frankivska, and Rivnenska *oblast*s in Western Ukraine). Freedom obtained the largest vote share in the Lvivska *oblast* in both the 2010 and 2012 electoral contests (becoming the parliamentary party in the latter case).

[35] In May 2010, a series of criminal investigations were launched on the party leader Yuliya Tymoshenko. In October 2011, she was sentenced for seven years in prison.

Fatherland was the frontrunner in ten regions where the Party of Regions, the ruling party, had obtained the largest vote shares in the 2010 regional elections.[36]

Next, I compared the parliamentary and municipal electoral arenas. In 12 out of 21 instances, the same parties obtained the largest vote shares in the 2012 parliamentary elections and the 2010 municipal council elections in the corresponding *oblast*s and *oblast* capitals. In other words, there were only nine cases of incongruence.

In the 2010 municipal council elections, non-parliamentary parties obtained the largest vote shares in six *oblast* capitals, including three *oblast* capitals where the frontrunner was Freedom, the party that gained parliamentary party status as a result of the 2012 parliamentary elections. In the 2015 municipal council elections, the number of such instances increased to eight; in the 2020 municipal council elections, it went up to 16.

In the 2010 contests, there was a limited number of non-parliamentary parties among the frontrunners in the municipal council elections. There was only the Conscience of Ukraine, led by Vinnytsia's incumbent city mayor, Volodymyr Hroysman, which obtained the largest vote shares in the 2010 municipal elections in two *oblast* capitals (Poltava and Vinnytsia in Central Ukraine). The party was able to take the lead only in the municipal elections; its electoral performance in the 2010 regional elections was modest.

When I compared the regional and municipal electoral arenas, I found more cases of vertical congruence between frontrunners in the simultaneous substate elections in the 2010/2012 electoral cycle than in the two subsequent cycles. In 13 out of 21 instances, the same parties obtained the largest vote shares in the regional and municipal electoral arenas. In most cases, the frontrunners were

---

36 Of these ten regions, eight regions are in Central Ukraine (the Vinnytska, Zhytomyrska, Kyivska, Kirovohradska, Poltavska, Sumska, Cherkaska, and Chernihivska *oblast*s) and two in Western Ukraine (the Khmelnytska and Chernivetska *oblast*s). It is worth keeping in mind that Fatherland was not able to contest the 2010 substate elections in two regions (the Lvivska and Kyivska *oblast*s) because it faced strict administrative barriers imposed by the authoritarian ruler in the Center.

parliamentary parties. In one case the frontrunner was Freedom, a non-parliamentary party in the 2010 elections that became a parliamentary party after the 2012 parliamentary elections.

Now I turn to measuring and comparing the extent of the fragmentation of the party system in regional and municipal electoral arenas (Table 4.5; Table 4.6).

Table 4.5. Average ENP in the regional and municipal electoral arenas in 2010, 2015, 2020.

Average ENP	The regional electoral arena	The municipal electoral arena
2010[37]	3.54	3.85
2015	5.64	5.22
2020	5.57	4.36

Note: I calculate ENP by taking the inverse of the sum of the fractional vote share of each party (Laakso and Taagepera 1979).

Source: Author's calculations on the basis of official data from the Central Electoral Commission.

2010 saw the lowest amount of fragmentation. The average ENP at the regional level was 3.54; the average ENP at the municipal level was 3.85. The least fragmented regional councils were found in the Donetska and Luhanska *oblast*s in Eastern Ukraine, while the most fragmented regional council was found in the Ivano-Frankivska *oblast* in Western Ukraine. In 2010, the principal determinant of the low party system fragmentation in the regional and municipal electoral arenas was the limited scope of political competition, which greatly benefited the ruling party in the Center. In the 2010 contests, the latter's electoral success was secured by employing substate actors as centrally appointed regional governors (more on that below) as well as by the full-scale application of administrative resources.

---

[37] Calculations comprise parties' vote shares obtained according to the proportional representation rules.

In 2015, the level of party system fragmentation in the regional and municipal electoral arenas increased. The average ENP in the regional electoral arena was 5.64, and the average ENP in the municipal electoral arena was 5.22. Arguably, this was determined by increased political competition after the change of the political regime in Ukraine.

When I turn to the 2020 contests, I find that party system fragmentation in the municipal electoral arena decreased when compared to the 2015 elections. The average ENP was 4.36. Simply put, the municipal councils elected in 2020 were less fragmented than those elected in the previous contests. The extent of party system fragmentation in the regional and municipal electoral arenas was no longer roughly the same. The average ENP in the regional electoral arena was 5.57. The extent of the fragmentation of the regional councils did not change significantly when compared to the previous electoral cycle. The different scope of party system fragmentation in the regional and municipal electoral arenas in 2020 suggests that the decentralization reform, which increased the "stakes" in the municipal contests, played a role. In this case, the decentralization reform contributed to the decrease of party system fragmentation in the municipal electoral arena.

Table 4.6. ENP in the regional and municipal electoral arenas in 2010, 2015, 2020: the regional dimension.

	The 2010 Regional Elections, ENP (according to PR)	The 2010 Municipal Elections, ENP (according to PR)	The 2015 Regional Elections, ENP	The 2015 Municipal Elections, ENP	The 2020 Regional Elections, ENP	The 2015 Municipal Elections, ENP
Vinnytska	6.0	4.3	5.6	4.4	3.5	2.2
Volynska	3.4	5.3	5.6	4.9	5.1	5.0

Dnipropetrovska	2.8	3.6	4.4	3.5	5.7	4.7
Donetska	1.3	1.3	-	-	-	-
Zhytomyrska	5.1	6.2	6.5	5.3	8.2	4.4
Zakarpatska	3.9	0.7	4.9	7.2	7.4	5.9
Zaporizka	2.3	3.6	5.5	5.6	5.6	5.3
Ivano-Frankivska	6.6	4.9	5.3	4.7	5.6	2.0
Kyivska	3.0	-	6.4	-	4.4	-
Kirovohradska	3.3	3.8	6.1	7.4	5.8	7.2
Lvivska	3.8	4.7	7	4.7	5.9	3.7
Luhanska	1.7	2.1				
Mykolaivska	2.2	3.5	5.5	3.1	5	4.6
Odeska	3.3	3.7	5	3.6	5.7	4.3
Poltavska	4.4	2.9	3.3	6.7	6.7	6.0
Rivnenska	5.0	7.0	4.9	6.3	6.7	6.3
Sumska	2.6	3.4	6.6	3.8	5.4	4.4
Ternopilska	-	-	5.6	5.4	0.9	3.8
Kharkivska	2.3	3.2	4	2.0	3.9	4.0
Khersonska	3.2	4.6	5.7	7.0	6	4.6
Khmelnytska	3.8	2.9	6.3	5.5	6.2	2.4
Cherkaska	3	-	6.8	7.5	5.2	6.5
Chernivetska	3.9	4.0	7.9	5.6	7.5	6.3
Chernihivska	4.5	5.7	7.2	5.4	6.1	2.4
Kyiv	-	-	3.7	-	5.6	-
Sevastopol	3.4	-	-	-	-	-

Now I proceed to capture the dynamics of dominant-party rule in substate councils over time. For this purpose, I identify cases in which a party obtains more than 50% of the votes (Table 4.7).

Table 4.7. Number of cases of dominant-party rule in regional and municipal councils elected in 2010, 2015, 2020.

	The 2010 elections	The 2015 elections	The 2020 elections
Number of cases of dominant-party rule in regional councils	8	0	0
Number of cases of dominant-party rule in municipal councils	4	1	4

Note: Cases of dominant-party rule qualify when a party obtains more than 50% of the votes in a regional or municipal council.

Source: Author's calculations on the basis of official data from the Central Electoral Commission.

In 2010, the ruling party won more than 50% (according to proportional representation rules) in eight regions (the Autonomous Republic of Crimea, the Dnipropetrovska, Donetska, Zaporizka, Luhanska, Mykolaivska, Odeska, Kharkivska, and Khersonska *oblasts*). When we add the electoral results in single-member electoral districts, we find that the number of regional councils with dominant-party rule increased to 14. The party obtained more than 50% (according to proportional representation rules) in four municipal councils in *oblast* capitals: Donetsk, Luhansk, Poltava, and Khmelnytsk. In two out of four cities, the Party of Regions, the Center's ruling party was the frontrunner: Donetsk and Luhansk in Eastern Ukraine. In Poltava (Central Ukraine), the Conscience of Ukraine gained more than 50% of the vote (according to proportional representation rules). Arguably, crucial to its electoral success was the effective electoral strategy of Oleksandr Mamai, the successful candidate in the 2010 mayoral elections, who ran under the party banner. In Khmelnytsk (Western Ukraine) Fatherland, the opposition parliamentary party, obtained 50% of the vote (according to proportional representation rules).

In contrast, the 2015 regional elections did not produce any cases of dominant-party rule in regional councils. In 2015, dominant party rule was established in only one municipal council, in the city of Kharkiv. The principal determinant for Renaissance—a non-parliamentary party—winning a majority of seats in the Kharkiv municipal council in Kharkiv was not the party's, but rather the popularity of the incumbent city mayor Kernes, who successfully ran in the 2015 mayoral elections under the Renaissance party banner.

As in 2015, there were no cases of dominant-party rule in the regional councils in 2020: no single party managed to win more than 50% of the vote. In the Vinnytska *oblast*, the Ukrainian Strategy of Hroysman came close, winning 47.6%. However, in 2020, single-party dominance was established in 4 out of 21 *oblast* capitals. In all four, a non-parliamentary party, which had prioritized the municipal electoral arena, gained more than 50% of the vote: Freedom in Ivano-Frankivsk; the Ukrainian Strategy of Hroysman in Vinnytsia; the Team of Symchyshyn in Khmelnytsk; and Native Home in Chernihiv. In three of these municipalities, the parties were led by incumbent city mayors: Serhiy Morhunov in Vinnytsia; Roman Martsynkiv in Ivano-Frankivsk; and Vladislav Atroshenko in Chernihiv.

The affiliation of the incumbent city mayors and the single-party majorities in their municipal councils implies the growing influence of the former over the latter. Clearly, in *oblast* capitals with dominant-party rule, the positions of city mayors in the system of local self-governance are strengthened.

Comparative analysis demonstrates that the political regime plays an important role. In 2010, during the authoritarian turn, dominant party rule was established in numerous regional councils. When political competition intensified in 2015, we do not see a single case of dominant-party rule in regional councils. If we trace the dynamics of municipal councils, we find four cases where dominant-party rule was established in 2010. Only two out of four these cases were a victory for the ruling party. This suggests that, during the authoritarian turn, political competition in the municipal electoral arena was less restricted than political competition in the regional arena.

This chapter has compared the electoral outcomes in multiple arenas (i) before and (ii) after the implementation of the post-2014 decentralization policy. The results of the comparative analysis demonstrate that the dissimilarity between the outcomes of parliamentary and municipal elections in the 2019/2020 multilevel electoral cycle doubled compared to the 2014/2015 electoral cycle. This finding indicates that decentralization played a role, and this corresponds to the theory-driven expectation that an increase of substate authority can drive multilevel voting apart.

The 2019/2020 electoral cycle witnesses the most striking extent of vertical incongruence between the frontrunners in the parliamentary and substate contests. In the 2019/2020 multilevel electoral cycle, there are no cases of vertical congruence between the frontrunners in the parliamentary elections, regional council elections, and municipal council elections in the same *oblasts*. Notably, there were three instances of this in the 2014/2015 electoral cycle and ten in the 2010/2012 electoral cycle. In no *oblast* capital did the same party come first in both the parliamentary and local council contests in the 2019/2020 electoral cycle. The two previous electoral cycles under study witnessed some extent of vertical congruence between the frontrunners in the parliamentary and municipal arenas.

The electoral performance of non-parliamentary parties improved, and this contributed to the extent of incongruence of multilevel elections on both the regional and municipal levels. In the 2020 contests, in 9 out of 23 regions, non-parliamentary parties obtained the largest vote shares in the regional council elections. The electoral performance of non-parliamentary parties in the municipal council elections was even more striking. They were frontrunners in 16 out of 21 *oblast* capitals. In as many as 9 out of 21 corresponding *oblasts* and *oblast* capitals, the same party obtained the largest vote shares in both the regional and municipal council elections. Still, in only three out of nine cases that the same party obtained the largest vote shares in the simultaneous regional and municipal council elections was the frontrunner a parliamentary party.

The extent of vertical congruence between frontrunners in the simultaneous regional and municipal council elections is higher than that between frontrunners in the parliamentary and substate electoral arenas. Non-parliamentary parties greatly contributed to the growing incongruence of the multilevel party system, but their electoral performance positively affected the scope of congruence between the observed outcomes of the regional and municipal contests.

The increase of incongruence of multilevel elections goes hand in hand with a decrease in the extent of party system fragmentation in the municipal electoral arena in Ukraine. The municipal councils elected in 2020 were less fragmented than those elected in the 2015 contests. The extent of fragmentation of the regional councils did not change significantly compared to the 2015 elections. Moreover, the 2020 contests reveal more instances of dominant-party rule at the municipal level compared to the previous elections under investigation.

Thus, Ukraine's parties — whether in power or in opposition — continue to obtain different vote shares in the multilevel elections in the same constituencies. Their regionalized electoral performance in Ukraine's general elections is still substantially different from their electoral performance in both the regional and municipal elections in the same *oblasts*.

5 Multilevel Competition and Decentralization

This chapter seeks to explain how party competition changes after implementation of the local amalgamation policy. It seeks to explain why the parliamentary parties associated with the central policymakers who initiated and completed the policy did not make impressive electoral gains in the 2020 substate contests.

The data analysis presented in the previous chapters compels me to suggest that the newly elected President Zelenskyy promoted decentralization, but did not work hard to improve his newly established party's electoral performance in advance of the 2020 contests.

However, compared to its electoral performance in the 2019 parliamentary elections, Servant of the People's 2020 electoral scores were not really poor. Although it did not perform well in the municipal council elections in *oblast* capitals, and although it obtained the largest vote shares in only four regional councils, Servant of the People still won a higher number of seats in all substate—i.e. regional, subregional, and local—councils (15.09%) than other political parties. Fatherland gained the second highest number of seats in all substate councils (10.53%). Opposition Platform came third (10.53%), followed by European Solidarity (9.20%) and For the Future, a non-parliamentary party, (9.20%). All parliamentary parties won approximately half of the seats in all local councils in 2020 (Romanova 2022). 15.42% seats in all local councils went to independent candidates.[38]

When we consider the presidential party's electoral performance in the 2019 parliamentary elections and the 2020 regional elections, we see that its electoral strongholds were not concentrated in one particular (macro)region. Instead, they were found in the Dnipropetrovska, Mykolaivska, and Sumska *oblast*s, the three

---

38 In 2020, independent candidates were allowed to stand for local elections only in constituencies with fewer than 10,000 voters. This change to the electoral rules was introduced in Summer 2020, a few months before the 2020 elections.

regions where its electoral performance was solid in both the 2019 parliamentary and 2020 regional elections. These three regions lie in Eastern, Southern, and Central Ukraine respectively. In contrast, the other major parliamentary parties continued to rely on their regionalized electoral strongholds concentrated in particular macroregions (Romanova forthcoming).

I propose that Zelenskyy's policymaking with respect to decentralization—completing local amalgamation and attempting to increase regional authority—had little to do with his expected electoral gains. I explain this puzzle in the following way. Contrary to expectations (e.g. Romanova 2020b), there would not have been very much "at stake" for Zelenskyy and his party in the 2020 substate elections, because the newly elected president started his tenure with all power in his hands in the Center. His predecessors invested effort and resources in party politics at the substate scales because they did not possess all the power resources in Kyiv. In contrast, Zelenskyy had already concentrated central power in the country: both the presidency and a single-party majority in parliament. I suggest that this is the principal reason why the president did not prioritize party building in advance of the 2020 substate elections. His party headquarters did not work very hard to enhance electoral gains in 2020 (Kravets 2020).

In addition, Zelenskyy won the 2019 presidential elections with no party. The brand-new party, which he established literally on the eve of the 2019 parliamentary elections, obtained the largest vote shares in every region where the elections were held, apart from Donetska and Luhanska *oblast*s in Eastern Ukraine, several electoral districts in the Lvivska *oblast* in Western Ukraine and one electoral district in the Odeska *oblast* in Southern Ukraine. The impressive electoral results of Servant of the People in the 2019 parliamentary elections testified to Zelenskyy's electoral support. This experience would have discouraged him from investing too much effort in institutionalizing his party at the substate scales. Prior to the 2020 regional elections, Servant of the People had established only 26 party branches in the regions.

Soon after Zelenskyy won the 2019 presidential elections, substate actors, i.e. the deputies in substate councils, attempted to join Servant of the People; however, the party ignored their appeals (Danutsa 2020). Vedernikova (2020) traces the attempts of numerous city mayors to switch to the political team of the newly elected President Zelenskyy in 2019. Arguably, the case of Hennadiy Kernes, the mayor of Kharkiv, is the most revealing. Immediately after the 2019 presidential elections, he showed his loyalty to Zelenskyy and could easily have been recruited into his political team in advance of the 2019 parliamentary contests. However, Zelenskyy largely ignored Kernes. This did not harm the electoral performance of Zelenskyy's newly established party: Servant of the People secured victory in all single-member districts in the Kharkivska *oblast* in the 2019 parliamentary elections. The outcomes of the subsequent substate contests were less favorable. In the 2020 mayoral elections, Servant of the People lost in the city of Kharkiv.[39] Nevertheless, in the 2020 regional elections, a Servant of the People candidate secured a seat as the head of the Kharkiv Regional Council.

It is an open question why President Zelenskyy decided not to co-opt substate elites when they wanted to join his party. His decision might have been guided by his previous positive experience recruiting inexperienced people into the party lists in the 2019 parliamentary elections. Voters who supported President Zelenskyy were also in favor[40] of candidates with no previous involvement in party politics. When President Zelenskyy recruited new and inexperienced people into his party, he enhanced his leadership and made the newcomers dependent on him. The Servant of the People parliamentary faction illustrates this. Despite its numerous internal divisions, President Zelenskyy remained the key decision-maker, capable of forcing the party faction to support his initiative to

---

39 Zelenskyy's candidate for the 2020 mayoral elections was Oleksandr Kucher, one of the MPs elected to parliament in the single-member district in Kharkiv region, who then served as a regional governor in the Kharkivska *oblast*.

40 The Committee of Voters of Ukraine (2020) found that the Servant of the People faction in municipal councils in Kyiv, Dnipro, and Kharkiv, elected in the 2020 contests, had no prior experience of serving in substate councils.

dismiss the parliamentary speaker Oleksandr Razumkov, even though Razumkov had been in charge of the party's 2019 parliamentary campaign (Minakov 2021b). "Members of the new party were recruited almost as if it were a competition. Deputy mandates were handed to people far removed from politics—and from any understanding of public administration. However, there were also competent, experienced people among the new faces" (Odarchenko 2020). Notably, in April 2020, the official leader of the president's party, Oleksandr Kornienko, addressed mayors with the following exhortation: '[Go ahead.] Establish your all-Ukrainian party of mayors. Become policymakers. Get engaged not only in local politics, but in all-Ukrainian politics. Represent the interests of local governance at the highest possible level [in parliament]' (Kornienko 2020). Presumably, at that point, Servant of the People did not believe that mayors would succeed in doing so in advance of the 2020 contests.

In addition, the new ruling party did not aggregate local incumbents into partner parties to compete against political opponents more effectively. As a result, the interactions between parliamentary parties and non-parliamentary parties changed compared to the two previous multilevel electoral cycles. In 2010 and 2015, the ruling party promoted the non-parliamentary parties that could effectively compete against the ruling party's opponents, i.e. the United Center in 2010; Our Land in 2015. A noteworthy exception was UKROP in the 2015 elections. Such strategic interactions between the party in power and non-parliamentary parties were not evident in the 2020 substate contests (Box 5.1.).

Box 5.1. Major non-parliamentary parties in 2010 and 2015

The Ukrainian Association of Patriots "UKROP" (*Ukrainske Obyednannia Patriotiv "UKROP"*), established on the eve of the 2015 elections, won seats in 18 regional councils across the country and came first at the regional elections in the Volynska *oblast*. Its candidate Boris Filatov won the mayoral election in the city of Dnipro, the Opposition Bloc electoral stronghold. Furthermore, UKROP gained 21 out of 64 seats in Dnipro City Council, the second-biggest electoral score after Opposition Bloc. The major factor in its electoral success was its direct link to the domestic oligarch Ihor Kolomoiskyi, who served as the regional governor in the UKROP electoral strongholds, the Dnipropetrovska *oblast,* in 2014-2015. Second, the party put forward an agenda that appealed to voters both in its electoral core and beyond. It paid special attention to the armed conflict in Donbas, actively supported the Ukrainian Army and volunteer battalions in Donbas. UKROP confronted parliamentary parties both in power and in opposition. It criticized President Poroshenko, who dismissed the regional governor Kolomoiskyi in March 2015. In addition, it appealed to voters who opposed Russia's annexation of Crimea and its engagement in the armed conflict in Donbas, and who were potential supporters of Opposition Bloc.

Renaissance (*Vidrodzhennia*) relied on a parliamentary group established by two MPs: (a) Anton Yatsenko, a Fatherland MP in parliament under the presidency of Viktor Yushchenko, who then joined the Party of Regions faction under the presidency of Viktor Yanukovych; (b) Vitaliy Khomutynnyk, an MP since 2002, who had previously benefited from connections with the oligarch Kolomoiskyi. Significantly, the party did not experience any administrative restrictions, whereas Opposition Bloc, a party with similar electoral appeal, was not able to contest elections in its electoral strongholds in the Kharkivska *oblast* because of barriers imposed. Renaissance recruited Hennadiy Kernes, the mayor of Kharkiv, who would otherwise have contested the 2015 elections under the Opposition Bloc banner, thus allowing Renaissance to become the frontrunner in the regional elections in the Kharkivska *oblast*. As Wilson puts it, "[i]n Kharkiv, Mayor Hennadiy Kernes seems to have been allowed a free run in return for agreeing not to run as part of the Opposition Block [sic] (the outstanding legal cases against him may have helped him make up his mind). Kyiv didn't put any strong candidates up against Kernes" (Wilson 2015). Another revealing example is the Sumska *oblast*. As Vedernikova (2020) points out, Yuriy Chmyr, who was very closely affiliated with the Party of Regions in 2006-2014 and served as a regional governor in the Sumska *oblast* in 2010-2013, contested the 2015 regional elections under the Renaissance banner, and then chaired its regional party branch in 2016-2020. Chmyr then contested the 2020 regional elections under the Opposition Platform banner; the latter party's electoral performance in the Sumska *oblast* greatly increased in 2020.

Our Land (*Nash Krai*) gained electoral representation in nine regional councils across Ukraine in the 2015 contests. "Our Land brings together lots of city mayors who used to support various 'parties of power' in the past" (Romanova 2015a). The party incorporated local policymakers, many of whom used to be associated with the Party of Regions, such as Anton Kisse and Sergiy Kaltsev. Unlike the Opposition Bloc, it did not face any administrative pressures during the electoral campaign. As Wilson puts it, "[t]he Presidential Administration covertly backed new clone parties against its main opponents. Nash Krai (Our Land) was developed explicitly to run against the Opposition Block [sic] — and was made up of local bosses in areas of the east and south adjacent to troublesome areas like the Donbas" (Wilson 2015). Notably, Our Land contested the 2020 substate elections without any prominent guidance from any parliamentary party and relied on affiliates it had recruited in the previous electoral cycles.

In the 2010/2012 electoral cycle, United Center benefited from connections with the Party of Regions, then the ruling party.[41] United Center was led by Viktor Baloha, the head of regional state administration in the Zakarpatska *oblast* (1999-2001 and 2005), the head of the Presidential Secretariat under President Yushchenko (2006-2009), and the minister in the central government under President Yanukovych. Some claim that Baloha contributed to Yanukovych's victory in the Zakarpatska *oblast* in the 2010 presidential elections and used administrative resources to ensure the electoral success of United Center in the 2010 regional elections (Kuzio 2010). In the 2010 regional elections, it was the only party (other than the Party of Regions) to nominate candidates in all 54 single-member districts in the Zakarpatska *oblast* (26 out of 54 candidates were elected) as well as in all 30 single-member districts in the municipal elections in the city of Uzhhorod (12 out of 30 candidates were elected). In addition, United Center won 24.3% according to proportional representation rules in the Zakarpatska *oblast* and became the largest party in the regional

---

41 In 2010, it performed best in the Zakarpatska *oblast*, even though the party contested elections in other regions, such as the Volynska *oblast*.

council, with 46 out of 108 seats. It is hard to believe that all this happened without administrative support from the regional governor, a member of the ruling party.[42] In the 2015 contests, United Center relied on local and regional interest groups and contested substate elections without visible guidance from central actors. The party employed a similar strategy in the 2020 contests, after it was re-registered as Andrii Baloha's Team (*Komanda Andriya Balohy*). This illustrates that non-parliamentary parties can successfully stand for elections even after losing guidance from the top, because they rely on regional and local interest groups.

Thus, in 2010 and 2015, non-parliamentary parties often benefited from the ruling party's support. The single exception was UKROP. In 2010 and 2015, the ruling party promoted non-parliamentary parties to undermine its major political opponents. However, neither the ruling party nor any other parliamentary party provided support to non-parliamentary parties in the 2020 contests.

The established opposition parliamentary parties were motivated to improve their electoral performance in the 2020 contests. In 2019, they failed to win the presidential race; then, they underperformed in the early parliamentary elections in 2019. Improved electoral performance at the substate levels would help strengthen them as an effective opposition to the newly elected president. European Solidarity (formed on the basis of the Petro Poroshenko Bloc), Opposition Platform (formed on the basis of the Opposition Bloc), and Fatherland had previous experience of contesting substate elections and winning political competitions when in opposition.

In 2020, the electoral performance of opposition parliamentary parties was better than that of the ruling party. Their vote shares often improved compared to their electoral record in the 2019 general contests. However, their electoral record in the 2020 substate

---

42 However, in the Donetska *oblast*, the Party of Regions and United Center did not collaborate at all in the 2010 regional elections, and United Center failed to pass the electoral threshold. Arguably, its active campaigning in the 2010 regional elections in the Donetska *oblast* and its criticism of the ruling party helped attract voters who would have cast their ballot for Fatherland.

elections was not impressive in comparison to the electoral performance of non-parliamentary parties.

European Solidarity was closely associated with the launch of the decentralization policy in 2014. The local amalgamation policy was launched under the presidency of Poroshenko. The policy of voluntary local amalgamation was implemented in 2015-2019. During his tenure, President Poroshenko made attempts to introduce constitutional amendments aimed at increasing regional authority in Ukraine. President Zelenskyy's subsequent decentralization policymaking relied greatly on the policy documents prepared under Poroshenko. Still, it does not look like the performance of European Solidarity in the 2020 contests — the elections held after local amalgamation was completed — reflected the input of the new president's party into the reform implementation. In the 2015 substate elections, its predecessor — the then ruling Petro Poroshenko Bloc — obtained reasonably high electoral scores.

It would not be an exaggeration to say that the leader of Fatherland is partly responsible for the post-2014 decentralization reform, because the central government prepared the initial policy drafts on decentralization during Tymoshenko's tenure as prime minister. When the reform was finally launched in 2014, Tymoshenko's party joined the parliamentary coalition that prioritized the decentralization reform in its coalition agreement. At that moment, Fatherland switched to criticizing the decentralization policy, especially, but not exclusively, with respect to local amalgamation. It is unlikely that Fatherland's vote shares in the 2020 contests reflect either the party's input into preparing the decentralization reform or opposition to its implementation.

The comparative analysis of major policy documents on decentralization presented in Chapter 2 revealed the input of Opposition Bloc-associated policymakers into the initial policy learning efforts related to decentralization in 2010-2013. After the decentralization reform was launched in 2014, Opposition Bloc and then its successor, Opposition Platform, criticized the process of policy implementation. The party's position to the decentralization reform had little to do with its electoral performance in the 2020 contests.

By 2020, with the exception of the president's party, no parliamentary party had affiliates among the centrally appointed regional governors. Previously, parliamentary parties' electoral performance used to benefit from the input of regional governors (See Box 'Regional governors and substate elections in 2010 and 2015'). Most critically, ambitious party affiliates of the three opposition parliamentary parties abandoned these parties on the eve of the 2020 contests and stood for election under the banners of non-parliamentary parties. This meant that the parliamentary parties could not sustain their networks of party affiliates with leading positions in local governance.

Opposition Platform faced this challenge before the 2020 substate contests, often in constituencies that could be regarded as its electoral strongholds. The incumbent mayor of Kharkiv, Kernes (who passed away in 2021), contested the 2015 elections under the banner of the non-parliamentary party Renaissance, because administrative barriers meant that Opposition Bloc was not able to stand for elections in Kharkiv. Instead of contesting the 2020 elections under the banner either of Opposition Platform or Trust Actions, Kernes campaigned under the party banner of Kharkiv Bloc—Successful Kharkiv. The latter's electoral performance was outstanding: the party became a frontrunner in both the regional and municipal contests in 2020.[43]

Another revealing example is the city of Zaporizzha. In the 2015 mayoral elections, Volodymyr Buryak[44] campaigned as an independent candidate, but largely relied on the support of Opposition Bloc. During his tenure as mayor, Buryak included various

---

43 This party was officially registered in 2016 under the name Unitary European Ukraine (*Unitarna Yevropeiska Ukraina*). In 2019, it was re-registered as Kharkiv Bloc—Successful Kharkiv; the new party leader was Hennadiy Kernes. According to Kharkiv Bloc's manifesto, the party's major objective was two-fold: improving the quality of life in (i) the city of Kharkiv and (ii) the Kharkiv *oblast*.
44 Prior to the 2015 contests, Volodymyr Buryak was a chief engineer in the "Zaporizhstal" industrial enterprise, owned by Rinat Akhmetov, a major domestic oligarch. While serving as mayor, Buryak appeared in the Opposition Bloc party list (No. 8) in the 2019 parliamentary elections. Opposition Bloc (led by Yevhen Murayev) did not pass the electoral threshold in 2019.

parties in his alliance in the municipal council (Vedernikova 2020), and then decided to stand for the 2020 contests elections under his own party banner: the Party of Volodymyr Buryak "Yednannya."[45] In the 2020 contests, the party's electoral performance was impressive: it won 25% of the vote in the municipal elections in Zaporizzha and 10.71% in the regional council elections in the Zaporizka *oblast*.

Fatherland faced a similar challenge, but only in the 2020 substate elections. The revealing piece of evidence is that Anatoliy Bondarenko,[46] the mayor of Cherkasy, who was a longstanding Fatherland affiliate, contested the 2020 substate elections under the banner of a non-parliamentary party, For the Future[47] — one of the most successful non-parliamentary parties in the 2020 substate contests and a frontrunner in the Volynska *oblast* as well as in three *oblast* capitals. For the Future came first (11.14%) and Fatherland

---

45 The party was first registered in November 2015 under the name Unity (*Yednannya*). In January 2019, the party was re-registered as the Party of Volodymyr Buryak "Yednannya."
46 In 2002-2005 Bondarenko was the mayor of Lysianska village council. In 2005-2006, he was the head of the Lysianska subregional state administration (subregional governor). In the 2006 regional elections, he became a councillor in the Cherkasy Regional Council (Fatherland). In 2010, he chaired the territorial party branch of Fatherland in the Cherkasy *oblast*. In the 2010 regional elections, he became a councillor in the Cherkasy Regional Council (Fatherland). In 2012 and 2014 he contested parliamentary elections (Fatherland), but did not succeed. As a result of the 2015 mayoral elections, he became mayor of Cherkasy (Fatherland). In the 2020 Cherkasy mayoral elections, he was re-elected (For the Future).
47 The party was registered in July 2008 under the name Ukraine of the Future (*Ukraina Maibutnyoho*). The party contested parliamentary elections in 2012 and 2014. In May 2020 the party was re-registered under the new name of For the Future.
    The party was closely linked to the parliamentary arena. It had the same title as the parliamentary group established in the *Verkhovna Rada* in August 2019. Its party leader was a parliamentary deputy, Ihor Palytsia, with close links to the oligarch Ihor Kolomoiskyi. For the Future was linked to the non-parliamentary parties that successfully contested the 2015 substate elections. Palytsia stood in the 2015 regional elections under the banner of another non-parliamentary party, UKROP, and then served as the head of the regional council in the Volynska *oblast* (2015-2019). Another important party affiliate, the MP Anton Yatsenko, had been one of the leaders of Renaissance in the previous electoral cycle.

came last (6.14%) in the 2020 municipal council elections in Cherkasy.

Prior to the 2020 contests, a few ambitious local incumbents left the parliamentary party led by President Poroshenko. The mayor of Chernihiv, Vladislav Atroshenko,[48] who had won the 2015 mayoral elections under banner of the president's party, the Petro Poroshenko Bloc, contested the 2020 elections under banner of Native Home.[49] In 2020, Native Home was the frontrunner in the municipal council elections, and had one of the best electoral performances when compared to other *oblast* capitals (61%). Moreover, Native Home obtained the largest vote shares in the regional council elections in the Chernihivska *oblast* (29%). Similarly, in 2015, Serhiy Sukhomlyn,[50] the mayor of Zhytomyr, and Andriy

---

48 In the 2002 parliamentary contests, Vladislav Atroshenko was elected in the single-member district No. 207 in the Chernihivska *oblast* (Our Ukraine Bloc). In February-December 2005, he was the head of the Chernihiv state administration (regional governor). In the 2006 parliamentary elections, he failed to become an MP (Our Ukraine). As a result of the 2010 regional contests, he became a councillor in the Chernihiv regional council (*Sylna Ukraina*). In the 2012 parliamentary elections, he was elected in the single-member district No. 207 in the Chernihivska *oblast* as an independent candidate. Once elected, he joined the Party of Regions faction. On 19 February 2014 he left the Party of Regions faction. After the victory of the Euromaidan Uprising, he led the territorial branch of the Petro Poroshenko Bloc in the Chernihivska *oblast*. In the 2014 parliamentary elections, he was elected MP in the single-member district No. 206 in the Chernihivska *oblast* (Petro Poroshenko Bloc). In 2015, he won the mayoral elections in the city of Chernihiv (Petro Poroshenko Bloc). In the 2020 mayoral elections in Chernihiv, he was re-elected (Native Home).
49 Native Home was officially registered as a party name in September 2015; previously the party, established in 2014, had been called the Capitalist Party of Ukraine (*Kapitalistychna Partia Ukrainy*). According to its party manifesto, Native Home's main objective is to stimulate the social and economic development of the city of Chernihiv and the Chernihivska *oblast*.
50 In 2006-2020 Sukhomlyn served as a councillor in the Zhyrtomyr City Council (Our Ukraine). In 2010-2014 he was a coucilor in Zhytomyr Regional Council ('Front of Change'). Sukhomlyn contested the 2012 parliamentary elections (Fatherland), but did not win a seat. In March 2014-November 2015, he was the deputy mayor of Zhytomyr. After winning the 2015 mayoral elections, he became mayor of Zhytomyr (Petro Poroshenko Bloc). In the 2020 mayoral elections in Zhytomyr, he was re-elected (Proposition).

Raikovych,[51] the mayor of Kropyvnytskyi, won their mayoral positions as affiliates of the ruling party, the Petro Poroshenko Bloc. In 2020, both mayors successfully contested elections under the banner of a non-parliamentary party, Proposition (*Propozitsia*).

Proposition expressed its eagerness to represent the collective desire of city mayors to contest the 2020 substate elections under a single party banner, thus presenting a unified appeal to voters across the country. Six city mayors of *oblast* capitals joined the party. Contrary to expectations, the mayor of Kyiv, Vitaliy Klitchko, did not. Without Klitchko—the head of the Association of Cities of Ukraine—the party looked less appealing to other local incumbents (e.g. Atroshenko 2021). Boris Filatov, the party leader, and mayor of Dnipro, contested the 2015 substate contests under the UKROP banner.[52] The Committee of Voters of Ukraine (2020: 22) found that the Proposition faction in Dniprovska City Council, elected in the 2020 contests, consisted of two merged factions, elected in the 2015 elections: UKROP and Our Land.

I acknowledge that other factors could have affected the electoral performance of the three parliamentary parties in the 2020 contests. For example, they could have made more strategic use of public funding, available to them in line with the 2015 Law on

---

51 Raikovych unsuccessfully contested parliamentary elections in 1998, 2002, 2006, and 2007. In 2010-2015 he served as a councillor in the Kirovohrad Regional Council (*Narodna Partia*). In 2015, he won the mayoral elections in the city of Kropyvnytskiy (Petro Poroshenko Bloc). In the 2020 mayoral elections in Kropyvnytskiy, he was re-elected (Proposition).
Since 1992, he has been the owner of "Yatran"—a medium-size enterprise that specializes in meat production.

52 Boris Filatov had successfully contested parliamentary and substate elections in the past. In the 2014 parliamentary elections, Filatov won in a single-member district in the city of Dnipro. In 2015, he won the mayoral election in Dnipro. At that time, he co-led UKROP, a party that benefited from the financial support of the oligarch Kolomoiskyi. The party leader and some affiliates had experience serving in regional state administrations. Filatov served as the deputy head of the Dnipripetrovska regional administration when Kolomoiskyi was the regional governor in 2014.
Proposition recruited Valentyn Reznichenko, the former regional governor of the Dnipropetrovska *oblast* (2015-2019), who led the party list in that region in the 2020 contests. In the 2020 contests, Dnipropetrovska *oblast* and the city of Dnipro were the party's electoral strongholds.

Public Funding for Political Parties. They could have invested these resources in improving their institutionalization at the substate scales. Fatherland had the highest number of territorial branches — in April 2016 there were as many as 16,862. However, the Committee of Voters of Ukraine (2021) finds that the Petro Poroshenko Bloc, Opposition Bloc and Fatherland spent most of the public finances on advertising (i.e. on TV). Of course, the amount of public funding available to parliamentary parties does not compare with the support that parties could receive from domestic oligarchs. Still, the way the parties used the available public funding suggests that party institutionalization at the substate scales was unlikely to be their core priority on the eve of the 2020 contests. European Solidarity had 2,174 substate branches in summer 2020; Opposition Platform had 225; and Fatherland had 7,333.

Why did local incumbents want to switch their affiliation to benefit the newly elected president and not the opposition parliamentary parties? In order to answer this question, I need to refer to Daria Platonova, who distinguishes between concentrated and diffused patronage between central and substate actors in Ukraine. As she argues, "the [substate] elites' main objectives are to remain in power, to keep their assets, and continue accessing resources in the centre" (Platonova 2020: 80). In her PhD research on politics in Donetsk and Kharkiv in March-April 2014, she categorized Donetsk as a concentrated patronage region; she categorized the city of Kharkiv as a diffused patronage unit. In a concentrated patronage system, substate actors can stay in power when they secure access to centrally distributed resources. In contrast, substate actors who operate within a diffused patronage system do not adhere to one patron in the center. They develop the capacity to adjust to the requirements of multiple patrons simultaneously or to frequent changes of patrons in the Center. Substate elites operating according to diffused patronage do not seek confrontation with the Center. Instead, they prefer negotiating and bargaining with the ruling party.

I observe that since 2014, in their interactions with the Center, most regions and municipalities in the government-controlled territories of Ukraine, including cities, operate in a diffused patronage system. Although President Zelenskyy did not recruit local incumbents into his party in the 2020 contests, or established any alternate non-parliamentary parties, as some ruling parties had in the past, local incumbents did not contest elections under the banners of the opposition parties. When they observed how harshly the Center confronted Klitchko, its major political opponent, the mayor of Kyiv (e.g. Vedernikova 2019; Vedernikova 2020a), they were probably discouraged from engaging in any rivalry with the president. In addition, standing for elections under the banners of parliamentary parties could imply that they were joining 'national patron-client networks that are manifested through the political party system' (USAID 2014: 19). Simply put, joining the party lists of well-established parliamentary parties on the eve of the 2020 contests would have required some form of costly bargaining with the leadership of the nationwide party branches.

I suggest that there was a lot "at stake" for non-parliamentary parties in the 2020 contests. The local amalgamation policy heavily decreased the number of substate councils at the local and subregional (*rayon*) levels. In the regular substate elections held in 2015, voters could elect 10,562 local—regional, subregional, and municipal—councils, with 108,941 seats. In 2020, electors could cast their ballots for 43,122 councilors in 1,577 local—regional, subregional, and municipal—councils. These drastic changes reduced the number of available seats and, thus, increased the scope of competition. The electoral rules, prescribed in the 2019 Electoral Code and again specified literally on the eve of the 2020 contests, require contestants in substate elections to stand for election under a party banner in all constituencies with more than 10,000 people.

In order to stay in office, substate incumbents made use of their major competitive advantage: the experience of serving in substate councils during the implementation of the decentralization policy. In centralized states, voting behavior is heavily guided by national issues, but when voters elect members of powerful institutions in regional elections, their voting preferences often depend on their assessment of the performance of regional rather than central authorities (Thorlakson 2007). I assume that this explanatory angle is not limited to the regional electoral arena. According to public polls, people across Ukraine tend to positively assess the performance of their local authorities, especially when compared to other officials (Council of Europe 2020b; IRI 2021). This is not surprising. Local authorities have had many opportunities to enhance public service delivery and foster local development since the launch of the post-2014 decentralization reform. Their efforts were the most beneficial for residents of cities and towns that constituted the administrative centers of ATCs (including all *oblast* capitals in Ukraine).

During the electoral campaign, central authorities and regional governors did not tackle the COVID-19 very effectively (Vedernikova 2020a). The former imposed severe quarantine measures, which were highly unpopular everywhere in the country, especially among those involved in business. The governors lacked the managerial skills required to implement the centrally directed policies. Tensions and conflicts between the state and local self-governance manifested in clashes between the Center and mayors, as well as between regional governors and mayors. Mass media and social media covered those clashes extensively, and voters had plenty of opportunities to learn which authorities imposed the unpopular quarantine measures and which authorities opposed them.

The relatively high level of appreciation of local authorities' performance explains why many voters cast their ballots for local incumbents in the 2020 substate contests, disregarding the changes in their party affiliation. The outcomes of the municipal elections in Ukraine demonstrated a relatively high number of re-elected local incumbents in the 2020 contests. Approximately one third of councillors in substate councils were re-elected;[53] the number of re-elected incumbent mayors was even higher (Torikai 2021). This accords with the comparative research in the field of territorial politics that proves that voters who vote for powerful substate

---

53 In the 2020 substate elections, approximately 40% incumbents were re-elected in city councils in Kyiv, Dnipro, Lviv, Odesa, and Kharkiv (Committee of Voters of Ukraine 2020: 15; 24; 29; 35; 40).

authorities tend to make electoral choices based on their assessment of the substate authorities' performance (e.g. Thorlakson 2007; Baumann et al 2020). Prior to the 2020 contests in Ukraine, voters were able to witness their ability to convert the advantages generated by the decentralization reform into improved public services and enhanced local development. The high level of public trust in local authorities in Ukraine as compared to that in central authorities can indirectly support this point.

As stated in chapters 1 and 2, local authorities gained experience in lobbying for their interests vis-à-vis the Center in 2015-2020. During the reform-implementation stage, they learned that no (parliamentary/national) political party could protect their interests when bargaining with the Center better than they could. I suggest that this was the critical reason why local incumbents preferred to stay away from parliamentary parties and contest local elections under their own party banners. Importantly, contesting elections under a new party banner does not require much effort and does not automatically lead to establishing a party from scratch. Several Ukrainian scholars have presented research that explains in detail how parties re-registered and re-branded themselves in advance of the 2020 contest (Seheda 2020; Bondarchuk and Savchuk 2021; Kryvko 2020). Domestic parties have exploited this technology for decades (Karmazina 2018).

Prior to the 2020 contests, most non-parliamentary parties, which performed better than parliamentary parties in substate contests, were often established in close cooperation with central policymakers and prioritized regional rather than municipal elections. This was not the case in 2020. First, the new ruling party did not make an effort to promote non-parliamentary parties in order to undermine the electoral performance of its competitors. Second, the 2020 contests witnessed the rise of non-parliamentary parties that prioritized municipal rather than regional electoral arenas. This is explained by the fact that the post-2014 decentralization reform greatly increased what was "at stake" in municipal council elections, but also brought many changes to the regional electoral arena. Such local and regional parties (non-statewide parties), mostly interested in municipal elections, were often, but not always, led by local incumbents. The notable exception is We Will Live Here—the frontrunner in the Khersonska *oblast* led by MP Ihor Kolykhayev (elected in 2019 in a single-member district) who contested the 2020 mayoral elections in the city of Kherson. Approximately 60 MPs contested the 2020 substate elections.

In four instances, non-parliamentary parties led by incumbent city mayors became frontrunners in both the regional and municipal council elections in 2020. I suggest that they managed to come first not only in the municipal elections, but also in the regional contests, because most voters reside in *oblast* capitals, in line with the urbanization trend evident in Ukraine. In Ukraine, the population of *oblast* capitals can account for 25-50 per cent of the population in the whole of the *oblast*. For example, approximately 1.5 million people reside in the city of Kharkiv, while approximately 2.6 million people reside in the Kharkiv *oblast*. My suggestion is tentatively supported by the case study of substate elections in the Zaporizka *oblast* presented in Zubchenko (2021: 170). In the 2020 contests, the Party of Volodymyr Buryak Yednannya obtained the overwhelming majority of their votes in the *oblast* capital; the share of the votes cast in the *oblast* capital and the periphery for the parliamentary parties (European Solidarity, Fatherland, Opposition Platform, Servant of the People) did not vary much. Further (comparative) research is required to verify my suggestion.

I acknowledge that other factors may have positively affected the electoral performance of non-parliamentary parties led by popular local incumbents. One of the first in-depth investigations of municipal elections in Ukraine—the comparative analysis of the 1994, 1998, and 2002 City Council elections in the city of Mykolaiv— discovered that "[w]hen voting for representatives of local government bodies, people consider the personal characteristics of every candidate. In other words, they support the ones they know, whose names they have heard, or whom they have seen in person, even if only once. These might be people who are part of the government structure (factory directors, representatives of housing and communal services departments, civil servants), or people who are supported by the state (school principals, hospital administrators)"

(Yatsunska 2004: 560). These research results are based on data from before 2014.

Since 2014, both academic and non-academic research has highlighted the increased input of local authorities, including city mayors, into conflict resolution during Russia's hybrid warfare (e.g. Smale 2014; Platonova 2020; Nitsova 2021). The mayors' active engagement in securing Ukraine's territorial integrity illustrates their increased input into vital nationwide issues. Simultaneously, regional elites' involvement in politics has been declining. Chapters 1 and 2 pointed out that regional councils did not take the lead in bargaining with the Center, when it came to either promoting or reversing the ongoing decentralization reform. The amended procedure for appointing regional governors in line with the 2015 civil service law (in force from December 2015 to November 2017) made regional governors' personal involvement in party politics slightly less popular.[54] The regional governors still contributed to the ruling parties' electoral gains in the 2015 substate elections. But the extent of their involvement in party politics heavily declined, (a) compared to the late 1990s, when they concentrated patronage resources—understood in the broad sense[55]—at the regional level,

---

54   In line with the 2015 civil service law, regional governors had to pass a specially designed civil service competition prior to being appointed. Despite this new procedure, the president and prime minister continued to negotiate the candidacies well in advance—but party affiliation and, thus, party subordination became a less crucial matter for regional governors. In late 2017, President Poroshenko managed to convince parliament to restore the procedure that allowed appointing regional governors without the need to pass the civil service competition. In March 2021, President Zelenskyy brought it back.

55   In its narrow sense, patronage is defined as the power of a party or parties to appoint people to positions in public and semi-public life (Kopecky et al. 2012). In the broad sense, patronage refers to electoral strategies that allow exchanging state resources for political support (Kopecky et al. 2012). Patronage is a type of "patronal politics"—the concept that was introduced by Henry Hale, defined as "politics in societies where individuals organize their political and economic pursuits primarily around the personalized exchange of concrete rewards and punishments through chains of actual acquaintance, and not primarily around abstract, impersonal principles such as ideological belief or categorizations like economic class that include many people one has not actually met in person" (Hale 2015: 9-10). Hale specifies that "the most powerful people in these relationships can be called patrons, and more subordinate ones clients. Politics in

largely to the benefit of the ruling party (Matsuzato 2001); (b) compared to the early 2000s, when they were not affiliated with a single ruling party exclusively;[56] and (c) when compared to 2010-2013, when most regional governors represented the ruling party (Romanova 2015b). According to Matsuzato's fieldwork in the Zakarpatska *oblast*, the input of city mayors into electoral politics at the substate scales has been in evidence since the 1990s; however, in the late 1990s, this was constrained by regional governors' engagement in electoral politics to the benefit of the party in power (Matsuzato 2002). His subsequent fieldwork carried out in two Ukrainian cities in 2015 (a) identified less significant input by regional governors into electoral politics, when compared to the previous period, and (b) revealed mayors' eagerness to stay away from national parties and agendas (Matsuzato 2018). Notably, in the 2015 substate contests the mayors' ability to freely choose their party affiliation was limited (Ogushi 2020). Clearly, this was not the case in 2020. Torikai (2021) finds a "geographical fragmentation of patronal politics" due to city mayors' increased engagement in patron-client relations, accompanied by corresponding drop in the input of regional governors, as evidenced in the 2020 mayoral and municipal elections. Based on empirical study of local patronage networks in Kharkiv, Mykolaiv, and Ivano-Frankivsk, Mazepus et al. (2020) identify different levels of patronage and different types of networks, which are not necessarily the same at the regional and local level (e.g. the city of Kharkiv vs the Kharkivska *oblast*).

Other possible factors can also be cited. Mykola Dobysh and Boris Yatsenko (2020) investigated longitudinal voting preferences for candidates with local roots in Ukraine: the "our man" effect, i.e.

---

patronalistic societies therefore revolves chiefly around personalized relationships joining extended networks of patrons and clients, and political struggle tends to take the form of competition among different patron-client networks" (Hale 2015: 21).

56 There were two main reasons for this state of affairs in 2005-2009: (a) if the president and the prime minister represented a single—Orange—political alliance, they attempted to follow the so-called "quota" principle when appointing the heads of regional state administrations; (b) if the president and the prime minister represented ideologically incongruent political parties, they had find compromises when appointing regional governors (Romanova 2015b).

"opportunities to use the symbolical capital of being known and even being associated with the places of different scales." Dobysh and Yatsenko (2020) explain: "[i]t is also about the use of administrative resources and local channels of communication to scale 'our man' effect. Because of poverty, lack of resources, weak democratic institutions and low civic engagement in politics it might lead to expressed by Allina-Pisano (2010) effect [sic] of corrupting changes in the social contract in society and patron-client relationships" (Dobysh and Yatsenko 2020: 10).

The enhanced collaboration between local authorities and civil society could have contributed to the improved electoral performance of parties with local profiles. Since 2014, the role of civil society at the central and substate scales has increased (Shapovalova and Burlyuk 2018). "[S]ince 2014, serious attempts to improve democratic governance in Cities of Oblast Significance in Ukraine have depended for the most part on the initiative of individual political actors, such as municipal mayors, in collaboration with local civil society groups and occasionally international NGOs, often on an ad hoc basis, and largely completely independently of the decentralization reform" (Dudley 2019: 25). Qualitative research on civic activism in the city of Kharkiv in advance of the 2020 contests identified two groups of local civic activists: those who considered standing for elections and those who preferred to stay outside of politics (Shapovalova 2019).

The comparative literature (Thorlakson 2007) proves that voters who elect more powerful substate authorities consider the performance of the corresponding authorities when casting their ballot. In the 2020 municipal council elections, voters, especially those who resided in ATC administrative centers (which include all *oblast* capitals), had many opportunities to positively assess the managerial ability of local self-governance to use its enhanced finances for the benefit of its community. Instead, the parliamentary parties — even those associated with the central policymakers who launched and completed the local amalgamation policy — did not make major electoral gains in the 2020 substate contests.

Substate incumbents attempted to get recruited into the new ruling party, when the political landscape shifted after the 2019 presidential and parliamentary elections, but did not succeed. The fact that Zelenskyy deliberately decided NOT to recruit well-established substate actors into the party lists of Servant of the People in the 2020 contests could have stimulated them to contest the elections under the banners of other parties. Instead of standing under the banners of opposition parliamentary parties, some ambitious incumbents opted to contest them under their own party banners. There could be many reasons why many ambitious local incumbents preferred to contest the 2020 elections under their own party banners. I propose the critical reason was that during the decentralization reform-implementation stage, they learned that no parliamentary political party would protect their interests when bargaining with the Center better than they could themselves.

6 The Aftermath of Regional Contests
The Indirect Elections of Regional Council Heads

This chapter explores the aftermath of substate elections: the indirect elections of the heads of regional councils. It pays special attention to instances when the party affiliations of the heads of regional councils did not align with that of the frontrunners in the regional elections. Finally, the chapter compares regional governors' engagement in the elections of the heads of regional councils across Ukraine over time.

The high fragmentation of regional councils creates fertile ground for compromises in the elections of the heads of regional councils. I am especially interested in instances where the party affiliation of the heads of regional councils does not align with the parties that came first at regional elections.

Such shifts can be illustrated by the following scheme:

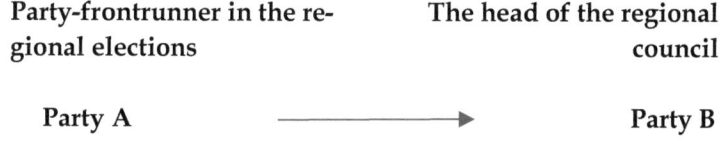

Party-frontrunner in the regional elections	The head of the regional council
Party A	Party B

Matsuzato (2002b) identifies two major strategies that parties employ to enable such shifts in elected councils:

- Strategy 1. The frontrunner voluntarily "steps down" and supports another candidate for the position of the head of regional council; this occurs when the frontrunner establishes an alliance with the party that wins the election to obtain some gains/benefits.
- Strategy 2. The frontrunner loses the election when other factions join efforts to disadvantage the frontrunner and support an alternate candidate for the position of the head of the regional council.

Apart from the two strategies, this chapter identifies Strategy 3, in which the frontrunner fails to secure leadership, but manages to disadvantage its major opponent; finally, the competing leaders agree to nominate a representative of a different faction as a head of a regional council.

In 2020, Strategy 1 was the most popular, whereas Strategy 2 had been actively employed in 2015. In 2020, there were ten instances when the party affiliation of the heads of regional councils did not align with the parties that came first in the regional elections. In eight of these, candidates belonging to the ruling party, the Servant of the People, won the positions of the heads of regional councils. In the remaining two instances, non-parliamentary parties won. In 2015, there were eleven cases where the party affiliation of the heads of regional councils did not align with the parties that came first in the regional elections. Based on this criterion, the scope of political competition did not change much. Notably, in 2010, there were only two instances when the party affiliation of the heads of regional councils did not align with the parties that came first in the regional elections, according to proportional representation rules. In both cases, the beneficiary was the ruling party, the Party of Regions.

Below I capture and compare the alliances in regional councils, along with the strategies that parties employed when electing the heads of regional councils in each of the electoral cycles under study.

Data for the analysis of the indirect elections of regional councils' heads in 2010 and 2015 is found in Dataset "Political elites in Ukrainian regions" (http://www.ukrregion.j.u-tokyo.ac.jp/). Data on the most recent electoral cycle has been collected from the official websites of regional councils.

In the 2020 regional elections, Servant of the People obtained the largest vote shares in only four regions, but won 11 positions of the heads of regional councils. Thus, it greatly enhanced its leadership at the regional scales.

Servant of the People obtained the positions in the Zaporizka, Mykolaivska, Khersonska, and Odeska *oblast*s in Southern Ukraine, where Opposition Platform gained the largest vote shares in the regional elections. In the Zaporizka *oblast*, the election of the head of the regional council provoked great conflict. Vitaliy Bohovin (Servant of the People), who led the party list in the 2020 regional elections and served as the regional governor of the Zaporizka *oblast* until his decision to be nominated for the position of the head of the regional council, was eager to win the election despite the sharp protests of the frontrunner, Opposition Platform. Bohovin managed to get elected as head of the regional council, but he was accused of violating procedure and had to resign after a few days. The Center did nothing to help. In addition, Bohovin was unable to resume his position as the regional governor, from which he was dismissed prior to the elections of the head of the regional council. However, Servant of the People did not lose leadership prospects in that regional council. It suggested a different Servant of the People candidate for the position of the head of the regional council, Olena Zhuk, who had served as Bohovin's subordinate in the regional state administration. To attract supporters, Zhuk nominated members of Opposition Platform, Fatherland, and For the Future to be deputy heads of the regional council. Such a strategy implied that the frontrunner had agreed to "step down," because it obtained institutional gains, the position of the deputy head of the regional council.

Box 6.1. Regional governors and elections in 2020.

Regional governors' input into electoral politics in the 2019/2020 multilevel electoral cycle was limited.

On the eve of the 2020 contests, Zelenskyy incorporated only five centrally appointed regional governors into the Servant of the People party lists: two in the Dnipropetrovska and Zaporizka *oblast*s in the east; and three in the Zakarpatska, Lvivska, and Ternopilska *oblast*s in the west of the country. In six other *oblast*s, the subordinates of the regional governors—deputy heads of regional state administrations, advisors to the heads of regional state administrations—joined the Servant of the People party lists. This was the case in the Vinnytska, Zhytomyrska, and Kyivska *oblast*s in Central Ukraine, in the Ivano-Frankivska and Rivnenska *oblast*s in Western Ukraine, in the Kharkivska *oblast* in Eastern Ukraine, and in the Khersonska *oblast* in Southern Ukraine.

I suggest that there was little incentive for the president to incorporate more regional governors into the ruling party, because most lacked the capacity to affect electoral performance, and there was no need to engage regional governors in electoral politics on the eve of the 2019 parliamentary contests. Servant of the People's solid electoral performance was guided by the same determinants as the electoral success of its leader in the 2019 presidential contests. On top of that, the party leader had assumed the presidency in advance of the parliamentary elections; thus, the new ruling party was supported by voters who favored the party in power.

I suggest that in 2019-2020 President Zelenskyy appointed regional governors in order to examine their potential suitability to serve in the central government. The regional governor in the Ivano-Frankivska *oblast* (July 2019 – February 2020), Denys Shmyhal, was first promoted to the position of minister for regional development (February 2020) and then appointed as prime minister (March 2020 –). The regional governor in the Kyivska *oblast* (October 2019-March 2020), Oleksiy Chernyshov, became the Minister for Regional Development (March 2020 – November 2021). Further proof that Zelenskyy perceived regional governors as candidates for positions in the central government, regardless of their political affiliation, was his decision to appoint Maxim Stepanov, head of the regional state administration in the Odeska *oblast* (January 2017-April 2019) under President Poroshenko, to serve as the Minister of Health, Labor, and Welfare (March 2020-May 2021).

In other southern regions, where Opposition Platform obtained the largest shares in the 2020 regional elections, Servant of the People gained the positions of the heads of regional councils without confronting the councillors. In all cases, Servant of the People nominated the representatives of Opposition Platform to be deputy heads of regional councils and thus obtained that party's support. In the Mykolaivska *oblast*, Servant of the People and Opposition Platform were the two largest factions and their alliance did not require much support from other factions. In the Odeska and Khersonska *oblast*s, Servant of the People had to rely on other factions' votes and thus nominated their representatives to be deputy heads of regional councils as well. The case of the Odeska *oblast* is perhaps the most interesting. Instead of bargaining for the position of deputy head of the regional council, Trust Action, the non-parliamentary party that obtained the third largest vote share in the 2020 regional council elections, lobbied for the appointment of its representative Serhiy Hrynevetskyi as the regional governor.

There are four other regions where Servant of the People did not obtain the largest vote shares in the regional contests, but its representatives became the heads of the regional councils: the Kyivska, Kirovohradska, and Chernihivska *oblast*s in Central Ukraine, and the Zakarpatska *oblast* in Western Ukraine. In the Zakarpatska *oblast*, the Servant of the People candidate, the regional governor Oleksiy Petrov, became the head of the regional council, while the representatives of Fatherland and European Solidarity became deputy heads. Furthermore, these three parties, along with Native Zakarpattya, the frontrunner in the 2020 regional council elections, chaired the permanent commissions of the regional councils. However, for eight months, the council's activities were heavily opposed by other parties. In those eight months, the balance of power in the regional council shifted. While the Servant of the People member stayed in power, he dismissed the two deputy heads of the regional council; the factions, which had been in opposition, now chaired the permanent commissions of the regional council. This case demonstrates that the consent of the frontrunner to "step down" in a highly fragmented regional council does not necessarily help maintain the balance of power for long. Moreover, the situation in the regional councils experienced further fluctuation, and the fragile balance of power collapsed in Fall 2021. On 21 October 2021 the councillors dismissed Petrov and elected the Native Zakarpattya representative, Volodymyr Chubirko, to serve as the regional council head, even as Petrov accused the councillors of violating procedures and refused to accept their decision. This demonstrates the challenges that the ruling party in the Center faces in a highly fragmented regional council.

In the Kirovohradska *oblast*, Fatherland, the frontrunner in the regional council elections, did not gain any leading position, because it failed to bargain with Servant of the People, nominated instead its own candidacy for the position of the head of the regional council. Servant of the People managed to form an alliance with three other parties, Opposition Platform, Proposition, and the Radical Party of Oleh Lyashko. This helped Servant of the People obtain leadership of the regional council without recruiting Fatherland into its team. This is a rare case of employing Strategy 2, in which other factions join their efforts to disadvantage the frontrunner, in the aftermath of the 2020 regional contests.

The elections of the heads of the regional councils in the Kyivska and Chernihivska *oblast*s followed the logic of Strategy 1: the frontrunner agreed to "step down" and obtained some gains from the head of the regional council. In the former case, European Solidarity was the frontrunner in the regional elections but managed to obtain only the position of the deputy head of the regional council. In the latter case, a non-parliamentary party that prioritized the municipal electoral arena, Native Home, won the most votes in the regional elections and secured the position of the deputy head of the regional council.

Notably, the ruling party in Kyiv failed to hold onto the leadership of the Chernivetska *oblast* in Western Ukraine. The regional council was one of the most fragmented in Ukraine. This inspired the leading parties to pursue their own ambitions and they refused to accept any candidacy other than their own. Finally, the leading parties agreed to support the candidate of the Agrarian Party, the non-parliamentary party that came fifth in the regional elections, in the election for the head of the regional council. For their part, the representatives of Servant of the People and European Solidarity obtained the positions of deputy heads. This case illustrates the need to identify Strategy 3, one that works well in a very fragmented council, in which the frontrunner obtains rather modest vote shares that do not form a solid competitive advantage when bargaining with other factions.

We see that the ruling party in Kyiv employed strategies of confrontation and compromise both to obtain the positions of the heads of regional councils. The case of the Zaporizka *oblast* demonstrates that the confrontation strategy failed, but the party still secured the leading position when it switched to a compromise strategy. In the Zakarpatska *oblast*, Servant of the People faced a change in the balance of power in the regional council, but still managed to secure leadership. In both *oblasts*, Servant of the People nominated regional governors as candidates for the positions of the heads of the regional councils. In the former case, the regional governor Bohovin failed to stay in power for more than a few days, while in the latter case Petrov succeeded, thanks to changing his alliances, on which he relied in the regional council.

Box 6.2. Regional governors and elections in 2010 and 2015.

> In the 2015 contests, the regional governors affiliated with the president's party often led the Petro Poroshenko Bloc's party lists in the regional council elections. They did not vehemently oppose the candidates of the Opposition Bloc, the party's main ideological rival, in the *oblasts* where it had reasonable electoral prospects; instead, they subsequently became the heads of the regional councils with the support of Opposition Bloc factions. Such cases were evident in the Zaporizka and Khersonska *oblasts*, where Hryhoriy Samardak and Anatoliy Putilov followed that path.
>
> When regional governors affiliated with the president's party did not lead the Petro Poroshenko Bloc party lists in the regional elections, they supported the president's party by other means. For example, the regional governor of the Zakarpatska *oblast*, Hennadiy Moskal, invested a lot of effort into bringing down United Center and securing the position of the head of the regional council for the representative of the Petro Poroshenko Bloc, despite United Center obtaining the largest vote shares in the 2015 regional elections.
>
> The Petro Poroshenko Bloc was not the only party that benefited from the affiliation of regional governors. Fatherland performed particularly well in regions where its party members were regional governors (the Mykolaivska, Potavska, Chernivetska *oblasts*) with the 2014/2015 electoral cycle.

In the 2010 substate elections, regional governors greatly contributed to the electoral success of the Party of Regions. When rotating regional governors, President Yanukovych appointed either (a) elites who had previously pursued careers in Donbas, the major electoral stronghold, or (b) well-established elites from the respective regions.

The most revealing example of the former category was the Autonomous Republic of Crimea. In 2010-2011 the Party of Region's Vasyl Dzharty was prime minister there. In 2000-2002 he was the mayor of Makiivka, Yanukovych's Donbas home town. The name of that town became a nickname for the local and regional Donbas elites who obtained leading positions in other regions of Ukraine (the so-called *makedontsy*, "Macedonians").

Cases in Western Ukraine mostly illustrate the second strategy. The regional governor in the Rivnenska *oblast*, Vasyl Bertash, previously served as the deputy head of the regional state administration (2002-2005), as councillor in the Rivnenska regional council (2006-2010; 2010-2014), and as an MP in 2006-2007 (elected as a member of the Party of Regions). The regional governor in the Volynska *oblast*, Borys Klimchuk, had established a reputation in the region and solid networks with local elites. In 1995-2002, he had been regional governor in the Volynska *oblast*. In 1992–1998, he was the head of the Volynska regional council. While chairing the regional state administration in 1995-2002, he showed loyalty to President Kuchma and effectively mobilized votes in his favor, despite previously (indirectly) demonstrating his support for then President Kravchuk.

In the 2015 regional elections, the Petro Poroshenko Bloc obtained the largest vote shares in 14 instances. Despite it being the frontrunner in the Zhytomyrska, Kyivska, Sumska, and Chernivetska *oblast*s, Fatherland managed to win the positions of the heads of regional councils there. In only the Sumska *oblast* did the Petro Poroshenko Bloc and Fatherland factions collaborate, jointly supporting the Fatherland candidate for the position of the head of the regional council. In most other instances, regional council factions joined efforts to disadvantage the frontrunners.

In the Zhytomyrska *oblast*, where the Petro Poroshenko Bloc came first in the 2015 regional elections, Fatherland formed an alliance with Opposition Bloc and Freedom factions and gained the position of the head of the regional council. It is interesting to explore the logic behind the action of the Fatherland allies. According to Sydor Kizin, the head of the Freedom faction in the Zhytomyrska regional council, who served as the head of the Zhytomyrska regional administration prior to the 2015 elections, supporting Fatherland was necessary to counterbalance the power of the newly appointed regional governor, a member of the Petro Poroshenko Bloc. Moreover, to avoid open confrontation with the ruling party in Kyiv, the newly elected head of the Zhytomyrska regional council, Anzhelika Labunska, ensured that two Petro Poroshenko Bloc representatives obtained the position of deputy head.

In contrast, the newly elected head of the Kyivska regional council, Hanna Starikova (Fatherland), made no effort to lobby for the representative of Petro Poroshenko Bloc to be one of the deputy heads of the council. Starikova relied on the support of Fatherland, UKROP, Self-Reliance, and the Radical Party of Lyashko. Those factions joined their efforts to disadvantage the frontrunner at the regional elections.

A similar case occurred in the Chernivetska *oblast*, where the councillors did not support the Petro Poroshenko Bloc candidate for the position of the head of the regional council. One reason for this may have been his simultaneous employment as regional governor. The newly elected head of the regional council, Ivan Muntian (Fatherland), ensured that the representative of the Radical Party of Oleh Lyashko became the first deputy head of the regional council, while the Freedom representative also became a deputy head of the regional council.

There was an interesting case in the Kirovohradska *oblast*. Both the Petro Poroshenko Bloc and Fatherland obtained 14 seats each out of the 64 seats on the regional council. Arguably, Fatherland obtained the position of the head of the regional council because its candidate, Oleksandr Chornoivanenko, was able to rely on the support of the major political parties, which he obtained in February 2014-October 2015, when he chaired the regional council.

In two instances, Petro Poroshenko Bloc failed to obtain other parties' support for its candidates in regional councils, but effectively blocked the leadership of Fatherland. In such cases, Strategy 3 was employed, as with the Chernivetska regional council elected in 2020.

In the Ivano-Frankivska regional council, Freedom, a non-parliamentary party, gained the position of head, even though the Petro Poroshenko Bloc was the frontrunner, and Freedom came third in the regional elections, winning 16 out of 84 seats. During the electoral campaign, the regional governor led the Petro Poroshenko Bloc party list, and some expected him to become the head of the regional council once elected. However, Fatherland chose not to support a candidate belonging to the ruling party in Kyiv. In these circumstances, the Freedom representative, Oleksandr Sych, emerged as a compromise candidate and gained the support of both the Petro Poroshenko Bloc and Fatherland. Sych had a well-established reputation among regional elites; he had chaired the regional council in 2010-2012, then served as an MP in 2012-2014, and was Vice Prime Minister between February and November 2014.

In the Rivnenska *oblast*, where the Petro Poroshenko Bloc came first in the 2015 regional elections, the representative of the Radical Party of Oleh Lyashko, Volodymyr Kovalchuk, obtained the post of the head of Rivnenska regional council. This might seem surprising, as the Radical party came third in the 2015 elections, winning 10 seats out of 64. However, the Petro Poroshenko Bloc and Fatherland agreed to support its candidate because they were not able to lobby for their own parties' representatives.

At the same time, the Petro Poroshenko Bloc secured the leadership of regional councils in six regions where it did not obtain the largest vote shares in the 2015 regional elections in the regions of two types. The first type was represented by the Dnipropetrovska, Zaporizka, Mykolayvska, and Odeska *oblast*s, where Opposition Bloc was the frontrunner. The Petro Poroshenko Bloc candidate in the Zaporizka *oblast* was the regional governor, Hryhoriy Samardak. Other party factions supported his candidacy only in the third session of the newly elected regional council, after Opposition Bloc lobbied for the position of the first deputy head of the regional council for its own candidate, Yehor Semenkov. This suggests that the ruling party representative made efforts to form an alliance with other factions to disadvantage the frontrunner. However, that strategy did not work very smoothly, and it was necessary to negotiate the conditions under which the frontrunner would agree to "step down" and indirectly support the proposed head of the regional council.

In contrast, in the Dnipropetrovska, Mykolaivska, and Odeska *oblasts*, Opposition Bloc was not successful in lobbying for its representative for the leading position in the regional council. The ruling party in Kyiv successfully formed alliances with other factions to disadvantage the frontrunner (Strategy 2).

In the Odeska *oblast*, the Petro Poroshenko Bloc and Opposition Bloc won almost the same number of seats: 23 and 22, respectively, out of the 84 seats in the regional council. Arguably, the regional governor, Mikhail Saakashvilli, made a big impact. He openly supported the ruling party and undermined Opposition Bloc's eager attempts to mount an effective opposition. The ruling party candidate, Anatoliy Urbanskiy, gained the support of 55 deputies. His Opposition Bloc opponent, Mykola Skoryk, was supported by 27 votes in the indirect elections for the head of the regional council. As a result, the Petro Poroshenko Bloc won the position, and Opposition Bloc failed to gain any leading position in the regional council.

In the Dnipropetrovska *oblast*, Opposition Bloc was well ahead of the Petro Poroshenko Bloc in the regional elections (38.33% and 11.67%, respectively). The Petro Poroshenko Bloc obtained the leadership of the regional council because it relied on the support of the second largest party, UKROP (20.83%). During the 2015 electoral campaign, UKROP ran against both the Petro Poroshenko Bloc and Opposition Bloc. Once elected to the regional council, it joined the alliance with the ruling party in Kyiv to oppose its major political competitor in the Dnipropetrovska *oblast*, Opposition Bloc. The latter failed to obtain any leading position in the regional council.

In the Mykolaivska *oblast*, Opposition Bloc failed to obtain either the position of the head of the regional council or any deputy head position. As in the Odeska *oblast*, the difference between the vote shares obtained by Opposition Bloc and the Petro Poroshenko Bloc was very modest: 22.8% vs. 20.0%. Here, the role of the regional governor was significant. Vadym Merikov, the regional governor in the Mykolaivska *oblast*, personally participated in negotiations between party factions and actively supported the Petro Poroshenko Bloc candidate, who had previously worked in one of the subregional state administrations. In addition, the post-electoral strategy employed by Opposition Bloc was ambiguous and confusing. Initially it declared that it would not nominate a candidate for the leading position in the council, only for Maksym Nevenchanniy, who contested the 2015 elections under the Opposition Bloc banner, then to nominate himself as an independent candidate with no party affiliation.

The second type of regional council is found in the Zakarpatska and Khmelnytska *oblast*s, where the non-parliamentary parties United Center and For Concrete Actions obtained the largest vote shares in the 2015 regional elections. Two different strategies were employed during the election of the heads of the regional councils.

In the Khmelnytska *oblast*, the regional governor, Myhailo Zahorodniy, who led the Petro Poroshenko Bloc party list in the 2015 regional elections, became the head of the regional council, largely due to the support of the frontrunner, For Concrete Actions. Arguably, For Concrete Actions supported Petro Poroshenko Bloc in the regional council, because the party leaders were MPs elected in single-member districts located in the Khmelnytska *oblast*, and were mostly interested in cooperating with the president.

In the case of the Zakarpatska *oblast*, the input of the regional governor, Hennadiy Moskal, was also important. Like his colleague in the Khmelnytska *oblast*, Moskal led the party list of the Petro Poroshenko Bloc when contesting the 2015 regional elections. However, in this case, the post-electoral strategies employed by the regional governors were different. Once the regional council was elected, Moskal did not attempt to ally himself with the frontrunner. Instead, he formed an alliance with the Party of Ukraine's Hungarians, a party that used to cooperate with United Center, Opposition Bloc and Renaissance. The alliance between the Petro Poroshenko Bloc and the Party of Ukraine's Hungarians undermined the position of the frontrunner, United Center, and the Petro Poroshenko Bloc representative, Mykhailo Rivis, who had worked as Moskal's subordinate in the Zakarpatska regional administration, obtained the position of the head of the regional council.

The elections of the heads of regional councils, in the 2010 contests, tell a different story. In 2010, the ruling party obtained leadership positions in the overwhelming majority of regions. In only two instances the heads of regional councils were members of Freedom: Oleh Pankevych in the Lvivska *oblast* and Oleksandr Sych in the Ivano-Frankivska *oblast*. In the Rivnenska and Chernivetska *oblast*s in Western Ukraine, the Party of Regions representatives chaired the regional councils. The role of regional governors was crucial in each instance under study. In the Chernivetska *oblast*, the regional governor, Mykhailo Papiev, consulted with the Fatherland and Our Ukraine factions to obtain their support for the candidacy of Vasyl Vatamanyuk, who used to chair the Party of Regions faction in the regional council in 2006-2010. In the Rivnenska *oblast*, Fatherland, the frontrunner according to proportional representation rules, initially proposed its own candidacy for the position of the head of the regional council. However, Fatherland had no chance of support for its candidacy, because the Party of Regions gained a majority in the regional council, due to its overwhelming victories in single-member districts. The elected head of the Rivnenska council, Yuriy Kichatyi, served as the deputy head of the regional state administration in April-October 2010.

Notably, the outcomes of the 2012 parliamentary elections affected the balance of power in some regional councils. Some heads of regional councils, all Freedom members, successfully contested the 2012 elections and decided to become MPs: Oleksiy Kaida in the Ternopilska *oblast* (the regional council was elected in 2009, prior to the 2010 presidential elections), Oleh Pankevych in the Lvivska *oblast*, and Oleksandr Sych in the Ivano-Frankivska *oblast*. Pankevych and Sych ensured that their successors on the positions of the head of the regional council were representative of Freedom. Instead, in the Ternopilska *oblast* the United Center faction refused to support the Freedom representative, and the regional council was led by the acting head Serhiy Tarashevskyi, who had served as the first deputy head of the regional council. Needless to say, he was a United Center representative.

This chapter traced instances of political competition in regional councils in the aftermath of the regional contests, during the elections of the heads of regional councils.

In 2020, there were ten instances when the party affiliation of the heads of regional councils did not align with the parties that came first in the regional elections. In eight of these, candidates belonging to the ruling party, the Servant of the People, won the positions of the heads of regional councils. In the remaining two instances, non-parliamentary parties won. In 2015, there were eleven cases where the party affiliation of the heads of regional councils did not align with the parties that came first at in the regional elections. In the 2020 regional elections, the Servant of the People, the ruling party, obtained the largest vote shares in the 2020 regional elections in only four regions, but secured the leadership of eleven regional councils. In 2015, the ruling Petro Poroshenko Bloc obtained the largest vote shares in the regional elections in 14 instances and, in the end, secured the leadership of 14 regional councils.

In the aftermath of the regional elections held during the authoritarian turn, there were only two changes, and both times to the benefit of the ruling party in the Center. After the regional council elections held under democratic rule in 2015 and 2020, the number of changes increased to 11 and 10, respectively.

Thus, in 2020, the ruling party's influence on regional councils increased. The ruling party in the Center could oppose substate elites during the 2020 electoral campaign, even lose electoral competitions in many instances, but still obtained the leadership of the elected regional councils in nearly half of the country. The high fragmentation of the regional councils stimulated party factions to make compromises when electing the heads of regional councils, and, in many instances, this benefited the ruling party in Kyiv. Presumably, this was due to the prevalence of the diffused patronage networks between central and substate actors evident in the government-controlled territories of Ukraine. Such networks manifest themselves in changes of power in the Center, when substate elites demonstrate their capacity to adjust to frequent changes in patrons.

Finally, comparative analysis reveals that regional governors' engagement in the indirect elections of the heads of regional councils declines over time.

Conclusion

This book pursued two goals. First, it aimed to explain how domestic reformers consolidated and strengthened local authority via local amalgamation, but failed to enhance regional authority in Ukraine. Second, it explored the implications of the post-2014 decentralization reform for multilevel electoral contests in Ukraine.

The Concept on Reforming Local Self-government and the Territorial Organization of Power adopted by Ukraine's government on 1 April 2014 promised local amalgamation, proposed establishing ATCs capable of executing local governance responsibilities, and introduced executive committees into the directly elected regional councils. By 2014, self-government bodies were being elected in regions (*oblasts*), subregions (*rayons*), and localities; while state executives—the centrally-appointed heads of regional and subregional state administration—operated at the regional and subregional levels. The self-government bodies in the regions and subregions are represented by directly elected councils, which do not have the constitutional right to establish their own executive committees.

In line with the 2014 Concept, the responsibilities of local governance were expected to increase, in accordance with the introduction of the principle of subsidiarity. This implied amending the division of responsibilities between substate authorities by strengthening the ATCs, which represented the local level. Such changes did not necessarily require amending the Constitution of Ukraine and could be introduced by parliamentary laws ratified by the president. In contrast, constitutional amendments were necessary to introduce policy changes with respect to regional authority and grant regional councils the right to establish their own executive committees.

Since 2014, there have been a few attempts to introduce decentralization-related changes into the constitution, but none has succeeded. On the other hand, reformers managed to complete local amalgamation in advance of the 2020 substate elections.

My research results regarding reform dynamics and multi-level elections support the argument that the post-2014 decentralization reform has consolidated Ukraine's center-periphery relations. If the post-2014 decentralization reform aimed at strengthening local authorities in relation to regional authorities, rather than the Centre (Tkachuk 2020), then the reformers mostly succeeded. As the OECD puts it, "[t]he most significant changes thus far observed primarily concern a reallocation of powers and resources across subnational levels of government rather than a true transfer of competences and resources from the central government to lower levels of government" (OECD 2018: 176).

Demands for regional autonomy have not been an issue for the government-controlled territories of Ukraine: regional councils have not demanded for an increase in their responsibilities vis-à-vis the Center or the local authorities. Unlike its earlier iteration, the debate on constitutional amendments with respect to decentralization engages strengthened local authorities. This debate reflects the ongoing process of bargaining between central, regional, and local actors with respect to the boundaries of local authority, and can lead to accommodating the shifting center-periphery relation in Ukraine.

Local authorities, even when represented by approximately 1,500 mayors, look less frightening to the Center than "one [absolute leader] on the central level, or 25 [absolute leaders] on the regional level" (Hanushchak 2021b). As Lennon puts it, "[a] direct link between Kyiv and local communities not only improved procedural efficiency but, more important, it reduced the political leverage and corruption of the middlemen in regional centers. In that way, decentralization has moved the cities' center of gravity from the regions to Kyiv … [and] is likely to prevent, not exacerbate, further fracturing along regional lines and to facilitate social cohesion and unity, critical to Ukraine's long-term stability" (Lennon 2021). Yet, in order to reach this objective, it is necessary to acknowledge, as Lutsevych argues, that "the strengthening of local elites via the local elections means Kyiv has serious thinking to do about how to create effective cooperation and trusted relations with regional actors" (Lutsevych 2020).

The post-2014 decentralization reform started as a top-down project initiated and implemented by the central government. In 2014, there was limited engagement of substate actors in agenda-setting and decision-making. At the stage of decision-implementation in 2015-2019, both regional and local actors participated in voluntary local amalgamation. Due to the different interests of substate actors, their input into local amalgamation policy was not consolidated. Some substate actors were recruited into the pro-reform advocacy coalition (e.g. the local actors who participated in voluntary local amalgamation), while others opposed it (e.g. numerous regional councils). Switching the local amalgamation policy from a voluntary to an administrative mode greatly reduced substate actors' opportunities to affect the implementation of the reform.

In contrast, the engagement of substate actors in the decision-making process became possible when negotiating constitutional reform related to decentralization. There were two core matters of importance for substate actors: (a) state supervision over the decisions made by local authorities and the role of both central and regional authorities in exercising state supervision over both delegated and own responsibilities; (b) granting the directly elected regional councils the constitutional right to establish their own executive committees. Clearly, only the first matter concerns the local authorities. However, the lengthy involvement of local authorities in discussions over that first matter delays the accomplishment of the second objective, because constitutional amendments refer to both issues. Regional actors—regional governors and regional councils—were able either to delay or speed up the implementation of the local amalgamation policy, thus consolidating and empowering local governance. Municipal authorities then managed to delay, though not to block, the constitutional provisions for regional self-government granting directly elected regional councils the right to establish executive committees. This demonstrates the ability of local authorities to affect constitutional reform on decentralization; their bargaining power has greatly increased.

The local amalgamation policy was implemented ahead of the 2020 local elections. The pro-reform advocacy coalition incorporated civil society actors with policy learning experience and policymakers with the political will to implement policy suggestions improved by the detailed professional feedback from the Council of Europe. Additionally, this success was possible because activities were facilitated by well-coordinated and substantial international support that helped identify shortcomings in the reform implementation process on the ground, informing the Center of these issues and sharing available policy solutions.

The increase of local authority also reflects an unexpected continuity in policy learning and policymaking efforts in Ukraine. I conducted a comparative analysis of major policy documents with respect to local amalgamation, prepared by the government in 2014 and earlier. I found that that these learning efforts comprise more than the policy documents prepared in 2008-2009. Apart from the previous attempt (the 2005 Concept), there were subsequent policy learning experiences (the drafts of the Concept prepared in 2012 and 2013), captured in policy documents and the appraisals by the Council of Europe. To be more precise, the drafts of the Concept on Reforming Local Self-government and the Territorial Organization of Power prepared by the government in 2012 and 2013 appear to be based on the 2009 Concept and look very similar to the 2014 Concept approved by the government on 1 April 2014. The most striking similarities refer to content and structure of the 2013 draft of the Concept and the 2014 Concept. This suggests that the long period dedicated to forming core policy beliefs and recruiting policymakers into the pro-reform advocacy coalition greatly contributed to launching the decentralization reform when the focusing event—the Euromaidan Uprising—occurred in 2014.

The alternate advocacy coalition opposed the reformers, but did not offer any plausible Plan B that the decentralization policy could follow. It managed to slow down local amalgamation and threatened its completion before the local elections scheduled for October 2020. I believe that the alternate advocacy coalition was short of policy suggestions because the leadership of the parties that contributed to challenging local amalgamation in 2015-2020 used to contribute to designing local amalgamation in 2005-2013. Because it lacked any alternative policy agenda backed by research-based insights and draft laws, however, its role was limited to blocking the existing policy proceedings and delaying their implementation. This was successful on those occasions when the pro-reform advocacy coalition lacked the political will to overcome such resistance.

The comparative analysis of major policy documents related to the increase of regional authority drafted in advance of the Euromaidan Uprising, along with the Council of Europe's feedback, shows that the new ruling elites that came to power in 2014 did not have a consensus on how to ensure the lack of overlap between the potential executive duties of regional self-governance (exercised by the executive committees of regional councils) and the executive duties of the state (exercised by regional executives). This explains why the pro-reform advocacy coalition was loosely united in the core policy belief of increasing regional authority and why the alternate coalition succeeded in redirecting attention away from the core policy issue to secondary, but still salient issues: (a) the attempt to grant special local self-government status to the temporarily non-government-controlled territories of the Donetsk and Luhansk *oblasts*; and (b) the intention to introduce state supervision over the strengthened local authorities' delegated and own responsibilities.

Notably, regional councils did not call for the increase of regional authority. Instead, mayors and local councils opposed the 2019 constitutional draft, which proposed granting regional councils the right to establish their own executive committees, so heavily that President Zelenskyy decided to withdraw it from parliament. After local authorities' interests were taken into consideration during the public debates regarding the constitutional amendments presented, they stopped criticizing the proposal of increasing regional authority.

As of January 2022, constitutional amendments related to the introduction of executive committees into regional councils are still being worked out. So far, regional authorities represent "both deconcentrated and decentralised entities. This means that parts of their budgets, although categorised as 'local government sector' in national accounts, should in reality be classified as 'central government sector', as executive committees are not elected, represent the central government and are responsible to a presidentially appointed oblast governor while oblast and rayon councils have very few powers" (OECD 2018: 177).

This book has identified the implications of decentralization on multilevel elections in Ukraine by investigating how and why parties' electoral performance changed across the parliamentary, regional, and municipal electoral arenas (i) before and (ii) after the implementation of the decentralization policy.

The Ukrainian government completed local amalgamation throughout the country prior to the 2020 regional and municipal elections; however, the scope of regional authority did not change much, despite a few attempts to introduce policy change. Based on the theoretical assumptions in the literature on multilevel elections, I expected to find an increased incongruence between parliamentary and municipal elections following the implementation of decentralization reform. At the same time, I did not expect to find any meaningful changes with respect to the incongruence between parliamentary and regional elections in the same regions.

The results of my comparative research indicate that decentralization made a difference with respect to Ukraine's multilevel elections. The dissimilarity between the outcomes of parliamentary and municipal elections in the 2019/2020 multilevel electoral cycle doubled compared to the 2014/2015 electoral cycle. This corresponds to the theory-driven expectation that an increase of substate authority would drive multilevel voting apart. The 2019/2020 electoral cycle witnessed the most striking extent of vertical incongruence between the frontrunners in the parliamentary and substate contests. In the 2019/2020 cycle, there are no cases of vertical congruence between the frontrunners in the parliamentary, regional council, and municipal council elections in the same *oblasts*. Notably, there were three such instances in the 2014/2015 electoral cycle and ten such cases in the 2010/2012 electoral cycle. This sharp increase was the result of the improved electoral performance of non-parliamentary parties in both the regional and municipal electoral arenas. Notably, the number of non-parliamentary parties that prioritized the municipal electoral arena, and which led in the regional and municipal elections, peaked in the 2020 contests.

The extent of the incongruence of the multilevel elections in the most recent electoral cycle does not undermine the integrity of Ukraine's polity as a whole. Non-parliamentary parties greatly contributed to the growing incongruence of the multilevel party system, but their electoral performance positively affected the scope of congruence between the observed outcomes of regional and municipal contests. I find that the extent of vertical congruence between frontrunners in the regional and municipal arenas did not change much over the three multilevel electoral cycles under investigation. After the 2020 substate contests, the extent of vertical congruence between frontrunners in the simultaneous regional and municipal council elections was higher than in the parliamentary and substate electoral arenas. Regional and local parties (non-statewide parties) greatly contributed to the sharp incongruence of the multilevel party system, and their outstanding electoral performance in both the regional and municipal contests positively affected the observed congruence between the outcomes of the regional and municipal contests.

Importantly, the extent of the party system's fragmentation in the municipal electoral arena decreased after the amalgamation policy was finalized. The municipal councils elected in 2020 were less fragmented than those elected in the 2015 contests. In 4 out of 21 instances, frontrunners in the 2020 municipal contests obtained more than 50% of the votes. Notably, in every case of dominant-party rule in the *oblasts*, the beneficiary was a regional or local party (non-statewide party) that prioritized the municipal electoral arena, one that gained more than 50% of the vote. Three out of four such cases occurred in municipalities where the frontrunners were led by incumbent city mayors. The latter's affiliation to the single-party majorities in the corresponding municipal councils likely strengthened their position in the system of local self-governance in *oblast* centers with dominant-party rule. In contrast, the extent of regional council fragmentation did not change significantly compared to the 2015 electoral cycle.

The 2020 substate elections did not witness particularly strong programmatic substance in the parties. I suggest that the new ruling party, Servant of the People, did not invest much effort into preparing for the 2020 substate contests, because there was not very much "at stake" for it in the regional and municipal council elections. Its leader — the president — had already concentrated central power in the unitary state. Unlike his predecessors, he did not have to compete against political opponents across the country in order to concentrate more power in the Center. The well-established parliamentary parties were motivated to increase their representation at the substate scales in the 2020 substate contests so as to mount a more effective opposition to the party in power. However, they found it difficult to maintain their clientelistic links when in opposition, and did little to foster programmatic mechanisms that would engage with voters.

Local incumbents attempted to get recruited into the new ruling party, but were not welcome. Instead of standing for the 2020 elections under the banners of opposition parliamentary parties, ambitious local incumbents decided to contest the substate elections under their own. Besides exploiting clientelistic linkages at the local scales, they presented their policy priorities for regional and local development, financially supported due to fiscal decentralization, and referred to their past performance as evidence of their ability to deliver on their promises. Although there might be many reasons why many local incumbents opted for contesting the 2020 elections under their own party banners, I propose that the following reason played a role: during the implementation of the post-2014 decentralization policy, local authorities gained experience of protecting their own interests when bargaining with the Center better that any parliamentary party.

Prior to the 2020 contests, most non-parliamentary parties, which performed better than parliamentary parties in the substate contests, were often established in close cooperation with central policymakers and prioritized regional rather than municipal elections. This was not the case in 2020. First, the new ruling party did not make an effort to promote non-parliamentary parties in order to undermine the electoral performance of its competitors. Second, the 2020 contests witnessed the rise of non-parliamentary parties that prioritized municipal rather than regional electoral arenas. This is explained by the fact that the post-2014 decentralization reform greatly increased what was "at stake" in municipal council elections, and brought many changes to the regional electoral arena.

In 2020, the ruling party managed to enhance its leadership in regional councils without the full engagement of regional governors in elections. The comparative analysis of the indirect elections of the heads of regional councils reflects the scope of post-electoral political competition at the regional scales. Because regional councils were fragmented, party factions had to bargain in order to gain support for the heads of regional councils, and in many instances, this benefited the ruling party in Kyiv. The indirect elections of regional councils heads helped the president to enhance the ruling party's influence at the substate scales. Servant of the People, the ruling party, came first at the 2020 regional elections in only four regions, but managed to secure the leadership of eleven regional councils. In turn, frontrunners agreed to "step down" and support the ruling party candidate for the position of the head of the regional council in order to obtain some gains/benefits, like being nominated to deputy head positions.

In contrast, in 2015, another strategy was popular. Frontrunners lost the election for the head of the regional council when other factions joined their efforts to support an alternate candidate. In 2015 the Petro Poroshenko Bloc obtained the largest vote shares in the regional elections in 14 instances and, in the end, secured 14 leadership positions in regional councils.

In 2020, there were ten cases when the party affiliation of the heads of regional councils did not align with the parties that came first in the regional elections. The number of such shifts highlights the scope of political competition in regional councils in the aftermath of the regional elections. The number of cases benefiting the ruling party signals both the leadership ability of the ruling party at the regional scales and the bargaining capacities of councillors in the regional councils. In 2020, in the overwhelming number of cases, the parties that opposed the ruling party in the Center failed to secure leadership positions in regional councils.

The next stage of the decentralization policy implies empowering regional councils by granting them the constitutional right to establish their own executive committees. If this happens, parties' alliances in regional councils would affect the composition of the corresponding executive committees. The ruling party has proved capable of securing leadership in regional councils without any active engagement of regional executives in elections. Under these circumstances, transforming regional governors into prefects with a status of civil servants is unlikely to undermine its power at regional scales. The Center and local authorities have already negotiated the mutually beneficial model of supervision over local authorities' decision-making. Bearing in mind that mayors and local councils used to oppose the constitutional reform in late 2019 – early 2020 the most heavily, the newly gained consensus suggests that the remaining obstacles for the constitutional change that will grant regional councils the right to establish their executive committees have been overcome.

For obvious reasons, Russia's fully-fledged military aggression against Ukraine has dramatically affected the domestic agenda and postponed any preparations of the constitutional amendments.

Bibliography

Aleksandrova, N. and Ihor Koliushko. 2011. (eds) *Rozvytok publichnoho prava v Ukraini (dopovid za 2009-2010)* [The Developments of Public Law in Ukraine (report on 2009-2010)]. Kyiv: Centre for Political and Legal Reforms.

Amendments to the Constitution of Ukraine. 2021. *Decentralization.gov.ua.* 30 November. https://decentralization.gov.ua/uploads/attachment/document/887/Constitutional_Amendments_NOV_30_ENG.pdf (accessed on 30 January 2022)

Arel, Dominique. 1995. "Language Politics in Independent Ukraine: Towards One or Two State Languages?" *Nationality Papers* 23 (3): 597-622.

Arel, Dominique and Valeri Khmelko. 1996. "The Russian Factor and Territorial Polarization in Ukraine." *Harriman Review* 9 (1–2): 81–91.

Arel, Dominique. 2018. "How Ukraine has become more Ukrainian." *Post-Soviet Affairs* 34 (2-3): 186-189.

Bader, Max. 2021. "The Risk of Local Elite Capture in Ukraine's Decentralization Reform." *Vox Ukraine* 25 January. https://voxukraine.org/en/the-risk-of-local-elite-capture-in-ukraine-s-decentralization-reform/ (accessed on 30 January 2022)

Bardi, Luciano and Peter Mair. 2008. "The Parameters of Party Systems." *Party Politics* 14 (2): 147-66.

Barrington, Lowell and Regina Faranda. 2009. "Reexamining Region, Ethnicity, and Language in Ukraine." *Post-Soviet Affairs* 25 (3): 232-256.

Baumann, Markus, Alejandro Ecker and Martin Gross. 2020. "Party competition and dual accountability in multi-level systems." *Journal of Elections, Public Opinion and Parties* 30 (4): 542-549.

Birch, Sarah. 1995. "The Ukrainian parliamentary and presidential elections of 1994." *Electoral Studies* 14 (1): 93–99.

Birch, Sarah. 1998. "Electoral systems, campaign strategies, and vote choice in the Ukrainian parliamentary and presidential elections of 1994." *Political Studies,* 46 (1): 96–114.

Bochsler, Daniel. 2010. Measuring party nationalisation: A new Gini-based indicator that corrects for the number of units, *Electoral Studies* 29 (1): 155-168.

Bondarchuk, Analtoliy and Andrii Savchuk. 2021. "Deshevo i serdyto: shcho treba znaty pro partii Zelenskoho, Poroshenka i vsih inshyh" [Cheaply and Angrily: What You should Know about the Parties of Zelenskyy, Poroshenko and all the Rest], *Dzerkalo Tyzhnia*, 29 October. https://zn.ua/internal/zapryhnut-v-poslednij-vahon-partii-optom-i-v-roznitsu.html (accessed on 30 January 2022)

Cabinet of Ministers of Ukraine. 2009a. Postanova vid 2 hrudnia 2009 r. No. 1456-r, Kyiv, 'Pro zatverdzhennia planu zahodiv shchodo realizatsii Koncepcii reformy miscevoho samovriaduvannia' [Decree issued on 2 December 2009 № 1456-r, Kyiv, 'On Approval of the Action Plan on the Implementation of the Concept of Local Government Reform']. https://zakon.rada.gov.ua/laws/show/1456-2009-%D1%80#Text (accessed on 30 January 2022)

Cabinet of Ministers of Ukraine. 2009b. Postanova vid 29 lypnia 2009. № 900-p, Kyiv, 'Pro shvalennia Koncepcii reformy miscevoho samovriaduvannia' [Decree issued on 29 July 2009 Order № 900-p, Kyiv, 'On Approving the Concept of Local Government Reform']. https://zakon.rada.gov.ua/laws/show/900-2009-%D1%80#Text (accessed on 30 January 2022)

Cabinet of Ministers of Ukraine. 2014. Postanova vid 8 kvitnya 2015 r. No. 214, Kyiv, 'Pro Zatverdzhennya Metodyky Formuvannya Spromozhnykh Terytorialnykh Hromad' [Decree issued on 8 April 2015 No. 214, Kyiv, 'On Approval of the Methodology for the Formation of Capable Territorial Communities'], https://zakon.rada.gov.ua/laws/show/214-2015-%D0%BF#n10 (accessed on 30 January 2022)

Chaisty, Paul and Stephen Whitefield. 2018. "Critical election or frozen cleavages? How voters chose parties in the 2014 Ukrainian parliamentary election." *Electoral Studies*, 56.

Chaisty, Paul and Stephen Whitefield. 2020. "How challenger parties can win big with frozen cleavages: Explaining the landslide victory of the Servant of the People party in the 2019 Ukrainian parliamentary elections." *Party Politics*. 1–12.

Chhibber, Pradeep and Ken Kollman. 2004. The Formation of National Party Systems: Federalism and Party Competition in Canada, Great Britain, India, and the United States. Princeton, New Jersey: Princeton University Press.

Chumak, Victor and Ihor Shevliakov. 2009. "Local Government Functioning and Reform in Ukraine." Norwegian Institute for Urban and Regional Research and ICPS. https://unece.org/fileadmin/DAM/hlm/prgm/cph/experts/ukraine/general_info/NIBR.local.government.pdf (accessed on 30 January 2022)

Clem, Ralph S. and Peter R. Craumer. 2008. "Orange, Blue and White, and Blonde: The Electoral Geography of Ukraine's 2006 and 2007 Rada Elections." *Eurasian Geography and Economics*, 49 (2): 127-151.

Committee of Voters of Ukraine. 2020. Formuvannia neformalnykh koalicii v radah mist-milyonnykiv [The Establishment of Informal Coalitions in City Councils with Population of over One Million]. 25 December. http://www.cvu.org.ua/nodes/view/type:news/slug:ormuvannia-neformalnykh-koalitsii-v-radakh-mist-milionnykiv (accessed on 30 January 2022)

Committee of Voters of Ukraine. 2021. Vplyv chotyryoh rokiv derzhavnoho finansuvannia na rozbudovu politychnyh partii v Ukraini [The Impact of Four-Year-Long Public Funding aimed at the Development of Political Parties in Ukraine], 29 September. http://cvu.org.ua/nodes/view/type:news/slug:doslidzhennia-komitetu-vybortsiv-ukrainy-vplyv-chotyrokh-rokiv-derzhavnoho-finansuvannia-na-rozbudovu-politychnykh-partii-v-ukraini (accessed on 30 January 2022)

Concept of Reforming Local Self-government and the Territorial Organization of Power in Ukraine. 2014.

Council of Europe. 2009. Appraisal of the Concept Paper and Draft Law on the Administrative-Territorial Reform of Ukraine. DPA/LEX 1/2009. Strasbourg. 16 February. http://www.slg-coe.org.ua/wp-content/uploads/2012/10/CoE-Appraisal-of-the-Concept-Paper-and-Draft-Law-on-the-Administrative-Terri.pdf (accessed on 30 January 2022)

Council of Europe. 2011. Appraisal of the Draft Law of Ukraine on Stimulation and State Support of Unification of Rural Territorial Communities. 22 February. Strasbourg. DPA/LEX 2/2011. http://www.slg-coe.org.ua/wp-content/uploads/2012/10/CoE-Appraisal-of-the-draft-Law-of-Ukraine-on-Stimulation-and-State-Support-of-Unification-of-Rural-Territorial-Communities_2011.pdf (accessed on 30 January 2022)

Council of Europe. 2012a. Appraisal of the draft of the law 'On Amalgamation of Territorial Communities.' CELGR/ LEX/ 1. Strasbourg. 13 March. http://www.slg-coe.org.ua/wp-content/uploads/2012/10/CoE-appraisal-of-the-draft-Law-of-Ukraine_On-Amalgamation-of-Territorial-Communities_2012.pdf (accessed on 30 January 2022)

Council of Europe. 2012b. Appraisal of the drafts of the Concept of Reforming Local Self-government and the Territorial Organisation of Power. CELGR/ LEX 4 / 2012. Strasbourg. 12 June.

Council of Europe. 2012c. Report of the Centre of Expertise for Local Governance Reform of the Council of Europe on the Roundtable Proceedings on the Reform of Local Self-governance in Ukraine (Sevastopol, 27-28 August 2012). CELGR/ LEX 6 / 2012. Strasbourg. 12 September.

Council of Europe. 2013a. Appraisal of the draft of the Concept of Reforming Local Self-government and the Territorial Organisation of Power. CELGR/ LEX 5/ 2013. 1 October.

Council of Europe. 2013b. Policy Advice "On the Revision of the Constitution of Ukraine: Provisions on the Territorial Organisation of State and Local Self-Government." Centre of Expertise for Local Government. CELGR/PAD 3/ 2013. 9 October.

Council of Europe. 2018. Meeting on supervision of local authorities' acts in Ukraine 26 April. http://www.slg-coe.org.ua/wp-content/uploads/2020/12/CEG GLEX20205.pdf (accessed on 30 January 2022)

Council of Europe. 2019. 'Reports: annual national opinion polls on decentralisation and local self-government reform'. 4 March. http://www.slg-coe.org.ua/p16423/?lang=en (accessed on 30 January 2022)

Council of Europe. 2020a. Preliminary comments on the Draft Law of Ukraine "On Amendments of the Constitution of Ukraine." CEGG/LEX(2020)2. Strasbourg. 20 February. http://www.slg-coe.org.ua/wp-content/uploads/2020/12/ CEGGLEX20205.pdf (accessed on 30 January 2022)

Council of Europe. 2020b. Draft Opinion on the draft law "On Amendments to the Law of Ukraine "On Local State Administrations" and Other Legislative Acts of Ukraine on Reforming Territorial Organisation of Executive Power in Ukraine" (#4298). CEGG/LEX(2020)5. Strasbourg. 27 November. http:// www.slg-coe.org.ua/wp-content/uploads/2020/12/CEGGLEX20205.pdf (accessed on 30 January 2022)

Council of Europe. 2020c. Decentralizatsia ta Reforma Miscevoho Samovriaduvannia. Rezultaty Piatoi Hvyli Sociolohichnoho Doslidjennia sered Zhyteliv Terytorialnyh Hromad, yaki Proishly Process Obiednannia v 2015-2018 Rokah. http://www.slg-coe.org.ua/wp-content/uploads/2020/11/2020Report_ATC_ukr.pdf (accessed on 30 January 2022)

D'Anieri, Paul. 2007. Understanding Ukrainian Politics: Power, Politics, and Institutional Design. Armonk, NY: ME Sharpe.

D'Anieri, Paul. 2019. "Gerrymandering Ukraine? Electoral Consequences of Occupation." *East European Politics and Societies* 33 (1): 89–108.

D'Anieri, Paul. 2021. Ukraine's 2019 Elections: Pro-Russian Parties and The Impact of Occupation. Presented at the ICCEES Conference, August 6.

Danutsa: "Na Mestnyh Vyborakh My Budem Voevat protiv Vsekh. Vse Strely Poletiat protiv Nas" [Danutsa: We Will Fight Everyone at the Local Elections. Everyone will Fight Us"], LB.UA, June, 25 2020, https://lb.ua/news/2020/06/25/460583_danutsa_na_mestnih_viborah.html (accessed on 30 January 2022)

DIIS (Danish Institute for International Studies). 2018. Decentralization in Ukraine: Supporting Political Stability by Strengthening Local Government.

Dobysh, Mykola and Boris Yatsenko. 2020. "Borders, Constituency Politics, and "Our Man" Voting in Electoral Geography of Ukraine." *Belgeo*, http://journals.openedition.org/belgeo/38851 (accessed on 30 January 2022)

Dopovidna Zapyska. 2012. Dopovidna Zapyska Kabinetovi Ministriv shchodo Koncepcii reformy miscevoho samovriaduvannia ta terytorialnoi orhanizacii vlady v Ukraini [Report addressed to the Cabinet of Ministers regarding the Concept of Reforming Local Self-government and the Territorial Organisation of Power in Ukraine]. Coordination Council on Civil Society Promotion. https://civil-rada.in.ua/dopovidna-zapiska-kabinetovi-ministriv-shhodo-koncepci%d1%97-reformi-miscevogo-samovryaduvannya-ta-teritorialno%d1%97-organizaci%d1%97-vladi-v-ukra%d1%97ni (accessed on 30 January 2022)

Draft of the Concept of Reforming Local Self-government and the Territorial Organization of Power in Ukraine. 2012. Coordination Council on Civil Society Promotion. https://civil-rada.in.ua/koncepciya-reformi-miscevogo-samovryaduvannya-ta-teritorialno%D1%97-organizaci%D1%97-vladi-v-ukra%D1%97ni (accessed on 30 January 2022)

Draft of the Concept of Reforming Local Self-government and the Territorial Organization of Power in Ukraine. 2013. Kharkiv City Council. https://dozvil.kh.ua/info_monitoring/21.html (accessed on 30 January 2022)

Draft of the Law of Ukraine "On Amendments to the Constitution of Ukraine" № 3207-1 registered in the parliament on 1 July 2003. http://w1.c1. rada.gov.ua/pls/zweb2/webproc4_1?pf3511=15410 (accessed on 30 January 2022)

Draft of the Law of Ukraine "On Amalgamation of Territorial Communities" № 9590 registered on 14 December 2011. http://w1.c1.rada.gov.ua/pls/zweb2/webproc4_2?id=&pf3516=9590&skl=7 (accessed on 30 January 2022)

Draft of the Law of Ukraine "On Amendments to the Constitution of Ukraine (On Decentralisation of Power)" №4178a registered in the parliament on 26 June 2014.

Draft of the Law of Ukraine "On Amendments to the Constitution of Ukraine (On Decentralisation of Power)" № 2598 registered in the parliament on 13 December 2019. http:// w1.c1.rada.gov.ua/pls/zweb2/webproc4_1?pf3511=67644 (accessed on 30 January 2022)

Draft of the Law of Ukraine 'On Amendments to the Law of Ukraine "On Local State Administrations" and Other Legislative Acts of Ukraine on Reforming Territorial Organization of Executive Power in Ukraine" № 4298 registered in the parliament on 30 October 2020.

Dudley, William. 2019. Ukraine's Decentralization Reform SWP Working Paper. https://www.swp-berlin.org/publications/products/arbeitspapiere/Ukraine_Decentralization_Dudley.pdf (accessed on 30 January 2022)

Ebinger, Falk, Kuhlmannb, Sabine and Joerg Bogumilc. 2019. "Territorial reforms in Europe: effects on administrative performance and democratic participation." *Local Government Srudies*, 45 (1): 1-23.

Fabre, Elodie. 2008. Party Organisation in a Multi-Layered Setting: Spain and the United Kingdom. PhD Dissertation. Leuven, Catholic University of Leuven. https://core.ac.uk/download/pdf/6264821.pdf (accessed on 30 January 2022)

Fedorenko, Kostyantyn, Olena Rybiy, and Andreas Umland. 2016. "The Ukrainian Party System before and after the 2013–2014 Euromaidan." *Europe-Asia Studies* 68 (4): 609–630.

Garaz, Stela. 2012. "Exploring the Link between Power Concentration and Ethnic Minorities' Mobilization in Post Soviet Georgia, Moldova, and Ukraine" PhD dissertation. Central European University.

Gendźwiłł, Adam, Kjaer, Ulrik and Kristof Steyvers. Eds. 2022. *The Routledge Handbook on Local Elections and Voting in Europe*. Routledge.

Gendźwiłł, Adam and Ulrik Kjaer. 2021. "Mind the gap, please! Pinpointing the influence of municipal size on local electoral participation." *Local Government Studies* 47(1): 11-30.

Gendźwiłł, Adam and Kristof Steyvers. 2021. "Guest editors' introduction: Comparing local elections and voting in Europe: lower rank, different kind... or missing link?" *Local Government Studies*, Special issue on comparing local elections and voting in Europe, 47(1): 1-10.

Golder, Sona, Lago, Ignacio, Blais, André, Gidengil, Elisabeth and Thomas Gschwend. 2017. *Multi-Level Electoral Politics. Beyond the Second-Order Election Model*. Oxford University Press.

Graeme, Boushey. 2013. "The punctuated equilibrium theory of agenda-setting and policy change." In *Routledge Handbook on Public Policy* edited by Eduardo Araral, Scott Fritzen, Michael Howlett, M. Ramesh, Xun Wu. Routledge.

Hale, Henry. 2015. Patronal Politics: Eurasian Regime Dynamics in Comparative Perspective. Cambridge University Press.

Hamanyuk, Oleksiy. 2018. "Subvencia na socialno-ekonomichniy rozvytok" [Subvention of Socio-Economic Development], *Centr Ekonomichnoi Stratehii*. https://ces.org.ua/subventsiia-na-sotsialno-ekonomichnyi-rozvytok/ (accessed on 30 January 2022)

Hanushchak, Yuri. 2013. *Reforma terytorialnoi orhanizatsii vlady*. DESPRO. Kyiv: Sofia.

Hanushchak, Yuri. 2019a. "Komentar do publichnoi zayavy miskyh holiv ta ekspertiv z pryvodu proektu zmin do Konstytucii" [Commentary on the Public Statement of Mayors and Experts regarding the Draft of the Constitutional Amendments], Decentralization.gov.ua, 26 December. https://decentralization.gov.ua/news/12027?page=13 (accessed on 30 January 2022)

Hanushchak, Yuri. 2019b. "Zminy do Konstytucii: zrada chy peremoha?" [The Constitutional Amendments: Betrayal or Victory?], Decentralization.gov.ua, 19 December. https://decentralization.gov.ua/news/12010?page=15 (accessed on 30 January 2022)

Hanushchak, Yuri. 2021a. "Missia MDA. Kak zarabotaet gosudarstvennyi nadzor v gromadah" [The Mission of Regional Administrations. How Would the State Oversight in Communities Work?], *Dzerkalo Tyzhnia*, 9 August. https://zn.ua/internal/missija-mha-kak-zarabotaet-hosudarstvennyj-nadzor-v-hromadakh.html (accessed on 30 January 2022)

Hanushchak, Yuri. 2021b. "God triumfa metsnoi elity. Chto dalshe?" [The Year of Triumph of Local Elites. What's Next?] *Dzerkalo Tyzhnia*, https://zn.ua/economics_of_regions/hod-triumfa-mestnoj-elity-chto-dalshe.html (accessed on 30 January 2022)

Henderson, Ailsa and Romanova, Valentyna. 2016. "Voting Behaviour and Party Competition in Simultaneous Multi-Level Elections." *Post-Soviet Affairs* 32 (3): 201-236.

Henderson, Ailsa, and Nicola McEwen. 2010. "A Comparative Analysis of Voter Turnout in Regional Elections." *Electoral Studies* 29 (3): 405–416.

Herron, Erik S. 2014. "The parliamentary elections in Ukraine, October 2012." *Electoral Studies* 33: 353-356.

Herron, Erik S. and Fredrik M. Sjoberg. 2016. "The Impact of 'Boss' Candidates and Local Political Machines on Elections in Ukraine." *Europe-Asia Studies* 68 (6): 985-1002.

Hesli, V., Reisinger, W. & Miller, A. 1998. "Party development in divided societies: The case of Ukraine." *Electoral Studies* 17 (2): 235-256.

Hesli, Vicky. 2007. "The 2006 Parliamentary Election in Ukraine." *Electoral Studies* 26: 507-533.

Hough, Daniel and Charlie Jeffery. 2006. "An introduction to multi-level electoral politics." In *Devolution and Electoral Politics* edited by Daniel Hough and Charlie Jeffery. Manchester, Manchester University Press, pp. 2-13.

Hrytsak, Yaroslav. 2019. "Ukraine in 2013-2014: A New Political Geography." In *Regionalism without Regions: Reconceptualizing Ukraine's Heterogeneity* edited by Ulrich Schmid and Oksana Myshlovska. Central European University Press, pp. 367-392.

IRI. 2021. Seventh Annual Ukrainian Municipal Survey. 12 May – 3 June. https://www.iri.org/sites/default/files/wysiwyg/seventh_municipal_survey_may_2021_eng_-_v2.pdf (accessed on 30 January 2022)

Jeffery, Charlie and Daniel Hough. 2003. "Regional elections in multi-level systems." *European Urban and Regional Studies*, 10(3): 199-212.

Jeffery, Charlie and Arjan Schakel. 2012. "Editorial: Towards a Regional Political Science." *Regional Studies* 43 (3): 299-302.

Jeffery, Charlie and Dan Hough. 2009. "Understanding Post-Devolution Elections in Scotland and Wales in Comparative Perspective." *Party Politics* 15 (2): 219-40.

Karmazina, Maria. 2018. *Regionalni politychni rezhymy v Ukraini: pidstavy formuvannia, specifika funkcionuvannia, osoblyvosti transformacii* [Regional political regimes in Ukraine: the causes of establishing, the specifics of functioning, the peculiarities of transformations], Visnyk Instytuta imeni I.F.Kurasa NAN Ukrainy. https://ipiend.gov.ua/wp-content/uploads/2018/11/karmazina_regionalni.pdf (accessed on 30 January 2022)

Katchanovski, Ivan. 2006. "Regional Political Divisions in Ukraine in 1991 – 2006." *Nationalities Papers* 34 (5): 507 – 532.

Kjaer, Ulrik and Elklit, J. 2010a. "Party Politisation of Local Councils." *European Journal of Political Research* 49(3): 337-358.

Kjaer, Ulrik and Jørgen Elklit. 2010b. "Local Party System Nationalisation: Does Municipal Size Matter?" *Local Government Studies* 36(3): 425-444.

Kjaer, Ulrik. 2013. "Local Political Leadership: The Art of Circulating Political Capital." *Local Government Studies* 39 (2): 253-272.

Kjaer, Ulrik and Robert Klemmensen. 2014. "What are the Local Political Costs of Centrally Determined Reforms of Local Government?" *Local Government Studies* (41)1: 100-118.

Koliushko, Ihor. 2019. "20 vysnovkiv pro proekt zmin do Konstytusii" [20 Conclusions on the Draft of the Constitutional Amendments], Decentralization.gov.ua, 24 December. https://decentralization.gov.ua/news/12017?page=14 (accessed on 30 January 2022)

Kopecky, Petr, Mair, Peter, and Maria Spirova. 2012. Party Patronage as an Organizational Resource in Party Patronage and Party Government in European Democracies. Oxford Scholarship Online.

Kozlov, Andriy and Michael Meyer-Resende. 2015. Constitutional Reforms in Ukraine: an Update on Recent Developments and Debates. *Democracy Reporting International.* Briefing Paper 56, June.

Kravets, Roman. 2020. "Chotyry Shtaby 'Sluhy Narodu': yak Orhanizovana Pidhotovka do Micevyh Vyboriv u Zelenskoho" [Four Headquarters of 'Servant of the People': How is Zelensky's Preparation for the Local Elections is Organized], *Ukrainska Pravda*, 12 May. https://www.pravda.com.ua/articles/2020/05/12/7251232/ (accessed on 30 January 2022)

Kryvko, Anton. 2020. "Kozhna druha partiya zminyue nazvu – osoblyvosti partbudivnytsva v Ukraini (onovleno)." *Chesno*, 11 June. https://www.chesno.org/post/4053/ (accessed on 30 January 2022)

Kulyk, Volodymyr. 2011. "Language Identity, Linguistic Diversity and Political Cleavages: Evidence from Ukraine." *Nations and Nationalism*, 17 (3).

Kuzio, Taras. 2014. "Impediments to the Emergence of Political Parties in Ukraine." *Politics* 34 (4): 309-323.

Kuzio, Taras. 1995. "The 1994 Parliamentary Elections in Ukraine." *Journal of Communist Studies and Transition Politics* 11 (4): 335–361.

Laakso, Markku and Rein Taagepera. 1979. "Effective number of parties: A measure with application to West Europe." *Comparative Political Studies* 12 (1): 3-27.

Ladner Andreas, Keuffer Nicolas and Harald Baldersheim. 2016. "Measuring Local Autonomy in 39 Countries (1990–2014)." *Regional & Federal Studies* 26 (3): 321–357.

Lago, Ignacio, André Blais, Sona N. Golder, Elisabeth Gidengil, and Thomas Gschwend. 2017. *Multi-Level Electoral Politics: Beyond the Second-Order Election Model.* Oxford Scholarship Online.

Law of Ukraine "On Amalgamation of Territorial Communities" 157-VIII approved on 5 February 2015. https://zakon.rada.gov.ua/laws/show/157-19#Text (accessed on 30 January 2022)

Leitch, Duncan. 2017. "International assistance to democratic reform in Ukraine: an opportunity missed or an opportunity squandered?" *Democratization* 24(6): 1142-1158.

Lennon, Olena. 2021. "Ukraine's Decentralization will Empower the Center, but Not in Ways You Think." *Wilson Centre.* https://www.wilsoncenter.org/blog-post/ukraines-decentralization-will-empower-center-not-ways-you-think (accessed on 30 January 2022)

Levitas, Tony and Jasmina Djikic. 2017. "Caught Mid-Stream: "Decentralization," Local Government Finance Reform, and the Restructuring of Ukraine's Public Sector 2014 to 2016." Swedish Association of Local and Regional Authorities (SKL). http://sklinternational.org.ua/wp-content/uploads/2017/10/UkraineCaughtMidStream-ENG-FINAL-06.10.2017.pdf (accessed on 30 January 2022)

Levitas, Tony. 2021. "How Should the Personal Income Tax be Shared with Ukrainian Local Governments?" Decentralisation.gov.ua 20 July. https://decentralization.gov.ua/en/news/13780 (accessed on 30 January 2022)

Lutsevych, Orysia. 2020. "Ukraine Local Elections Challenge Zelenskyy's Plans." *Chatham House*, 3 November. https://www.chathamhouse.

org/2020/11/ukraine-local-elections-challenge-zelenskyys-plans (accessed on 30 January 2022)

Madoian, Karen. 2020. "Devil in the Detail. Local versus regional approaches to peace in Donbas." *European Union Institute for Security Studies*, Brief 2, February. https://www.iss.europa.eu/sites/default/files/EUISSFiles/Brief%202%20Ukraine_0.pdf (accessed on 30 January 2022)

Makarov, Hlib and Yulia Kaplan. 2015. "Miscevi vybory 2015." Kyiv: NISS. https://niss.gov.ua/sites/default/files/2016-01/vuboru-f2365.pdf (accessed on 30 January 2022)

Malynovskiy, Valentyn. 2013. "Stan i Perspektyvy Administratyvnoi Reformy v Ukraini" [The State and Perspectives of the Administrative Reform in Ukraine], *Naukovi Pratsi Petro Mohyla Black Sea National University, Series: Political Science*, 212 (200): 18-22. https://evnuir.vnu.edu.ua/bitstream/123456789/6890/3/Npchdupol_2013_212_200_5.pdf (accessed on 30 January 2022)

Marlin, Marguerite. 2016. "Concepts of "Decentralization" and "Federalization" in Ukraine: Political Signifiers or Distinct Constitutionalist Approaches for Devolutionary Federalism?" *Nationalism and Ethnic Politics* 22 (3): 278-299.

Matsuzato, Kimitaka. 2000. "Local Reforms in Ukraine 1990–1998: Elite and Institutions." In *The Emerging Local Governments in Eastern Europe and Russia: Historical and Post-Communist Development* edited by Osamu Ieda. Hiroshima: Keisuisha, pp. 25–54.

Matsuzato, Kimitaka. 2001a. "All Kuchma's men: The reshuffling of Ukrainian governors and the presidential election of 1999." *Post-Soviet Geography and Economics* 42 (6): 416–439.

Matsuzato, Kimitaka. 2001b. "From Ethno-Bonapartism to Centralized Caciquismo: Characteristics and Origins of the Tatarstan Political Regime, 1990–2000." *The Journal of Communist Studies and Transition Politics* 17 (4): 43–77.

Matsuzato Kimitaka. 2002a. "Elites and the Party System of Zakarpattya Oblast': Relations among Levels of Party Systems in Ukraine." *Europe-Asia Studies* 54 (8), 1267-1299.

Matsuzato, Kimitaka. 2002b. "The Last Bastion of Unitarism? Local Institutions, Party Politics, and Ramifications of EU Accession in Lithuania." *Eurasian Geography and Economics* 43 (5).

Matsuzato, Kimitaka. 2005. "Semipresidentialism in Ukraine: Institutionalist Centrism in Rampant Clan Politics." *Demokratizatsiya: The Journal of Post-soviet Democratization* 1: 453–74.

Matsuzato, Kimitaka. 2018. "The Donbas War and Politics in Cities on the Front: Mariupol and Kramatorsk." *Nationalities Papers* 46 (6): 1008–1027.

Maynzyuk, Kateryna and Yuriy Dzhygyr. 2010. "The Evolution of Ukraine's Administrative and Territorial Structure: Trends, Issues, and Risks." In *Territorial Consolidation Reforms in Europe* edited by P. Swianiewicz. Open Society Institute–Budapest, pp. 265-278.

Mazepus, Honorata, Frear, Matthew. Toshkov, Dimiter and Nina Onopriychuk. 2020. "When Business and Politics Mix: Local Networks and Socio-political Transformations in Ukraine." *East European Politics and Societies and Cultures* 35 (2): 437–459.

Mefford, Brian. 2020. "National parties lose out to local candidates in Ukraine's 2020 municipal elections." *Atlantic Council*. https://www.atlanticcouncil.org/blogs/ukrainealert/national-parties-lose-out-to-local-candidates-in-ukraines-2020-municipal-elections/ (accessed on 30 January 2022)

Melvin, Hinich, Khmelko, Valerii, Klochko, Marianna and Peter C. Ordeshook. 2008. "A Coalition Lost, Then Found: A Spatial Analysis of Ukraine's 2006 and 2007 Parliamentary Elections." *Post-Soviet Affairs* 24 (1): 63-96.

Melvin, Hinich, Khmelko, Valerii and Peter C. Ordeshook. 1999. "Ukraine's 1998 Parliamentary Elections: A Spatial Analysis." *Post-Soviet Affairs* 15 (2): 149-185.

Melvin, Hinich, Khmelko, Valerii and Peter C. Ordeshook. 2002. "Ukraine's 1999 Presidential Election: A Spatial Analysis." *Post-Soviet Affairs* 18 (3): 250-269.

Mierzejewski-Voznyak, Melanie. Forthcoming. "The Effects of Decentralization on Party Politics in Ukraine" In *Ukraine's Decentralization: Challenges and Implications of the Local Governance Reform after the Euromaidan Revolution* edited by Valentyna Romanova and Andreas Umland. Stuttgart: ibidem-Verlag.

Minakov, Myhailo. 2021a. "Zelensky's Presidency at the Two-Year Mark." *Focus Ukraine*, 3 June. https://www.wilsoncenter.org/blog-post/zelenskys-presidency-two-year-mark (accessed on 30 January 2022)

Minakov, Myhailo. 2021b. "Just Like All the Others: The End of the Zelensky Alternative?" *Focus Ukraine*, 2 November. https://www.wilsoncenter.org/blog-post/just-all-others-end-zelensky-alternative (accessed on 30 January 2022)

Monitorynh protsesu detsentralizatsiyi vlady ta reformuvannya mistsevoho samovryaduvannya stanom na 10 veresnya 2020 roku. 2020. Ministerstvo rozvytku hromad ta terytoriy Ukrayiny. URL: https://decentralization.gov.ua/uploads/library/file/593/%D0%9C%D0%BE%D0%BDi%D1%82%D0%BE%D1%80%D0%B8%D0%BD%D0%B3__10.09.2020.pdf (accessed on 30 January 2022)

Neljas, Aap. 2020. Administrative Reform and Local Elections in Ukraine 2020. Estonian Centre for Eastern Partnership. https://eceap.eu/wp-content/uploads/2020/10/eceap_dok48.pdf (accessed on 30 January 2022)

Niland, Paul. 2016. "Making Sense of Minsk: Decentralization, Special Status, and Federalism." *The Atlantic Council*, 27 January.

Nitsova, Silviya. 2021. "Why the Difference? Donbas, Kharkiv and Dnipropetrovsk After Ukraine's Euromaidan Revolution." *Europe-Asia Studies* 1-25.

O'Connell, Sean and Deborah Wetzel. 2003. "Systemic Soft Budget Constraints in Ukraine." In *Fiscal Decentralization and the Challenge of Hard Budget Constraints* edited by Jonathan Rodden, Gunnar S. Eskeland, and Jennie Litvack. The MIT Press. pp. 353-393.

Odarchenko, Kateryna. 2020. "The Map of Political Forces in Today's Ukraine." *Focus Ukraine, Kennan Institute*, 1 July. https://www.wilsoncenter.org/blog-post/map-political-forces-todays-ukraine (accessed on 30 January 2022)

OECD. 2014. OECD Territorial Reviews: Ukraine 2013. Paris: OECD Publishing.

OECD. 2018. *Maintaining the Momentum of Decentralisation in Ukraine.* OECD: Multi-level Governance Studies. Paris: OECD Publishing.

Ogushi, Atsushi. 2020. "The Opposition Bloc in Ukraine: A Clientelistic Party with Diminished Administrative Resources." *Europe-Asia Studies* 72 (10): 1639–1656.

OPORA. 2015. *Local Elections: Preliminary Observation Summary From OPORA,* 26 October. https://www.oporaua.org/en/report/vybory/mistsevi-vybory/mistsevi-vybory-2015/41080-618-1446984481-miscevi-vybory-promizhni-pidsumky-sposterezhennja-opory (accessed on 30 January 2022)

Ordeshook, Peter. 1996. "Russia's Party System: Is Russian Federalism Viable?" *Post-Soviet Affairs* 12 (3): 195-217.

Palermo, Francesco. 2020. "The Elephant in the Room: Ukraine between Decentralization and Conflict." *Ethnopolitics* 19: 369–82.

Pallares, Francesc and Michael Keating. 2003. "Multi-level electoral competition: regional elections and party systems in Spain." *European Urban and Regional Studies* 10 (3): 239-255.

Parlamentski Sluhannia. 2005. Decentralizacia Vlady v Ukraini. Rozshyrennia Prav Samovriaduvannia [Decentralisation of Power in Ukraine. To Strengthen the Rights of Local Self-governance]. 12 October. https://static.rada.gov.ua/zakon/skl4/par_sl/sl121005.htm (accessed on 30 January 2022)

Pavlenko, Iryna. 2020. "Analiz Rezultativ Vyborchoi Kampanii do Miscevyh Orhaniv Vlady 25 Zhovtnia 2020 r." [The Analysis of the results of the local elections' campaign held on 25 October 2020.] Kyiv: National Institute for Strategic Studies.

Platonova, Daria. 2020. "Local elites and the Donbas conflict a comparative case study of Kharkiv city and Donets'k region." PhD thesis. King's College London.

Podolian, Olena and Valentyna Romanova. 2018. "Ukraine: The Dynamics of Cross-Cutting Cleavages During Quadruple Transition." In: *Crises in the Post-Soviet Space* edited by Felix Jaitner, Tina Olteanu and Tobias Spori. Routledge.

Podolian, Olena. 2020. The Challenge of 'Stateness' in Estonia and Ukraine. PhD Thesis. Sodotorn University.

Pop-Eleches Grigore and Graeme B. Robertson. 2018. "Identity and political preferences in Ukraine—before and after the Euromaidan." *Post-Soviet Affairs* 34 (2-3): 107-118.

Presidential Decree of Ukraine of 22 July 1998 № 810/98 'Pro Zahody shchodo Vprovadjennia Administratyvnoi Reformy' ['On Measures regarding the Implementation of the Administrative Reform']. https://zakon.rada.gov.ua/laws/show/810/98#Text (accessed on 30 January 2022)

Rabinovych, Maryna, Levitas, Anthony and Andreas Umland. 2018. "Revisiting Decentralisation After Maidan: Achievements and Challenges of Ukraine's Local Governance Reform." *Kennan Cable*, no. 34, https://www.wilsoncenter.org/publication/kennan-cable-no-34-revisiting-decentralization-after-maidan-achievements-and-challenges (accessed on 30 January 2022)

Rabinovych, Maryna. 2020. "Introduction: Regional Diversity, Decentralization, and Conflict in and around Ukraine." In *Decentralization, Regional Diversity, and Conflict: The Case of Ukraine* edited by Hanna Shelest and Maryna Rabinovych. Palgrave Macmilan, pp. 1-14.

Rakhmanin, Serhiy. 2014. "Novaya Konstitutsia. Eskiz Neizvestnogo Avtora" [The New Constitution. The Draft of the Unknown Author], *Dzerkalo Tyzhnia*, 16 May. https://zn.ua/internal/novaya-konstituciya-eskiz-neizvestnogo-avtora-_.html (accessed on 30 January 2022)

Razumkov Centre. 2007. "The Constitutional Reform in Ukraine: Proceedings and Perspectives." *National Security and Defence* 1 (85). https://razumkov.org.ua/uploads/journal/ukr/NSD85_2007_ukr.pdf (accessed on 30 January 2022)

Razumkov Centre. 2016. Ukraine 2015-2016: The Reform Challenge (assessments). Kyiv: Razumkov Centre. https:// razumkov.org.ua/uploads/article/2015-2016_Pidsumky.pdf (accessed on 30 January 2022)

Riabchuk, Mykola. 2015. "The 'Two Ukraines' Reconsidered: The End of Ukrainian Ambivalence?" *Studies in Ethnicity and Nationalism* 15 (1).

Romanova, Valentyna. 2010. The Party Politics of Territorial Reforms in Ukraine, International Workshop on the Party Politics of Territorial Reforms, University of Edinburgh, 26-27 November.

Romanova, Valentyna. 2011a. "The Role of Centre–Periphery Relations in the 2004 Constitutional Reform in Ukraine." *Regional & Federal Studies* 21 (3): 321-339.

Romanova, Valentyna. 2011b. "Regionalist Origins of Centralisation." *Sfera Politicii*. 167. http://revistasferapoliticii.ro/sfera/167/art07-Romanova.php#_ftn22 (accessed on 30 January 2022)

Romanova, Valentyna. 2013. "Regional Elections in Ukraine in 2006 and 2010." *Perspectives on European Politics and Society* 14 (1): 36–62.

Romanova, Valentyna. 2015a. "Challenges of Ukraine's Oct 25 local elections." *KyivPost,* 21 October. https://www.kyivpost.com/article/opinion/op-ed/valentyna-romanova-challenges-of-ukraines-oct-25-local-elections-400335.html (accessed on 30 January 2022)

Romanova, Valentyna. 2015b. "The Regional Level of Ukraine's Party System in 2005-2012." *Kyiv-Mohyla Law and Politics Journal,* 1.

Romanova, Valentyna and Andreas Umland. 2019. "Ukraine's Decentralization Reforms Since 2014: Initial Achievements and Future Challenges." *Chatham House: International Affairs Think Tank.* https://www.chathamhouse.org/sites/default/files/2019-09-24-UkraineDecentralization.pdf (accessed on 30 January 2022)

Romanova, Valentyna. 2020a. "The Post-Euromaidan Decentralisation Reform in Ukraine." In *Center(s) and Peripheries in the Post-Soviet Space* edited by Alexander Filippov, Nicolas Hayoz and Jens Herlth. Peter Lang — Interdisciplinary series on Central and Eastern Europe.

Romanova, Valentyna. 2020b. "Caricature of Policy-Making in Ukraine under President Z: the Case of Decentralisation." Workshop of Japan Association of Ukrainian Studies, 17 July.

Romanova, Valentyna. 2022. "Ukraine: The first experiences with voting in the amalgamated territorial communities." In *The Routledge Handbook on Local Elections and Voting in Europe* edited by Gendźwiłł, Adam, Kjaer, Ulrik and Kristof Steyvers. Routledge.

Romanova, Valentyna. Forthcoming. "The 2020 Regional Elections in Ukraine." *Regional and Federal Studies.*

Ross, Cameron and Petr Panov. 2019. "The range and limitation of subnational regime variations under electoral authoritarianism: The case of Russia." *Regional and Federal Studies,* Issue 3: Second Annual Review of Regional Elections, pp. 355-380.

Ross, Cameron. 2011a. "Regional elections and electoral authoritarianism in Russia." *Europe–Asia Studies* 63 (4): 641–662.

Ross, Cameron. 2011b. "The rise and fall of political parties in Russia's regional assemblies." *Europe–Asia Studies,* Special Issue: Russian Regional Politics under Putin and Medvedev, 63 (3): 429–448.

Rozumnyi, Maksym and Iryna Pavlenko. 2015. Partiine zakonodavstvo ta rozvytok politychnyh partii v Ukraini [Legislature of Parties and the Development of Political Parties in Ukraine]. Kyiv: NISS. http://old2.niss.gov.ua/content/articles/files/partii-95fc5.pdf (accessed on 30 January 2022)

Sabatier, Paul and Christopher M. Weible. 2007. "The advocacy coalition framework: Innovations and clarifications." In *Theories of the Policy Process* edited by Paul Sabatier. 2nd edn. Boulder, CO: Westview Press, pp. 189–222.

Sabatier, Paul. 1998. "The advocacy coalition framework: revisions and relevance for Europe." *Journal of European Public Policy* 5 (March): 98–130.

Samoorg. 2018. "Analitychnyi daidzhest #10: Konflikty v OTH" [Analytical Digest No. 10: Conflicts in ATCs], http://samoorg.com.ua/blog/2018/12/20/analitichniy-daydzhest-10-konflikti-v-obyednanih-teritorialnih-gromadah (accessed on 30 January 2022)

Sasse, Gwendolyn. 2001. "The 'New' Ukraine: A State of Regions." *Regional and Federal Studies* 11 (3).

Savchuk, Andrii. 2021. "Shcho ne Tak z "Rynkom" Partii." *OPORA*, 30 June. https://www.oporaua.org/article/vybory/partii/23225-shcho-ne-tak-z-rinkom-partii (accessed on 30 January 2022)

Schakel, Arjan H. 2013a. "Congruence Between Regional and National Elections." *Comparative Political Studies* 46 (5): 631–662.

Schakel, Arjan H. 2013b. "Nationalisation of multilevel party systems: A conceptual and empirical analysis." *European Journal of Political Research* 52 (2): 212-236.

Schakel, Arjan H. 2015. "Nationalisation of regional elections in Central and Eastern Europe." *East European Politics* 31 (2): 229-247.

Schakel, Arjan H. and Valentyna Romanova (eds). 2018. First Annual Review of Regional Elections, *Regional & Federal Studies* 28 (3).

Schakel, Arjan H. and Valentyna Romanova (eds). 2019. Second Annual Review of Regional Elections, *Regional & Federal Studies* 29 (3).

Schakel, Arjan H. and Valentyna Romanova (eds). 2020. Third Annual Review of Regional Elections, *Regional & Federal Studies* 30 (3).

Schakel, Arjan H. and Valentyna Romanova (eds). 2021. Fourth Annual Review of Regional Elections, *Regional & Federal Studies* 31 (3).

Seheda, Halyna. 2020. "Regionalni politychni partii iz vseukrainskym statusom abo "My sami (ne) miscevi"" [Regional Political Parties with all-Ukrainian Status or "We are (not) Local]. OPORA. 17 August. https://www.oporaua.org/blog/vybory/mistsevi-vybory/mistsevi_2020/20301-regionalni-partiyi-zi-vseukrayinskim-statusom-abo-mi-sami-ne-mistsevi (accessed on 30 January 2022)

Shapovalova and Burlyuk (eds.). 2018. *Civil Society in Post-Euromaidan Ukraine. From Revolution to Consolidation.* ibidem Press.

Shapovalova, Natalia 2019. "Assessing Ukrainian Grassroots Activism Five Years After Euromaidan." *Carnegie Europe.* https://carnegieendowment.org/files/2-6_Shapovalova_Five_Years.pdf (accessed on 30 January 2022)

Shapovalova, Natalia and Valentyna Romanova. 2020. "Second-Class Citizens? Kyiv's Policy Towards the Residents of the Conflict-torn Eastern Regions of Ukraine through the Lens of Citizenship." In *Center(s) and Peripheries in the Post-Soviet Space* edited by Alexander Filippov, Nicolas Hayoz and Jens Herlth. Peter Lang—Interdisciplinary series on Central and Eastern Europe.

Shevchenko Olha, Romanova, Valentyna, Yaroslav Zalilo. 2020. *Decentralizatsia i Formuvannia Polityky Regionalnogo Rozvytku v Ukraini* [Decentralisation and the Formation of Regional Development Policy in Ukraine]. Kyiv: National Institute for Strategic Studies. https://niss.gov.ua/sites/default/files/2020-09/decentralizatsiya-i-formuvannya-polityky-regionalnogo-rozvytku-v-ukraini_0.pdf (accessed on 30 January 2022)

Shevel, Oxana. 2015. "The parliamentary elections in Ukraine, October 2014." *Electoral Studies* 39: 153-177.

Smale, Alison. 2014. "2 Ukrainian Mayors Play Different Hands in Crisis." *New York Times*, 28 February. https://www.nytimes.com/2014/03/01/world/europe/ukrainian-cities-reflect-nations-deep-divisions.html (accessed on 30 January 2022)

Snyder, Richard. 2001. "Scaling Down: The Subnational Comparative Method." *Comparative International Development*, 36: 93–110.

Söller-Winkler, Manuela. 2021. "Financial autonomy: At the heart of local government!" Decentralization.gov.ua. 3 June. https://decentralization.gov.ua/
en/news/13610?page=3 (accessed on 30 January 2022)

Solougub, Ilona. 2019. "Zelensky's New Constitution: What Is On The Table?" *VoxUkraine*, 27 December. https:// voxukraine.org/en/zelensky-s-new-constitution-what-is-on-the-table/ (accessed on 30 January 2022)

Swenden, Wilfred and Bart Maddens. 2009. "Introduction: Territorial Party Politics in Western Europe: a Framework for Analysis." In *Territorial Party Politics in Western Europe* edited by Wilfred Sweden and Bart Maddens. Basingstoke, Palgrave Macmillan, pp. 1-30.

Swianiewicz, Pawel, 2018. "If territorial fragmentation is a problem, is amalgamation a solution?—Ten years later." *Local Government Studies* 44 (1): 1-10.

Swianiewicz, Paweł. 2010. "If Territorial Fragmentation is a Problem, is Amalgamation a Solution? An East European Perspective." *Local Government Studies* 36 (2): 183-203.

Syroid, Oksana. 2014. "Opinion on the Draft Law Amending the Constitution of Ukraine." *Vox Ukraine*, 24 August. https://voxukraine.org/en/opinion-on-the-draft-law-amending-the-constitution-of-ukraine-submitted-by-oksana-syroyid/ (accessed on 30 January 2022)

Thorlakson, Lori. 2007. "An institutional explanation of party system congruence: Evidence from six federations". *European Journal of Political Research* 46 (1): 69–95.

Thorlakson, Lori. 2009. "Patterns of party integration, influence and autonomy in seven federations." *Party Politics* 15 (2): 157–177.

Timothy, Frye. 2014. "What Do Voters in Ukraine Want? A Survey Experiment on Candidate, Language, Ethnicity and Policy Orientation." *SSRN*, 8 August. https://papers.ssrn.com/sol3/papers.cfm?abstract_id=2477440 (accessed on 30 January 2022)

Tkachuk, Analtoliy. 2007. "Terytorialna Reforma: Vchora, Syohodni, Zavtra" [The Territorial Reform: Yesterday, Today, Tomorrow]. Civil Society Institute, Kyiv: Lesta. https://www.csi.org.ua/wp-content/uploads/2007/05/atu-vchora-sogodni-zavtra.pdf (accessed on 30 January 2022)

Tkachuk, Anatoliy. 2014. "Pro Proekt Zakonu pro Vnesennia Zmin do Konstitucii Ukrainy vid Prezidenta Poroshenka P.O." [On the Draft of Constitutional Amendments from President Poroshenko P.O.], Civil Society Institute. 1 July. https://www.csi.org.ua/publications/pro-proekt-zakonu-pro-vnesennya-zmin-do/ (accessed on 30 January 2022)

Tkachuk, Anatoliy. 2015. "Zminy do Konstytucii: Panatseya chy Novyi Etap Reformy?" [The Constitutional Amendments: Panacea or the New Stage of the Reform]. Civil Society Institute, 28 August. https://www.csi.org.ua/publications/zminy-do-konstytutsiyi-panatseya-chy-novyj/ (accessed on 30 January 2022)

Tkachuk, Anatoliy. 2017. "Pro Detsentralizatsiyu, Uspikhy, Ryzyky i Rol Parlamentu." *Dzerkalo Tyzhnia*, 13 January. https://dt.ua/internal/pro-decentralizaciyu-uspihi-riziki-i-rol-parlamentu-_.html (accessed on 30 January 2022)

Tkachuk, Anatoliy. 2020. "Decentralizatsia. Stratehiya Meniaetsia?" [Decentralisation. Is the Strategy being Changed?] *Dzerkalo Tyzhnia*, 19 June. https://zn.ua/internal/decentralizaciya-strategiya-menyaetsya-358111_.html (accessed on 30 January 2022)

Tkachuk, Anatoliy. 2021. "Chomu zaraz ne mozhna vnosyty zminy do Konstytucii" [Why We should not introduce the Constitutional Amendments Now?], *Dzerkalo Tyzhnia*, 26 January. https://zn.ua/internal/pochemu-sejchas-nelzja-vnosit-izmenenija-v-konstitutsiju.html (accessed on 30 January 2022)

Torikai, Masatomo. 2021. "Growing localization and fragmentation of patronal politics: Ukrainian local elections since 2010." *Eurasian Geography and Economics*. November.

UCIPR. 2017. Decentralisation in Ukraine: Achievements, expectations and concerns. https://www.international-alert.org/sites/default/files/Ukraine_Decentralisation_EN_2017.pdf (accessed on 30 January 2022)

UNDP. 2019. Integrity and Inclusiveness of the Democratic Process in Ukraine - Analysis of Interim Research Findings in the Regions. https://www.ua.undp.org/content/ukraine/en/home/library/democratic_governance/integrity-and-inclusiveness-of-the-democratic-process-in-Ukraine.html (accessed on 30 January 2022)

USAID. 2014. Local Governance and Decentralization Assessment: Implications of Proposed reforms in Ukraine. 3 September. https://2012-2017.usaid.gov/documents/1863/local-governance-and-decentralization-assessment-implications-proposed-reforms (accessed on 30 January 2022)

Vedernikova, Inna. 2019. "Avtor Reformy Decentralizatsii Analtoliy Tkachuk: 'Zaraz ne mozhna zminyuvaty konstytuciu. Posylymo Regiony—Vtratymo Krainu'" [The Author of the Decentralization Reform Analtoliy Tkachuk: 'We should not Change the Constitution Now. If We Strengthen the Regions—We will Lose the Country], *Dzerkalo Tyzhnia*, 21 September. https://zn.ua/ukr/internal/avtor-reformi-decentralizaciyi-anatoliy-tkachuk-zaraz-ne-mozhna-zminyuvati-konstituciyu-posilimo-regioni-vtratimo-krayinu-324152_.html (accessed on 30 January 2022)

Vedernikova, Inna. 2020a. "Kraina po Polychkakh" [The State on the Shelves]. *Dzerkalo Tyzhnia*. https://zn.ua/project/miscevivybory2020/ (accessed on 30 January 2022)

Vedernikova, Inna. 2020b. "Interview with Oleksandr Kornienko." *Dzerkalo Tyzhnia*, 26 April. https://zn.ua/internal/aleksandr-kornienko-my-v-lyubom-sluchae-vystroim-s-merami-dialog-ne-s-etimi-tak-s-drugimi-352347_.html

Vedernikova, Inna. 2020c. "Partiya Meriv: Otvetka Tsentru." *Dzerkalo Tyzhnia*, May 9. https://zn.ua/ukr/internal/partiya-meriv-otvetka-centru-346412_.html (accessed on 30 January 2022)

Vedernikova, Inna. 2021. "Zelenskyy idyot na vtoroi srok i stroit set." [Zelenskyy aims at the second [presidential] tenure and develops a network [of subordinates in regions], *Dzerkalo Tyzhnia.*, 10 December,https://zn.ua/internal/zelenskij-idet-na-vtoroj-srok-i-stroit-set.html

Venice Commission. 2014. Opinion on the Draft Law Amending the Constitution of Ukraine Submitted by the President of Ukraine on 2 July 2014. Endorsed by the Venice Commission at its 100th plenary session (Rome, 10-11 October 2014). Strasbourg, 27 October 2014. Opinion no. 766/2014.

Venice Commission. 2015. Opinion on the Amendments to the Constitution of Ukraine regarding the Territorial Structure and Local Administration as Proposed by the Working Group of the Constitutional Commission in June 2015. Endorsed by the Venice Commission at its 104th Plenary Session (Venice, 23-24 October 2015). Strasbourg, 26 October 2015. Opinion No. 803/2015. https://www.venice.coe.int/webforms/documents/default.aspx?pdffile=CDL-AD(2015)028-e (accessed on 30 January 2022)

Verkhovna Rada of Ukraine. 2015. 'Proekt Zakonu pro vnesennya zmin do Konstytutsiyi Ukrainy (shchodo detsentralizatsii vlady)' [Draft Law 'On Amendments to the Constitution of Ukraine (Regarding the Decentralization of Power)'], http://w1.c1.rada.gov.ua/pls/zweb2/webproc4_1?pf3511=55812

Way, Lucan 2015. *Pluralism by Default. Weak Autocrats and the Rise of Competitive Politics.* Johns Hopkins University Press.

Weible, Christopher M. and Daniel Nohrstedt. 2013. "The advocacy coalition framework Coalitions, learning and policy change." In *Routledge Handbook on Public Policy* edited by Eduardo Araral, Scott Fritzen, Michael Howlett, M. Ramesh, Xun Wu. Routledge.

Frosiniak, R. 2021. "Micevi Vybory yak Chynnyk Rozvytku Regionalnyh Politychnyh Partii v Ukraini" [Local elections as the development factor of regional political parties in Ukraine], *Public Administration and Customs Administration*, 1 (28): 88-93. http://customs-admin.umsf.in.ua/archive/2021/1/16.pdf (accessed on 30 January 2022)

Whitmore, Sarah. 2014. Political party development in Ukraine. Helpdesk Research Report. 25 September. https://gsdrc.org/docs/open/hdq1146.pdf (accessed on 30 January 2022)

Wilson, Andrew. 2015. "Five lessons from the local elections in Ukraine." *European Council on Foreign Relations.* https://ecfr.eu/article/commentary_five_lessons_from_the_local_elections_in_ukraine4087/ (accessed on 30 January 2022)

Wolczuk, Kataryna. 2002. "Catching up with 'Europe'? Constitutional Debates on the Territorial-Administrative Model in Independent Ukraine." *Regional & Federal Studies* 12 (2): 65-88.

World Bank. 2008. Ukraine - Improving Intergovernmental Fiscal Relations and Public Health and Education Expenditure Policy. Selected Issues. Washington, DC. https://openknowledge.worldbank.org/handle/10986/8006 (accessed on 30 January 2022)

World Bank. 2017. Ukraine Public Finance Review. June 27. https://documents1.worldbank.org/curated/en/476521500449393161/pdf/117583-WP-P155716-final-output-PUBLIC-2017-06-28-23-16.pdf (accessed on 30 January 2022)

Wyn Jones, Richard and Roger Scully. 2006. "Devolution and electoral politics in Wales." *Publius: The Journal of Federalism*, 36 (1): 115-134.

Yatsenyuk, Arseniy. 2014. Yatsenyuk Vvazhaye Zavdanniam Kabminu Decentralizatsiu Vlady. *LB.ua*, 5 March https://lb.ua/news/2014/03/05/258233_yatsenyuk_schitaet_zadachey_kabmina.html (accessed on 30 January 2022)

Yatsunska, Olena. 2004. "Local elections in independent Ukraine: the case study of Nikolayev." *Nationalities Papers* 32 (3): 551-563.

Zhalilo, Yaroslav, Shevchenko Olha, Romanova Valentyna. 2019. Decentralizacia vlady: poriadok dennyi na seredniostrokovu perspektyvu [Decentralisation of power: middle term agenda]. Kyiv: National Institute for Strategic Studies.

Zubchenko, Oleksandr. 2021. "Socio-Political Cleavages in Local Elections." *Knowledge, Education, Law, Management* № 3 (39), vol. 1: 165-172. http://kelmczasopisma.com/en/viewpdf/6360 (accessed on 30 January 2022)

Appendix

Table A1. Dissimilarity indices: the congruence of parliamentary and municipal contests within the 2010/2012 multilevel elections.

	Party of Regions, vote shares in the parliamentary elections, %	Party of Regions, vote shares in the municipal elections, %	Fatherland, vote shares in the parliamentary elections, %	Fatherland, vote shares in the parliamentary elections, %	UDAR, vote shares in the parliamentary elections, %	UDAR, vote shares in the municipal elections, %	KPU, vote shares in the parliamentary elections, %	KPU, vote shares in the local elections, %	Freedom, vote shares in the parliamentary elections, %	Freedom, vote shares in the municipal elections, %	Dissimilarity Index
Vinnytska	17.38	12	45.01	20	13.38	8	8.86	0	8.4	8	21.635
Volynska	12.92	12	39.46	32	15.96	0	0	0	17.98	20	17.99
Dnipropetrovska	35.79	46.7	18.38	13.3	14.61	0	19.38	13.3	5.19	0	19.725
Donetska	65.09	88.9	5.26	0	0	0	18.85	6.7	0	0	9.05
Zhytomyrska	21.61	20	36.15	23.3	14.19	6.7	12.82	6.7	7.47	0	19.76
Zakarpatska	30.87	20	27.69	23.3	20.03	6.7	5.03	0	8.35	0	29.245
Zaporizka	40.95	43.2	14.93	22.7	12.4	0	21.16	15.9	0	0	12.04

Ivano-Frankivska	5.18	10.3	38.21	13.8	15.25	6.9	0	0	33.79	34.5	12.285
Kirovohradska	26.25	36.8	32.17	31.6	14.87	0	13.46	5.3	6.22	0	27.42
Lvivska	0	11.1	35.48	0	14.44	6.7	0	0	38.02	40	23.8
Luhanska	57.06	63.2	5.49	0	0	0	25.14	26.3	0	0	2.845
Mykolaivska	40.51	48.9	16.93	8.9	12.51	0	19.09	13.3	0	0	14.26
Odeska	41.9	43.9	15.49	0	13.77	0	18.16	5.3	0	0	23.99
Poltavska	21.91	20	30.14	16	18.47	0	13.49	4	0	0	22.43
Rivnenska	15.8	14.8	36.59	22.2	17.25	7.4	6.21	0	16.63	18.5	12.44
Sumska	21.09	12.8	36.27	30.8	16.71	0	12.24	5.1	6.37	0	24.05
Kharkivska	40.98	48	15.21	22	12.82	0	20.84	16	0	0	13.265
Khersonska	29.34	39.5	21.8	15.8	13.63	5.3	23.34	13.2	0	0	16.665
Khmelnytska	18.69	13.8	37.71	55.2	16.33	0	8.81	0	11.79	10.3	29.075
Chernivetska	20.77	26.7	39.6	26.7	19.13	0	5.46	0	8.71	10	24.06

| Cherni-hivska | 20.09 | 24 | 30.73 | 24 | 12.91 | 12 | 13.2 | 12 | 5.98 | 0 | 10.875 |

Note: In Table A1, Table A2, Table A3, Table A4, Table A5, and Table A6, I calculated the dissimilarity index by adding the differences between parties' vote shares gained at in the parliamentary and the substate elections in each oblast and then dividing the sum by two, following academic literature in the field of territorial politics (Palares and Keating 2003; Jeffery and Hough 2009; Schakel 2015). I used parties' vote shares scored according to proportional representation rules.

Table A2. Dissimilarity indices: the congruence of parliamentary and regional contests within the 2010/2012 multilevel elections.

	Party of Regions, vote shares in the parliamentary elections, %	Party of Regions, vote shares in the regional elections, %	Fatherland, vote shares in the parliamentary elections, %	Fatherland, vote shares in the regional elections, %	UDAR, vote shares in the parliamentary elections, %	KPU, vote shares in the parliamentary elections, %	KPU, vote shares in the local elections, %	UDAR, vote shares in the municipal elections, %	Freedom, vote shares in the parliamentary elections, %	Freedom, vote shares in the regional elections, %	Dissimilarity index
AR Crimea	52.34	80	13.09	0	7.17	19.41	5	0	0	0	31.165
Vinnytska	17.38	23	45.01	22	13.38	8.86	0	0	8.4	0	29.635
Volynska	12.92	18.86	39.46	23.36	15.96	0	0	0	17.98	7.5	24.24
Dnipropetrovska	35.79	40.53	18.38	9.55	14.61	19.38	8.9	0	5.19	0	21.925
Donetska	65.09	65.78	5.26	0	0	18.85	4.4	0	0	0	10.2
Zhytomyrska	21.61	28.2	36.15	24.3	14.19	12.82	6.5	0	7.47	0	23.21

186 APPENDIX

Zakar-patska	30.87	18.15	27.69	8.63	20.03	5.03	0	0	8.35	0	32.595
Zaporizka	40.95	46.9	14.93	15.4	12.4	21.16	8.4	0	0	0	15.79
Ivano-Frankivska	5.18	19.2	38.21	35.3	15.25	0	0	1.8	33.79	15.8	24.185
Kyivska	21	26.3	36.63	0	18.73	6.11	0	7.5	10.84	3.4	33.355
Kirovohr-adska	26.25	33.99	32.17	14.32	14.87	13.46	5	0	6.22	0	27.57
Lvivska	0	6.36	35.48	0	14.44	0	0	3.4	38.02	34.5	28.2
Luhanska	57.06	55.7	5.49	0	0	25.14	10.5	0	0	0	10.745
Mykola-ivska	40.51	41.3	16.93	7.5	12.51	19.09	11.7	0	0	0	15.06
Odeska	41.9	30.59	15.49	5.45	13.77	18.16	3	0	0	0	25.14
Poltavska	21.91	24.16	30.14	15.49	18.47	13.49	5.8	0	0	0	21.53
Rivnenska	15.8	19.2	36.59	29.3	17.25	6.21	0	0	16.63	6.3	22.24
Sumska	21.09	22.9	36.27	20.2	16.71	12.24	5	0	6.37	0	24.1
Kharkivska	40.98	34.59	15.21	17.69	12.82	20.84	5.9	0	0	0	18.315
Kher-sonska	29.34	31.9	21.8	9.5	13.63	23.34	10.7	2.4	0	0	19.365
Khmelnytska	18.69	42.3	37.71	29.8	16.33	8.81	0	0	11.79	3.9	32.275

Cherkaska	18.65	28.92	37.78	17.16	17.23	9.29	3.8	0	9.48	1.9	30.595
Chernivetska	20.77	22.9	39.6	16.91	19.13	5.46	0	0	8.71	2.9	27.61
Chernihivska	20.09	21.62	30.73	18.6	12.91	13.2	5	3	5.98	0	18.875
Sevastopol	46.9	32.08	5.86	0	5.04	29.46	10.5	0	0	0	22.34

Table A3. Dissimilarity indices: the congruence of parliamentary and municipal contests within the 2014/2015 multilevel elections.

	Petro Poroshenko Bloc "Solidarnist," vote shares in the parliamentary elections, %	Petro Poroshenko Bloc "Solidarnist," vote shares in the municipal elections, %	Fatherland, vote shares in the parliamentary elections, %	Fatherland, vote shares in the municipal elections, %	Self-Reliance, vote shares in the parliamentary elections, %	'Self-Reliance', vote shares in the municipal elections, %	Radical Party of Oleh Lyashko, vote shares in the parliamentary elections, %	Radical Party of Oleh Lyashko, vote shares in the municipal elections, %	Opposition Bloc, vote shares in the parliamentary elections, %	Opposition Bloc, vote shares in the parliamentary elections, %	Dissimilarity index
Vinnytska	37.45	18.52	6.6	16.67	7.59	9.26	6.09	10.71	0	7.41	20.515
Volynska	16.89	19.05	7.48	9.52	11.46	9.52	9.7	7.14	0	0	3.38

188 APPENDIX

Dnipropet-rovska	19.48	9.38	0	0	8.59	7.81	7.59	0	24.27	39.06	16.24
Zhytomy-rska	23.03	26.19	6.52	23.81	9.12	16.67	10.63	9.52	0	11.9	16.73
Zakar-patska	28.05	13.89	5.12	8.33	9.63	8.33	6.83	0	0	0	12.1
Zaporizka	16.94	12.5	0	9.38	8.59	9.38	5.92	0	22.18	31.25	14.405
Ivano-Frankivska	18.25	21.43	6.19	9.52	14.69	14.29	0	0	0	0	3.255
Kirovohr-adska	21.73	21.43	8.34	14.29	7.9	7.14	11.67	7.14	7	11.9	7.84
Lvivska	20.42	15.63	0	0	18.78	37.5	5.35	0	0	0	5.07
Mykola-ivska	20.64	16.67	0	0	7.71	18.52	7.78	0	15.88	48.15	22.01
Odeska	19.63	21.88	0	0	7.23	7.81	5.41	0	18.05	18.75	4.47
Poltavska	23.24	19.05	6.22	11.9	9.22	9.52	10.85		5.33	0	13.175
Rivnenska	24.21	21.43	6.65	19.05	11.08	14.29	7.91	9.52	0	0	9.955
Sumska	25.09	21.43	7.19	42.86	8.28	9.52	10.61	0	0	9.52	30.35
Terno-pilska	19.73	16.67	6.31	9.52	11.3	16.67	11.3	7.14	0	0	7.9
Kharkivska	15.17	8.33	0	0	7.49	15.48	6.38	0	32.16	0	26.685

Khersonska	22.26	20.37	5.68	11.11	6.7	12.96	8.98	5.56	10.39	16.67	11.64
Khmelnytska	24.98	16.67	7.65	14.29	10.39	21.43	9.33	0	0	0	17.66
Cherkaska	22.5	14.29	6.44	14.29	9.83	11.9	10.05	7.14	0	0	10.52
Chernivetska	21.2	21.43	7.45	16.67	8.56	14.29	8.79	0	0	0	11.985
Chernihivska	21.46	21.43	7.43	16.67	7.63	11.9	16.42	7.14	0	7.14	14.98

Table A4. Dissimilarity indices: the congruence of parliamentary and regional contests within the 2014/2015 multilevel elections.

	Petro Poroshenko Bloc "Solidarnist," vote shares in the parliamentary elections, %	Petro Poroshenko Bloc "Solidarnist," vote shares in the regional elections, %	Fatherland, vote shares in the parliamentary elections, %	Fatherland, vote shares in the parliamentary elections, %	Self-Reliance, vote shares in the parliamentary elections, %	Self-Reliance, vote shares in the municipal elections, %	Radical Party of Oleh Lyashko, vote shares in the parliamentary elections, %	Radical Party of Oleh Lyashko, vote shares in the municipal elections, %	Opposition Bloc, vote shares in the parliamentary elections, %	Opposition Bloc, vote shares in the parliamentary elections, %	Dissimilarity index
Vinnytska	37.45	32.14	6.6	19.05	7.59	8.33	6.09	10.71	0	7.14	15.13
Volynska	16.89	20.31	7.48	18.75	11.46	7.81	9.7	9.38	0	0	9.33

190 APPENDIX

Dnipro-petrovska	19.48	11.67	0	7.5	8.59	6.67	7.59	6.67	24.27	38.33	16.105
Zhytomy-rska	23.03	26.56	6.52	20.31	9.12	9.38	10.63	9.38	0	10.94	14.885
Zakar-patska	28.05	23.44	5.12	10.94	9.63	0	6.83	0	0	6.25	16.57
Zaporizka	16.94	15.48	0	9.52	8.59	7.14	5.92	7.14	22.18	33.33	12.4
Ivano-Frankivska	18.25	27.38	6.19	20.24	14.69	9.52	0	0	0	0	14.175
Kyivska	24.28	26.19	6.56	19.05	13.13	11.9	6.91	10.71	0	7.14	13.285
Kirovohr-adska	21.73	21.88	8.34	21.88	7.9	6.25	11.67	9.38	7	20.31	15.47
Lvivska	20.42	23.81	0	10.71	18.78	16.67	5.35	5.95	0	0	8.405
Mykola-ivska	20.64	23.44	0	10.94	7.71	0	7.78	0	15.88	26.56	19.955
Odeska	19.63	26.19	0	13.1	7.23	0	5.41	0	18.05	27.38	20.815
Poltavska	23.24	17.86	6.22	15.48	9.22	0	10.85	9.52	5.33	7.14	13.5
Rivnenska	24.21	29.69	6.65	25	11.08	0	7.91	15.63	0	0	21.315
Sumska	25.09	21.88	7.19	21.88	8.28	0	10.61	10.94	0	7.81	17.16

Ternopilska	19.73	28.13	6.31	15.63	11.3	9.38	11.3	7.81	0	0	11.565
Kharkivska	15.17	16.67	0	6.67	7.49	10	6.38	0	32.16	0	24.61
Khersonska	22.26	28.13	5.68	14.06	6.7	7.81	8.98	9.38	10.39	20.31	12.84
Khmelnytska	24.98	20.24	7.65	13.1	10.39	9.52	9.33	9.52	0	0	5.625
Cherkaska	22.5	21.43	6.44	15.48	9.83	0	10.05	11.9	0	0	10.895
Chernivetska	21.2	23.44	7.45	18.75	8.56	7.81	8.79	7.81	0	6.25	10.76
Chernihivska	21.46	18.75	7.43	17.19	7.63	0	16.42	18.75	0	6.25	14.345
Kyiv	23.95	43.33	5.22	14.17	21.39	18.33	0	0	0	0	15.695

192 APPENDIX

Table A5. Dissimilarity indices: the congruence of parliamentary and municipal contests within the 2019/2020 multilevel elections.

	Servant of the People, vote shares in the parliamentary elections, %	Servant of the People, vote shares in the municipal elections, %	Opposition Platform – For Life, vote shares in the parliamentary elections, %	Opposition Platform – For Life, vote shares in the municipal elections, %	Fatherland, vote shares in the parliamentary elections, %	Fatherland, vote shares in the municipal elections, %	European Solidarity, vote shares in the parliamentary elections, %	'European Solidarity', vote shares in the municipal elections, %	Voice, vote shares in the parliamentary elections, %	Voice, vote shares in the municipal elections, %	Dissimilarity index
Vinnytska	37.91	11.11	5.41	9.26	10.03	0	8.29	16.67	3.4	0	26.205
Volynska	41.76	11.9	3.78	0	13.08	9.52	8.02	21.43	6.96	0	28.785
Dnipropetrovska	56.7	14.06	15.17	20.31	4.7	0	4.64	10.94	2.22	0	30.5
Zhytomyrska	47.04	16.67	8.16	14.29	9.96	7.14	7.04	14.29	3.71	0	25.14
Zakarpatska	49.86	18.42	8.01	15.79	10.04	21.05	4.58	15.79	4.38	0	32.91
Zaporizka	48.39	20.31	21.79	20.31	4.4	0	5.2	17.19	2.25	0	24.1
Ivano-Frankivska	33.81	0	1.37	0	14.67	9.52	11.94	23.81	13.25	0	32.725
Kirovohradska	51.4	14.29	9.73	9.52	11.84	11.9	5.88	14.29	2.5	0	24.145

Lvivska	22.03	0	1.71	0	9.44	0	19.87	40.63	23.09	12.5	32.265
Mykola-ivska	52.18	16.67	18.99	31.48	4.68	0	5.03	9.26	2.32	0	29.615
Odeska	47.03	15.63	23.35	28.13	4.55	0	4.19	15.63	2.41	0	27.29
Poltavska	52.53	21.43	10.12	9.52	10.31	0	5.36	14.29	3.06	0	27
Rivnenska	41.87	16.67	4.21	0	10.56	11.9	9.65	23.81	7.96	11.9	24.425
Sumska	50.94	19.05	11.9	21.43	10.08	30.95	5.04	21.43	2.83	0	40.755
Terno-pilska	31.51	7.14	1.7	0	12.23	0	12.59	21.43	13.07	0	30.105
Kharkivska	42.72	10.71	26.55	22.62	3.56	0	4.95	10.71	2.67	0	23.965
Kher-sonska	49.71	18.52	17.97	20.37	5.29	0	6	12.96	2.82	0	24.69
Khmelnytska	46.77	9.52	5.35	0	10.67	9.52	6.92	9.52	4.1	0	25.225
Cherkaska	51.03	19.05	6.28	9.52	9.23	9.52	6.43	16.67	3.75	14.29	28.145
Cherni-vetska	50.67	11.9	8.87	0	10.26	0	6.71	14.29	4.55	0	35.015
Cherni-hivska	44.26	9.52	8.23	9.52	14.28	0	5.84	9.52	2.66	0	28.325
Kyiv	36.46	43.16	7.79	13.05	8.42	8.18	16.68	8.1	9.92	5.82	12.44

Table A6. Dissimilarity indices: the congruence of parliamentary and regional contests within the 2019/2020 multilevel elections.

	Servant of the People, vote shares in the parliamentary elections, %	Servant of the People, vote shares in the regional elections, %	Opposition Platform – For Life, vote shares in the parliamentary elections, %	Opposition Platform – For Life, vote shares in the regional elections, %	Fatherland, vote shares in the parliamentary elections, %	Fatherland, vote shares in the regional elections, %	European Solidarity, vote shares in the parliamentary elections, %	European Solidarity, vote shares in the regional elections, %	Voice, vote shares in the parliamentary elections, %	Voice, vote shares in the regional elections, %	Dissimilarity index
Vinnytska	37.91	9.52	5.41	8.33	10.03	13.1	8.29	13.1	3.4	0	21.295
Volynska	41.76	12.5	3.78	0	13.08	14.06	8.02	14.06	6.96	0	23.51
Dnipropetrovska	56.7	25	15.17	22.5	4.7	6.67	4.64	10.83	2.22	0	24.705
Zhytomyrska	47.04	17.19	8.16	10.94	9.96	9.38	7.04	14.06	3.71	0	21.97
Zakarpatska	49.86	17.19	8.01	9.38	10.04	12.5	4.58	9.38	4.38	0	22.84
Zaporizka	48.39	22.62	21.79	27.38	4.4	8.33	5.2	11.9	2.25	0	22.12
Ivano-Frankivska	33.81	10.71	1.37	0	14.67	16.67	11.94	20.24	13.25	0	24.01
Kyivska	46.48	26.19	6.16	10.71	11.07	16.67	9.86	29.76	5.82	0	28.08

Kirovohr-adska	51.4	21.88	9.73	17.19	11.84	23.44	5.88	14.06	2.5	0	29.63
Lvivska	22.03	10.71	1.71	0	9.44	8.33	19.87	33.33	23.09	8.33	21.18
Mykola-ivska	52.18	25	18.99	28.13	4.68	0	5.03	12.5	2.32	0	25.395
Odeska	47.03	19.05	23.35	28.57	4.55	8.33	4.19	11.9	2.41	0	23.55
Poltavska	52.53	16.67	10.12	13.1	10.31	14.29	5.36	10.71	3.06	0	25.615
Rivnenska	41.87	18.75	4.21	0	10.56	14.06	9.65	20.31	7.96	0	24.725
Sumska	50.94	25	11.9	21.88	10.08	15.63	5.04	14.06	2.83	0	26.66
Terno-pilska	31.51	12.5	1.7	0	12.23	12.5	12.59	26.56	13.07	0	24.01
Kharkivska	42.72	14.17	26.55	24.17	3.56	0	4.95	9.17	2.67	0	20.69
Kher-sonska	49.71	17.19	17.97	23.44	5.29	9.38	6	10.94	2.82	0	24.92
Khmelnytska	46.77	15.63	5.35	0	10.67	10.94	6.92	10.94	4.1	0	22.44
Cherkaska	51.03	18.75	6.28	0	9.23	10.94	6.43	14.06	3.75	0	25.825
Cherni-vetska	50.67	18.75	8.87	9.38	10.26	0	6.71	0	4.55	0	26.975
Cherni-hivska	44.26	12.5	8.23	7.81	14.28	9.38	5.84	7.81	2.66	0	20.855

Table A7. Parties-frontrunners at the three multilevel elections under study.

	The 2012 parliamentary elections	The 2010 regional elections	The 2010 municipal elections	The 2014 parliamentary elections	The 2015 regional elections	The 2015 municipal elections	The 2019 parliamentary elections	The 2020 regional elections	The 2020 municipal elections
Kyiv	36.46	7.79	10	8.42	16.68	25.83	9.92	7.5	20.91
AR Crimea	Party of Regions	Party of Regions	-	-	-	-	-	-	-
Vinnytska	Fatherland	Party of Regions	*Sovist Ukrainy*	Petro Poroshenko Bloc	Petro Poroshenko Bloc	Vinnytska European Strategy	Servant of the People	The Ukrainian Strategy of Hroysman	The Ukrainian Strategy of Hroysman
Volynska	Fatherland	Fatherland	Fatherland'	People's Front	UKROP	UKROP	Servant of the People	For the Future	For the Future
Dnipropetrovska	Party of Regions	Party of Regions	Party of Regions	Opposition Bloc	Opposition Bloc	Opposition Bloc	Servant of the People	Servant of the People	Proposition
Donetska	Party of Regions	Party of Regions	Party of Regions				The Opposition Platform – For Life	-	-
Zhytomyrska	Fatherland	Party of Regions	Party of Regions	People's Front	Petro Poroshenko Bloc	Petro Poroshenko Bloc	Servant of the People	Servant of the People	Proposition
Zakarpatska	Party of Regions	United Center	Party of Regions	Petro Poroshenko Bloc	United Center	Renaissance	Servant of the People	*Native Zakarpattya*	Fatherland
Zaporizka	Party of Regions	Party of Regions	Party of Regions	Opposition Bloc	Opposition Bloc	Opposition Bloc	Servant of the People	Opposition Platform – For Life	Party of Volodymyr Buryak Yednannya

Ivano-Frankovska	Fatherland	Fatherland	Fatherland	Freedom	People's Front	Petro Poroshenko Bloc	Freedom	Servant of the People	Freedom	Freedom
Kyivska	Fatherland	Party of Regions	Party of Regions	-	People's Front	Petro Poroshenko Bloc	-	Servant of the People	European Strategy	-
Kirovohradska	Fatherland	Party of Regions	Party of Regions	Party of Regions	People's Front	Petro Poroshenko Bloc	Petro Poroshenko Bloc	Servant of the People	Fatherland	Proposition
Luhanska	Party of Regions	Party of Regions	Party of Regions	Party of Regions	-	-	-	Opposition Platform – For Life	-	-
Lvivska	Freedom	Freedom	Freedom	Freedom	People's Front	Petro Poroshenko Bloc	Self-Reliance	Holos	European Strategy	European Strategy
Mykolaivska	Party of Regions	Party of Regions	Party of Regions	Party of Regions	Petro Poroshenko Bloc	Opposition Bloc	Opposition Bloc	Servant of the People	Opposition Platform – For Life	Opposition Platform – For Life
Odeska	Party of Regions	Party of Regions	Party of Regions	Party of Regions	Petro Poroshenko Bloc	Opposition Bloc	Trust Actions	Servant of the People	Opposition Platform – For Life	Trust Actions
Poltavska	Fatherland	Fatherland	Party of Regions	Sovist Ukrainy	People's Front	Petro Poroshenko Bloc	Petro Poroshenko Bloc	Servant of the People	Trust	For the Future
Rivnenska	Fatherland	Fatherland	Fatherland	Fatherland	People's Front	Petro Poroshenko Bloc	Petro Poroshenko Bloc	Servant of the People	European Strategy	European Strategy
Sumska	Fatherland	Fatherland	Party of Regions	Ridne Misto	Petro Poroshenko Bloc	Petro Poroshenko Bloc	Fatherland	Servant of the People	Servant of the People	Fatherland
Ternopilska	Fatherland	Fatherland	-	-	People's Front	Petro Poroshenko Bloc	Freedom	Servant of the People	European Strategy	Proposition

198 APPENDIX

	Party of Regions	Party of Regions	Party of Regions	Party of Regions	Opposition Bloc	Renaissance	Renaissance	Servant of the People	Kharkiv Bloc – Successful Kharkiv	Kharkiv Bloc – Successful Kharkiv
Kharkivska	Party of Regions	Party of Regions	Party of Regions	Party of Regions	Opposition Bloc	Renaissance	Renaissance	Servant of the People	Kharkiv Bloc – Successful Kharkiv	Kharkiv Bloc – Successful Kharkiv
Khersonska	Party of Regions	Party of Regions	Party of Regions	Party of Regions	Petro Poroshenko Bloc	Petro Poroshenko Bloc	Petro Poroshenko Bloc	Servant of the People	Opposition Platform – For Life	We will live here
Khmelnytska	Fatherland	Party of Regions	Fatherland	Fatherland	People's Front	For Concrete Actions	Freedom	Servant of the People	The Team of Symchyshyn	The Team of Symchyshyn
Cherkaska	Fatherland	Party of Regions	Fatherland	-	People's Front	Petro Poroshenko Bloc	*Patriya Vilnyh Demokrativ*	Servant of the People	The Cherkasy People	For the Future
Chernivetska	Fatherland	Party of Regions	Fatherland	*Front Zmin*	People's Front	Petro Poroshenko Bloc	*Ridne Misto*	Servant of the People	Servant of the People	The Only Alternative
Chernihivska	Fatherland	Party of Regions	Fatherland	Party of Regions	Petro Poroshenko Bloc	Petro Poroshenko Bloc	Our Land	Servant of the People	Native Home	Native Home
Kyiv	Fatherland	-	Fatherland	-	-	Petro Poroshenko Bloc	-	Servant of the People	European Strategy	-
Sevastopol	Party of Regions	Party of Regions	-	-	Petro Poroshenko Bloc	-	-	-	-	-

Source: Based on official data from the Central Electoral Commission.

Index

1995 Constitutional Agreement 63
1996 Constitution 63, 65, 66
1998 Concept 39
    and local self-government 39
    not carried out 39
2005 Concept 40, 43
    and Council of Europe 41
    as model for decentralization 40–41
    criticisms of 41
2009 Concept 42–43, 43, 46, 61, 66, 67, 154
2014 Concept 15–16, 16, 22, 48, 55, 61, 63, 69, 81, 151, 154
2019 Electoral Code 126
ACF (Advocacy Coalition Framework) 21–22, 37, 39
alternate advocacy coalition 62
    and executive committees 22
    and local amalgamation 61, 154
    and local authorities 80, 82
    and regional authority 82
    criticisms of pro-reform advocacy coalition 82
    criticizes pro-reform advocacy coalition 25
    lack of evidence-based policy agenda 62
ATC (Amalgamated Territorial Community) 44, 49–53, 54, 57, 60, 151
    and administrative centers 52, 53, 56, 58, 127, 132
    and budget relations 50, 51
    and infrastructure 49, 50
    and local elections 58, 60
    and perspective plans 53, 59
    and public services 49, 54
    and regional development 50
    and voluntary amalgamation 52
    criteria for amalgamation 51
Atroshenko, Vladislav 110, 123
Baloha, Viktor 118
Bertash, Vasyl 142
Bezsmertnyi, Roman 40, 41, 48, 65
bipolar political divide (ethnic/linguistic & geopolitical) 83–88
Bohovin, Vitaliy 137
Bondarenko, Anatoliy 122
Buryak, Volodomyr 121–22, 129
center-periphery relations 19, 25, 83, 152
Chaisty, Paul 33, 87, 88
Chernyshov, Oleksiy 138
Chhibber, Pradeep 29
Chmyr, Yuriy 117–18
Chornoivanenko, Oleksandr 143
Chubirko, Volodymyr 139
COVID-19 127
    and political divisions 77
D'Anieri, Paul 33, 87
decentralization 39, 50, 59, 62, 80, 91, 111, 126, 130, 133, 156
    and 2005 Concept 41
    and 2009 Concept 46, 66
    and 2012 draft Concept 46
    and 2014 Concept 15, 69
    and Action Plan 55
    and ATCs 54
    and center-periphery relations 152

and constitutional amendments 69, 73, 77, 80, 151, 152, 153
and Council of Europe Appraisal 47, 67–68
and fragmentation 36, 106
and incongruence 92, 111, 156
and international support 24, 56
and local amalgamation 48
and local authorities 26, 31, 82, 127, 153
and multilevel elections 15, 25, 27, 28, 31, 35, 38, 128, 151, 156, 159
and party politics 25, 29, 36, 38, 120
and policy learning 120
and policymaking 22–23, 49
and Poroshenko 55, 75, 120
and prioritization of substate agendas 29
and pro-reform advocacy coalition 154
and public engagement 76
and public services 128
and regional councils 160
and ruling elites 16
and Russia's hybrid war against Ukraine 17
and state supervision of local authorities 81
and the Euromaidan 25
and the Euromaidan Uprising 16
and Zelenskyy 55, 61, 75, 113, 114, 120
as strenghtening local self-governance 152
as strengthening local self-governance 15
as top-down project 153
fiscal 49, 51, 54, 59, 158
pre-Euromaidan reforms 48
Dobysh, Mykola 132
Dudley, William 57
Dzharty, Vasyl 142

elites 30, 35, 142
business 88, 89
local 72, 142, 152
regional 130, 142, 144
ruling 24, 44, 53, 55, 66, 155
substate 115, 125, 148, 149
Euromaidan
change of elites 48
change of political alliances 85, 86, 87
leadership 84
post-Euromaidan change of elites 81
Uprising 25, 39, 48, 84, 85, 87, 155
European Charter of Local Self-Government 20, 25, 39, 68, 75
executive committees 20, 64, 67, 151, 153, 160
and constitutional amendments 69
and 1995 Constitutional Agreement and 1996 Constitution 63
and 2014 Concept 151
and alternate advocacy coalition 22
and constitutional amendments 77, 80, 151, 155
and Council of Europe 67, 68
and directly elected councils 15
and Euromaidan 25
and lack of consensus 69, 70, 72, 75, 155
and regional councils 15, 16, 17, 24, 37, 63, 66, 67, 69, 70, 71, 80, 81
and regional executives 20
and Russia's hybrid war against Ukraine 24
and subregional councils 66
and substate actors 153
and Ukrainian SSR 19
Filatov, Boris 116, 124

fragmentation 27, 105, 131
   and regional councils 37, 106, 112, 135, 149, 158
   and the party system 35, 36, 38, 91, 105–6, 112, 157
Frye, Timothy 87
Hanushchak, Yuri 49, 72, 73, 78
Hough, Daniel 28, 29
Hroysman, Volodymyr 16, 49, 55, 100, 104
Hynevetskyi, Serhiy 139
incongruence 27, 34, 35, 92, 93, 99, 104, 111, 112, 157
   in parliamentary and municipal elections 31, 91, 156
   in parliamentary and regional elections 27, 31, 35, 92, 93, 111, 156
   vertical 36, 99, 102, 156
Jeffery, Charlie 28, 29
Kaida, Oleksiy 147
Kaltsev, Sergiy 118
Keating, Michael 29
Kernes, Hennadiy 110, 115, 117, 121
Khomutynnyk, Vitaliy 117
Kichatyi, Yuriy 147
Kisse, Anton 118
Kizin, Sydor 143
Klimchuk, Borys 142
Klitchko, Vitaliy 84, 124, 126
Koliushko, Ihor 42, 43, 49, 72
Kollmann, Ken 29
Kolomoiskyi, Ihor 117
Kolykhayev, Ihor 129
Kovalchuk, Volodymyr 144
Kuchma, Leonid 39, 64, 142
Labunska, Anzhelika 143

local amalgamation 24, 31, 63, 80, 92, 113, 114, 132, 151, 154
   and 1998 Concept 39
   and alternate advocacy coalition 61, 154
   and cities of *oblast* significance 58
   and constitutional amendments 49
   and Council of Europe Appraisal 43, 45, 47
   and education and healthcare 56
   and financial incentives 49, 51
   and geographical boundaries 32
   and local elections 58, 60
   and Ministry of Regional Development and Construction 42
   and parliament 48, 59, 60
   and party politics 25
   and perspective plan 45
   and policy learning 23–24
   and policymaking 17, 23, 46, 48, 61
   and political party competition 38
   and pro-reform advocacy coalition 22, 24, 37, 61
   and regional actors 153
   and regional councils 59
   and substate councils 126
   and urban communities 45
   as strengthening local self-governance 15, 17, 151
   completion of 151, 154, 156
   contrasted with regional authority 16
   inconsistent decision-making 54–56
   launched under Poroshenko 120
   opposition to 24, 60, 61, 62, 120
   procedures 51–54

voluntary vs. administrative 54–56, 61, 153
Madoian, Karen 17
Mamai, Oleksandr 110
Martsynkiv, Roman 110
Matsuzato, Kimitaka 19, 30, 35, 131, 135
    Strategy 1 135, 136, 140
    Strategy 2 135, 136, 140, 145
Merikov, Vadym 146
Minsk Agreements 74
Morhunov, Serhiy 110
Moskal, Hennadiy 141, 146–47
Neljas, Aap. 26
Nevenchanniy, Maksym 146
OECD 50, 57, 152
Orange revolution 64
Ordeshook, Peter 30
Pallarés, Francesc 29
Pankevych, Oleh 147
Papiev, Mykhailo 147
Pavlenko, Iryna 26, 27
perspective plans (ATCs) 45, 46, 53, 59
Petrov, Oleksiy 139, 141
Platonova, Daria 125
Poroshenko, Petro 16, 49, 74, 75, 84, 117, 120, 123, 138
    and constitutional amendments 70, 71, 73, 76, 120
    and decentralization 55
    and local amalgamation policy 120
    and pro-reform advocacy coalition 82
prefects 73, 76, 78, 79
    civil servant status 80
    subordinated to the Center 78

pro-reform advocacy coalition 22, 23, 53, 56, 60, 61, 62, 69, 76, 77, 80, 82, 154, 155
    and civil society actors 154
    and international support 24, 55
    and lack of consensus 82
    and lack of political will 155
    and parliament 60
    and policy learning 24, 37, 55
    and Poroshenko 82
    and regional authority 155
    and regional councils 53, 69, 82
    and substate actors 153
    and Zelenskyy 61, 82
    criticisms of 25, 82
Putilov, Anatoliy 141
Rabinovych, Maryna 17
Raikovych, Andriy 124
regional authority 23, 63, 151
    and alternate advocacy coalition 82
    and constitutional amendments 151
    and Constitutional Assembly 67, 68
    and executive committees 25
    and party politics 25
    and policymaking 21, 37, 63, 65, 81, 114
    and pro-reform advocacy coalition 80, 82, 155
    as contest between president and parliament 20
    first attempt to change status 64
    in relation to 2019/2020 electoral cycle 91
    increase of 15, 29, 67
    lag in implementation 16, 24
    local opposition to increase of 81, 82
    second attempt to change status 75
Riabchuk, Mykola 86

Rivis, Mykhailo 147
Rozumnyi, Maksym 26
Russia's hybrid war against Ukraine 17, 24, 33, 83, 84, 130
Saakashvilli, Mikhail 145
Samardak, Hryhoriy 141, 144
Scully, Roger 28, 29
Semenkov, Yehor 145
Skoryk, Mykola 145
Söller-Winkler, Manuela 75
Starikova, Hanna 143
State Fund for Regional Development 50
state supervision 25, 74, 76, 77, 81, 153, 155
Stepanov, Maxim 138
Sukhomlyn, Serhiy 123
Sych, Oleksandr 144, 147
Tarashevskyi, Serhiy 148
Thorlakson, Lori 29
Tkachuk, Anatoliy 17, 22, 40, 41, 42, 45, 47, 49, 68, 72
Torikai, Masatomo 27, 131
Turchynov, Oleksandr 16
Tymoshenko, Yulia 22, 40, 42, 64, 65, 84, 120
Urbanskiy, Anatoliy 145
Vedernikova, Inna 117
Venice Commission 74
    and constitutional amendments 71–72, 74
Whitefield, Stephen 33, 87, 88
Wilson, Andrew 26, 117, 118
World Bank 57
Wyn Jones, Richard 28, 29
Yanukovych, Viktor 25, 66, 67, 81, 117, 118, 142

Yatsenko, Anton 117
Yatsenko, Boris 132
Yatsenyuk, Arseniy 16
Yushchenko, Viktor 48, 64, 81, 117, 118
Zahorodniy, Myhailo 146
Zelenskyy 84
Zelenskyy, Volodymyr 26, 84, 88, 126
    and 2020 substate elections 114
    and clientelistic linkages 88
    and concentration of central power 114
    and constitutional amendments 75, 76, 120
    and decentralization 55, 61, 113, 114
    and pro-reform advocacy coalition 82
    and regional authority 75
    and regional governors 138
    and Servant of the People 114–16, 133, 137
Zhuk, Olena 137
Zubchenko, Oleksandr 129

SOVIET AND POST-SOVIET POLITICS AND SOCIETY
Edited by Dr. Andreas Umland | ISSN 1614-3515

1 Андреас Умланд (ред.) | Воплощение Европейской конвенции по правам человека в России. Философские, юридические и эмпирические исследования | ISBN 3-89821-387-0

2 Christian Wipperfürth | Russland – ein vertrauenswürdiger Partner? Grundlagen, Hintergründe und Praxis gegenwärtiger russischer Außenpolitik | Mit einem Vorwort von Heinz Timmermann | ISBN 3-89821-401-X

3 Manja Hussner | Die Übernahme internationalen Rechts in die russische und deutsche Rechtsordnung. Eine vergleichende Analyse zur Völkerrechtsfreundlichkeit der Verfassungen der Russländischen Föderation und der Bundesrepublik Deutschland | Mit einem Vorwort von Rainer Arnold | ISBN 3-89821-438-9

4 Matthew Tejada | Bulgaria's Democratic Consolidation and the Kozloduy Nuclear Power Plant (KNPP). The Unattainability of Closure | With a foreword by Richard J. Crampton | ISBN 3-89821-439-7

5 Марк Григорьевич Меерович | Квадратные метры, определяющие сознание. Государственная жилищная политика в СССР. 1921 – 1941 гг | ISBN 3-89821-474-5

6 Andrei P. Tsygankov, Pavel A. Tsygankov (Eds.) | New Directions in Russian International Studies | ISBN 3-89821-422-2

7 Марк Григорьевич Меерович | Как власть народ к труду приучала. Жилище в СССР – средство управления людьми. 1917 – 1941 гг. | С предисловием Елены Осокиной | ISBN 3-89821-495-8

8 David J. Galbreath | Nation-Building and Minority Politics in Post-Socialist States. Interests, Influence and Identities in Estonia and Latvia | With a foreword by David J. Smith | ISBN 3-89821-467-2

9 Алексей Юрьевич Безугольный | Народы Кавказа в Вооруженных силах СССР в годы Великой Отечественной войны 1941-1945 гг. | С предисловием Николая Бугая | ISBN 3-89821-475-3

10 Вячеслав Лихачев и Владимир Прибыловский (ред.) | Русское Национальное Единство, 1990-2000. В 2-х томах | ISBN 3-89821-523-7

11 Николай Бугай (ред.) | Народы стран Балтии в условиях сталинизма (1940-е – 1950-е годы). Документированная история | ISBN 3-89821-525-3

12 Ingmar Bredies (Hrsg.) | Zur Anatomie der Orange Revolution in der Ukraine. Wechsel des Elitenregimes oder Triumph des Parlamentarismus? | ISBN 3-89821-524-5

13 Anastasia V. Mitrofanova | The Politicization of Russian Orthodoxy. Actors and Ideas | With a foreword by William C. Gay | ISBN 3-89821-481-8

14 Nathan D. Larson | Alexander Solzhenitsyn and the Russo-Jewish Question | ISBN 3-89821-483-4

15 Guido Houben | Kulturpolitik und Ethnizität. Staatliche Kunstförderung im Russland der neunziger Jahre | Mit einem Vorwort von Gert Weisskirchen | ISBN 3-89821-542-3

16 Leonid Luks | Der russische „Sonderweg"? Aufsätze zur neuesten Geschichte Russlands im europäischen Kontext | ISBN 3-89821-496-6

17 Евгений Мороз | История «Мёртвой воды» – от страшной сказки к большой политике. Политическое неоязычество в постсоветской России | ISBN 3-89821-551-2

18 Александр Верховский и Галина Кожевникова (ред.) | Этническая и религиозная интолерантность в российских СМИ. Результаты мониторинга 2001-2004 гг. | ISBN 3-89821-569-5

19 Christian Ganzer | Sowjetisches Erbe und ukrainische Nation. Das Museum der Geschichte des Zaporoger Kosakentums auf der Insel Chortycja | Mit einem Vorwort von Frank Golczewski | ISBN 3-89821-504-0

20 Эльза-Баир Гучинова | Помнить нельзя забыть. Антропология депортационной травмы калмыков | С предисловием Кэролайн Хамфри | ISBN 3-89821-506-7

21 Юлия Лидерман | Мотивы «проверки» и «испытания» в постсоветской культуре. Советское прошлое в российском кинематографе 1990-х годов | С предисловием Евгения Марголита | ISBN 3-89821-511-3

22 Tanya Lokshina, Ray Thomas, Mary Mayer (Eds.) | The Imposition of a Fake Political Settlement in the Northern Caucasus. The 2003 Chechen Presidential Election | ISBN 3-89821-436-2

23 Timothy McCajor Hall, Rosie Read (Eds.) | Changes in the Heart of Europe. Recent Ethnographies of Czechs, Slovaks, Roma, and Sorbs | With an afterword by Zdeněk Salzmann | ISBN 3-89821-606-3

24 *Christian Autengruber* | Die politischen Parteien in Bulgarien und Rumänien. Eine vergleichende Analyse seit Beginn der 90er Jahre | Mit einem Vorwort von Dorothée de Nève | ISBN 3-89821-476-1

25 *Annette Freyberg-Inan with Radu Cristescu* | The Ghosts in Our Classrooms, or: John Dewey Meets Ceauşescu. The Promise and the Failures of Civic Education in Romania | ISBN 3-89821-416-8

26 *John B. Dunlop* | The 2002 Dubrovka and 2004 Beslan Hostage Crises. A Critique of Russian Counter-Terrorism | With a foreword by Donald N. Jensen | ISBN 3-89821-608-X

27 *Peter Koller* | Das touristische Potenzial von Kam''janec'–Podil's'kyj. Eine fremdenverkehrsgeographische Untersuchung der Zukunftsperspektiven und Maßnahmenplanung zur Destinationsentwicklung des „ukrainischen Rothenburg" | Mit einem Vorwort von Kristiane Klemm | ISBN 3-89821-640-3

28 *Françoise Daucé, Elisabeth Sieca-Kozlowski (Eds.)* | Dedovshchina in the Post-Soviet Military. Hazing of Russian Army Conscripts in a Comparative Perspective | With a foreword by Dale Herspring | ISBN 3-89821-616-0

29 *Florian Strasser* | Zivilgesellschaftliche Einflüsse auf die Orange Revolution. Die gewaltlose Massenbewegung und die ukrainische Wahlkrise 2004 | Mit einem Vorwort von Egbert Jahn | ISBN 3-89821-648-9

30 *Rebecca S. Katz* | The Georgian Regime Crisis of 2003-2004. A Case Study in Post-Soviet Media Representation of Politics, Crime and Corruption | ISBN 3-89821-413-3

31 *Vladimir Kantor* | Willkür oder Freiheit. Beiträge zur russischen Geschichtsphilosophie | Ediert von Dagmar Herrmann sowie mit einem Vorwort versehen von Leonid Luks | ISBN 3-89821-589-X

32 *Laura A. Victoir* | The Russian Land Estate Today. A Case Study of Cultural Politics in Post-Soviet Russia | With a foreword by Priscilla Roosevelt | ISBN 3-89821-426-5

33 *Ivan Katchanovski* | Cleft Countries. Regional Political Divisions and Cultures in Post-Soviet Ukraine and Moldova | With a foreword by Francis Fukuyama | ISBN 3-89821-558-X

34 *Florian Mühlfried* | Postsowjetische Feiern. Das Georgische Bankett im Wandel | Mit einem Vorwort von Kevin Tuite | ISBN 3-89821-601-2

35 *Roger Griffin, Werner Loh, Andreas Umland (Eds.)* | Fascism Past and Present, West and East. An International Debate on Concepts and Cases in the Comparative Study of the Extreme Right | With an afterword by Walter Laqueur | ISBN 3-89821-674-8

36 *Sebastian Schlegel* | Der „Weiße Archipel". Sowjetische Atomstädte 1945-1991 | Mit einem Geleitwort von Thomas Bohn | ISBN 3-89821-679-9

37 *Vyacheslav Likhachev* | Political Anti-Semitism in Post-Soviet Russia. Actors and Ideas in 1991-2003 | Edited and translated from Russian by Eugene Veklerov | ISBN 3-89821-529-6

38 *Josette Baer (Ed.)* | Preparing Liberty in Central Europe. Political Texts from the Spring of Nations 1848 to the Spring of Prague 1968 | With a foreword by Zdeněk V. David | ISBN 3-89821-546-6

39 *Михаил Лукьянов* | Российский консерватизм и реформа, 1907-1914 | С предисловием Марка Д. Стейнберга | ISBN 3-89821-503-2

40 *Nicola Melloni* | Market Without Economy. The 1998 Russian Financial Crisis | With a foreword by Eiji Furukawa | ISBN 3-89821-407-9

41 *Dmitrij Chmelnizki* | Die Architektur Stalins | Bd. 1: Studien zu Ideologie und Stil | Bd. 2: Bilddokumentation | Mit einem Vorwort von Bruno Flierl | ISBN 3-89821-515-6

42 *Katja Yafimava* | Post-Soviet Russian-Belarussian Relationships. The Role of Gas Transit Pipelines | With a foreword by Jonathan P. Stern | ISBN 3-89821-655-1

43 *Boris Chavkin* | Verflechtungen der deutschen und russischen Zeitgeschichte. Aufsätze und Archivfunde zu den Beziehungen Deutschlands und der Sowjetunion von 1917 bis 1991 | Ediert von Markus Edlinger sowie mit einem Vorwort versehen von Leonid Luks | ISBN 3-89821-756-6

44 *Anastasija Grynenko in Zusammenarbeit mit Claudia Dathe* | Die Terminologie des Gerichtswesens der Ukraine und Deutschlands im Vergleich. Eine übersetzungswissenschaftliche Analyse juristischer Fachbegriffe im Deutschen, Ukrainischen und Russischen | Mit einem Vorwort von Ulrich Hartmann | ISBN 3-89821-691-8

45 *Anton Burkov* | The Impact of the European Convention on Human Rights on Russian Law. Legislation and Application in 1996-2006 | With a foreword by Françoise Hampson | ISBN 978-3-89821-639-5

46 *Stina Torjesen, Indra Overland (Eds.)* | International Election Observers in Post-Soviet Azerbaijan. Geopolitical Pawns or Agents of Change? | ISBN 978-3-89821-743-9

47 *Taras Kuzio* | Ukraine – Crimea – Russia. Triangle of Conflict | ISBN 978-3-89821-761-3

48 *Claudia Šabić* | „Ich erinnere mich nicht, aber L'viv!" Zur Funktion kultureller Faktoren für die Institutionalisierung und Entwicklung einer ukrainischen Region | Mit einem Vorwort von Melanie Tatur | ISBN 978-3-89821-752-1

49 *Marlies Bilz* | Tatarstan in der Transformation. Nationaler Diskurs und Politische Praxis 1988-1994 | Mit einem Vorwort von Frank Golczewski | ISBN 978-3-89821-722-4

50 *Марлен Ларюэль (ред.)* | Современные интерпретации русского национализма | ISBN 978-3-89821-795-8

51 *Sonja Schüler* | Die ethnische Dimension der Armut. Roma im postsozialistischen Rumänien | Mit einem Vorwort von Anton Sterbling | ISBN 978-3-89821-776-7

52 *Галина Кожевникова* | Радикальный национализм в России и противодействие ему. Сборник докладов Центра «Сова» за 2004-2007 гг. | С предисловием Александра Верховского | ISBN 978-3-89821-721-7

53 *Галина Кожевникова и Владимир Прибыловский* | Российская власть в биографиях I. Высшие должностные лица РФ в 2004 г. | ISBN 978-3-89821-796-5

54 *Галина Кожевникова и Владимир Прибыловский* | Российская власть в биографиях II. Члены Правительства РФ в 2004 г. | ISBN 978-3-89821-797-2

55 *Галина Кожевникова и Владимир Прибыловский* | Российская власть в биографиях III. Руководители федеральных служб и агентств РФ в 2004 г.| ISBN 978-3-89821-798-9

56 *Ileana Petroniu* | Privatisierung in Transformationsökonomien. Determinanten der Restrukturierungs-Bereitschaft am Beispiel Polens, Rumäniens und der Ukraine | Mit einem Vorwort von Rainer W. Schäfer | ISBN 978-3-89821-790-3

57 *Christian Wipperfürth* | Russland und seine GUS-Nachbarn. Hintergründe, aktuelle Entwicklungen und Konflikte in einer ressourcenreichen Region| ISBN 978-3-89821-801-6

58 *Togzhan Kassenova* | From Antagonism to Partnership. The Uneasy Path of the U.S.-Russian Cooperative Threat Reduction | With a foreword by Christoph Bluth | ISBN 978-3-89821-707-1

59 *Alexander Höllwerth* | Das sakrale eurasische Imperium des Aleksandr Dugin. Eine Diskursanalyse zum postsowjetischen russischen Rechtsextremismus | Mit einem Vorwort von Dirk Uffelmann | ISBN 978-3-89821-813-9

60 *Олег Рябов* | «Россия-Матушка». Национализм, гендер и война в России XX века | С предисловием Елены Гощило | ISBN 978-3-89821-487-3

61 *Ivan Maistrenko* | Borot'bism. A Chapter in the History of the Ukrainian Revolution | With a new Introduction by Chris Ford | Translated by George S. N. Luckyj with the assistance of Ivan L. Rudnytsky | Second, Revised and Expanded Edition ISBN 978-3-8382-1107-7

62 *Maryna Romanets* | Anamorphosic Texts and Reconfigured Visions. Improvised Traditions in Contemporary Ukrainian and Irish Literature | ISBN 978-3-89821-576-3

63 *Paul D'Anieri and Taras Kuzio (Eds.)* | Aspects of the Orange Revolution I. Democratization and Elections in Post-Communist Ukraine | ISBN 978-3-89821-698-2

64 *Bohdan Harasymiw in collaboration with Oleh S. Ilnytzkyj (Eds.)* | Aspects of the Orange Revolution II. Information and Manipulation Strategies in the 2004 Ukrainian Presidential Elections | ISBN 978-3-89821-699-9

65 *Ingmar Bredies, Andreas Umland and Valentin Yakushik (Eds.)* | Aspects of the Orange Revolution III. The Context and Dynamics of the 2004 Ukrainian Presidential Elections | ISBN 978-3-89821-803-0

66 *Ingmar Bredies, Andreas Umland and Valentin Yakushik (Eds.)* | Aspects of the Orange Revolution IV. Foreign Assistance and Civic Action in the 2004 Ukrainian Presidential Elections | ISBN 978-3-89821-808-5

67 *Ingmar Bredies, Andreas Umland and Valentin Yakushik (Eds.)* | Aspects of the Orange Revolution V. Institutional Observation Reports on the 2004 Ukrainian Presidential Elections | ISBN 978-3-89821-809-2

68 *Taras Kuzio (Ed.)* | Aspects of the Orange Revolution VI. Post-Communist Democratic Revolutions in Comparative Perspective | ISBN 978-3-89821-820-7

69 *Tim Bohse* | Autoritarismus statt Selbstverwaltung. Die Transformation der kommunalen Politik in der Stadt Kaliningrad 1990-2005 | Mit einem Geleitwort von Stefan Troebst | ISBN 978-3-89821-782-8

70 *David Rupp* | Die Rußländische Föderation und die russischsprachige Minderheit in Lettland. Eine Fallstudie zur Anwaltspolitik Moskaus gegenüber den russophonen Minderheiten im „Nahen Ausland" von 1991 bis 2002 | Mit einem Vorwort von Helmut Wagner | ISBN 978-3-89821-778-1

71 *Taras Kuzio* | Theoretical and Comparative Perspectives on Nationalism. New Directions in Cross-Cultural and Post-Communist Studies | With a foreword by Paul Robert Magocsi | ISBN 978-3-89821-815-3

72 *Christine Teichmann* | Die Hochschultransformation im heutigen Osteuropa. Kontinuität und Wandel bei der Entwicklung des postkommunistischen Universitätswesens | Mit einem Vorwort von Oskar Anweiler | ISBN 978-3-89821-842-9

73 *Julia Kusznir* | Der politische Einfluss von Wirtschaftseliten in russischen Regionen. Eine Analyse am Beispiel der Erdöl- und Erdgasindustrie, 1992-2005 | Mit einem Vorwort von Wolfgang Eichwede | ISBN 978-3-89821-821-4

74 *Alena Vysotskaya* | Russland, Belarus und die EU-Osterweiterung. Zur Minderheitenfrage und zum Problem der Freizügigkeit des Personenverkehrs | Mit einem Vorwort von Katlijn Malfliet | ISBN 978-3-89821-822-1

75 *Heiko Pleines (Hrsg.)* | Corporate Governance in post-sozialistischen Volkswirtschaften | ISBN 978-3-89821-766-8

76 *Stefan Ihrig* | Wer sind die Moldawier? Rumänismus versus Moldowanismus in Historiographie und Schulbüchern der Republik Moldova, 1991-2006 | Mit einem Vorwort von Holm Sundhaussen | ISBN 978-3-89821-466-7

77 *Galina Kozhevnikova in collaboration with Alexander Verkhovsky and Eugene Veklerov* | Ultra-Nationalism and Hate Crimes in Contemporary Russia. The 2004-2006 Annual Reports of Moscow's SOVA Center | With a foreword by Stephen D. Shenfield | ISBN 978-3-89821-868-9

78 *Florian Küchler* | The Role of the European Union in Moldova's Transnistria Conflict | With a foreword by Christopher Hill | ISBN 978-3-89821-850-4

79 *Bernd Rechel* | The Long Way Back to Europe. Minority Protection in Bulgaria | With a foreword by Richard Crampton | ISBN 978-3-89821-863-4

80 *Peter W. Rodgers* | Nation, Region and History in Post-Communist Transitions. Identity Politics in Ukraine, 1991-2006 | With a foreword by Vera Tolz | ISBN 978-3-89821-903-7

81 *Stephanie Solywoda* | The Life and Work of Semen L. Frank. A Study of Russian Religious Philosophy | With a foreword by Philip Walters | ISBN 978-3-89821-457-5

82 *Vera Sokolova* | Cultural Politics of Ethnicity. Discourses on Roma in Communist Czechoslovakia | ISBN 978-3-89821-864-1

83 *Natalya Shevchik Ketenci* | Kazakhstani Enterprises in Transition. The Role of Historical Regional Development in Kazakhstan's Post-Soviet Economic Transformation | ISBN 978-3-89821-831-3

84 *Martin Malek, Anna Schor-Tschudnowskaja (Hgg.)* | Europa im Tschetschenienkrieg. Zwischen politischer Ohnmacht und Gleichgültigkeit | Mit einem Vorwort von Lipchan Basajewa | ISBN 978-3-89821-676-0

85 *Stefan Meister* | Das postsowjetische Universitätswesen zwischen nationalem und internationalem Wandel. Die Entwicklung der regionalen Hochschule in Russland als Gradmesser der Systemtransformation | Mit einem Vorwort von Joan DeBardeleben | ISBN 978-3-89821-891-7

86 *Konstantin Sheiko in collaboration with Stephen Brown* | Nationalist Imaginings of the Russian Past. Anatolii Fomenko and the Rise of Alternative History in Post-Communist Russia | With a foreword by Donald Ostrowski | ISBN 978-3-89821-915-0

87 *Sabine Jenni* | Wie stark ist das „Einige Russland"? Zur Parteibindung der Eliten und zum Wahlerfolg der Machtpartei im Dezember 2007 | Mit einem Vorwort von Klaus Armingeon | ISBN 978-3-89821-961-7

88 *Thomas Borén* | Meeting-Places of Transformation. Urban Identity, Spatial Representations and Local Politics in Post-Soviet St Petersburg | ISBN 978-3-89821-739-2

89 *Aygul Ashirova* | Stalinismus und Stalin-Kult in Zentralasien. Turkmenistan 1924-1953 | Mit einem Vorwort von Leonid Luks | ISBN 978-3-89821-987-7

90 *Leonid Luks* | Freiheit oder imperiale Größe? Essays zu einem russischen Dilemma | ISBN 978-3-8382-0011-8

91 *Christopher Gilley* | The 'Change of Signposts' in the Ukrainian Emigration. A Contribution to the History of Sovietophilism in the 1920s | With a foreword by Frank Golczewski | ISBN 978-3-89821-965-5

92 *Philipp Casula, Jeronim Perovic (Eds.)* | Identities and Politics During the Putin Presidency. The Discursive Foundations of Russia's Stability | With a foreword by Heiko Haumann | ISBN 978-3-8382-0015-6

93 *Marcel Viëtor* | Europa und die Frage nach seinen Grenzen im Osten. Zur Konstruktion ‚europäischer Identität' in Geschichte und Gegenwart | Mit einem Vorwort von Albrecht Lehmann | ISBN 978-3-8382-0045-3

94 *Ben Hellman, Andrei Rogachevskii* | Filming the Unfilmable. Casper Wrede's 'One Day in the Life of Ivan Denisovich' | Second, Revised and Expanded Edition | ISBN 978-3-8382-0044-6

95 *Eva Fuchslocher* | Vaterland, Sprache, Glaube. Orthodoxie und Nationenbildung am Beispiel Georgiens | Mit einem Vorwort von Christina von Braun | ISBN 978-3-89821-884-9

96 *Vladimir Kantor* | Das Westlertum und der Weg Russlands. Zur Entwicklung der russischen Literatur und Philosophie | Ediert von Dagmar Herrmann | Mit einem Beitrag von Nikolaus Lobkowicz | ISBN 978-3-8382-0102-3

97 *Kamran Musayev* | Die postsowjetische Transformation im Baltikum und Südkaukasus. Eine vergleichende Untersuchung der politischen Entwicklung Lettlands und Aserbaidschans 1985-2009 | Mit einem Vorwort von Leonid Luks | Ediert von Sandro Henschel | ISBN 978-3-8382-0103-0

98 *Tatiana Zhurzhenko* | Borderlands into Bordered Lands. Geopolitics of Identity in Post-Soviet Ukraine | With a foreword by Dieter Segert | ISBN 978-3-8382-0042-2

99 *Кирилл Галушко, Лидия Смола (ред.)* | Пределы падения – варианты украинского будущего. Аналитико-прогностические исследования | ISBN 978-3-8382-0148-1

100 *Michael Minkenberg (Ed.)* | Historical Legacies and the Radical Right in Post-Cold War Central and Eastern Europe | With an afterword by Sabrina P. Ramet | ISBN 978-3-8382-0124-5

101 *David-Emil Wickström* | Rocking St. Petersburg. Transcultural Flows and Identity Politics in the St. Petersburg Popular Music Scene | With a foreword by Yngvar B. Steinholt | Second, Revised and Expanded Edition | ISBN 978-3-8382-0100-9

102 *Eva Zabka* | Eine neue „Zeit der Wirren"? Der spät- und postsowjetische Systemwandel 1985-2000 im Spiegel russischer gesellschaftspolitischer Diskurse | Mit einem Vorwort von Margareta Mommsen | ISBN 978-3-8382-0161-0

103 *Ulrike Ziemer* | Ethnic Belonging, Gender and Cultural Practices. Youth Identitites in Contemporary Russia | With a foreword by Anoop Nayak | ISBN 978-3-8382-0152-8

104 *Ksenia Chepikova* | ‚Einiges Russland' - eine zweite KPdSU? Aspekte der Identitätskonstruktion einer postsowjetischen „Partei der Macht" | Mit einem Vorwort von Torsten Oppelland | ISBN 978-3-8382-0311-9

105 *Леонид Люкс* | Западничество или евразийство? Демократия или идеократия? Сборник статей об исторических дилеммах России | С предисловием Владимира Кантора | ISBN 978-3-8382-0211-2

106 *Anna Dost* | Das russische Verfassungsrecht auf dem Weg zum Föderalismus und zurück. Zum Konflikt von Rechtsnormen und -wirklichkeit in der Russländischen Föderation von 1991 bis 2009 | Mit einem Vorwort von Alexander Blankenagel | ISBN 978-3-8382-0292-1

107 *Philipp Herzog* | Sozialistische Völkerfreundschaft, nationaler Widerstand oder harmloser Zeitvertreib? Zur politischen Funktion der Volkskunst im sowjetischen Estland | Mit einem Vorwort von Andreas Kappeler | ISBN 978-3-8382-0216-7

108 *Marlène Laruelle (Ed.)* | Russian Nationalism, Foreign Policy, and Identity Debates in Putin's Russia. New Ideological Patterns after the Orange Revolution | ISBN 978-3-8382-0325-6

109 *Michail Logvinov* | Russlands Kampf gegen den internationalen Terrorismus. Eine kritische Bestandsaufnahme des Bekämpfungsansatzes | Mit einem Geleitwort von Hans-Henning Schröder und einem Vorwort von Eckhard Jesse | ISBN 978-3-8382-0329-4

110 *John B. Dunlop* | The Moscow Bombings of September 1999. Examinations of Russian Terrorist Attacks at the Onset of Vladimir Putin's Rule | Second, Revised and Expanded Edition | ISBN 978-3-8382-0388-1

111 *Андрей А. Ковалёв* | Свидетельство из-за кулис российской политики I. Можно ли делать добро из зла? (Воспоминания и размышления о последних советских и первых послесоветских годах) | With a foreword by Peter Reddaway | ISBN 978-3-8382-0302-7

112 *Андрей А. Ковалёв* | Свидетельство из-за кулис российской политики II. Угроза для себя и окружающих (Наблюдения и предостережения относительно происходящего после 2000 г.) | ISBN 978-3-8382-0303-4

113 *Bernd Kappenberg* | Zeichen setzen für Europa. Der Gebrauch europäischer lateinischer Sonderzeichen in der deutschen Öffentlichkeit | Mit einem Vorwort von Peter Schlobinski | ISBN 978-3-89821-749-1

114 *Ivo Mijnssen* | The Quest for an Ideal Youth in Putin's Russia I. Back to Our Future! History, Modernity, and Patriotism according to Nashi, 2005-2013 | With a foreword by Jeronim Perović | Second, Revised and Expanded Edition | ISBN 978-3-8382-0368-3

115 *Jussi Lassila* | The Quest for an Ideal Youth in Putin's Russia II. The Search for Distinctive Conformism in the Political Communication of Nashi, 2005-2009 | With a foreword by Kirill Postoutenko | Second, Revised and Expanded Edition | ISBN 978-3-8382-0415-4

116 *Valerio Trabandt* | Neue Nachbarn, gute Nachbarschaft? Die EU als internationaler Akteur am Beispiel ihrer Demokratieförderung in Belarus und der Ukraine 2004-2009 | Mit einem Vorwort von Jutta Joachim | ISBN 978-3-8382-0437-6

117 *Fabian Pfeiffer* | Estlands Außen- und Sicherheitspolitik I. Der estnische Atlantizismus nach der wiedererlangten Unabhängigkeit 1991-2004 | Mit einem Vorwort von Helmut Hubel | ISBN 978-3-8382-0127-6

118 *Jana Podßuweit* | Estlands Außen- und Sicherheitspolitik II. Handlungsoptionen eines Kleinstaates im Rahmen seiner EU-Mitgliedschaft (2004-2008) | Mit einem Vorwort von Helmut Hubel | ISBN 978-3-8382-0440-6

119 *Karin Pointner* | Estlands Außen- und Sicherheitspolitik III. Eine gedächtnispolitische Analyse estnischer Entwicklungskooperation 2006-2010 | Mit einem Vorwort von Karin Liebhart | ISBN 978-3-8382-0435-2

120 *Ruslana Vovk* | Die Offenheit der ukrainischen Verfassung für das Völkerrecht und die europäische Integration | Mit einem Vorwort von Alexander Blankenagel | ISBN 978-3-8382-0481-9

121 *Mykhaylo Banakh* | Die Relevanz der Zivilgesellschaft bei den postkommunistischen Transformationsprozessen in mittel- und osteuropäischen Ländern. Das Beispiel der spät- und postsowjetischen Ukraine 1986-2009 | Mit einem Vorwort von Gerhard Simon | ISBN 978-3-8382-0499-4

122 *Michael Moser* | Language Policy and the Discourse on Languages in Ukraine under President Viktor Yanukovych (25 February 2010–28 October 2012) | ISBN 978-3-8382-0497-0 (Paperback edition) | ISBN 978-3-8382-0507-6 (Hardcover edition)

123 *Nicole Krome* | Russischer Netzwerkkapitalismus Restrukturierungsprozesse in der Russischen Föderation am Beispiel des Luftfahrtunternehmens „Aviastar" | Mit einem Vorwort von Petra Stykow | ISBN 978-3-8382-0534-2

124 *David R. Marples* | 'Our Glorious Past'. Lukashenka's Belarus and the Great Patriotic War | ISBN 978-3-8382-0574-8 (Paperback edition) | ISBN 978-3-8382-0675-2 (Hardcover edition)

125 *Ulf Walther* | Russlands „neuer Adel". Die Macht des Geheimdienstes von Gorbatschow bis Putin | Mit einem Vorwort von Hans-Georg Wieck | ISBN 978-3-8382-0584-7

126 *Simon Geissbühler (Hrsg.)* | Kiew – Revolution 3.0. Der Euromaidan 2013/14 und die Zukunftsperspektiven der Ukraine | ISBN 978-3-8382-0581-6 (Paperback edition) | ISBN 978-3-8382-0681-3 (Hardcover edition)

127 *Andrey Makarychev* | Russia and the EU in a Multipolar World. Discourses, Identities, Norms | With a foreword by Klaus Segbers | ISBN 978-3-8382-0629-5

128 *Roland Scharff* | Kasachstan als postsowjetischer Wohlfahrtsstaat. Die Transformation des sozialen Schutzsystems | Mit einem Vorwort von Joachim Ahrens | ISBN 978-3-8382-0622-6

129 *Katja Grupp* | Bild Lücke Deutschland. Kaliningrader Studierende sprechen über Deutschland | Mit einem Vorwort von Martin Schulz | ISBN 978-3-8382-0552-6

130 *Konstantin Sheiko, Stephen Brown* | History as Therapy. Alternative History and Nationalist Imaginings in Russia, 1991-2014 | ISBN 978-3-8382-0665-3

131 *Elisa Kriza* | Alexander Solzhenitsyn: Cold War Icon, Gulag Author, Russian Nationalist? A Study of the Western Reception of his Literary Writings, Historical Interpretations, and Political Ideas | With a foreword by Andrei Rogatchevski | ISBN 978-3-8382-0589-2 (Paperback edition) | ISBN 978-3-8382-0690-5 (Hardcover edition)

132 *Serghei Golunov* | The Elephant in the Room. Corruption and Cheating in Russian Universities | ISBN 978-3-8382-0570-0

133 *Manja Hussner, Rainer Arnold (Hgg.)* | Verfassungsgerichtsbarkeit in Zentralasien I. Sammlung von Verfassungstexten | ISBN 978-3-8382-0595-3

134 *Nikolay Mitrokhin* | Die „Russische Partei". Die Bewegung der russischen Nationalisten in der UdSSR 1953-1985 | Aus dem Russischen übertragen von einem Übersetzerteam unter der Leitung von Larisa Schippel | ISBN 978-3-8382-0024-8

135 *Manja Hussner, Rainer Arnold (Hgg.)* | Verfassungsgerichtsbarkeit in Zentralasien II. Sammlung von Verfassungstexten | ISBN 978-3-8382-0597-7

136 *Manfred Zeller* | Das sowjetische Fieber. Fußballfans im poststalinistischen Vielvölkerreich | Mit einem Vorwort von Nikolaus Katzer | ISBN 978-3-8382-0757-5

137 *Kristin Schreiter* | Stellung und Entwicklungspotential zivilgesellschaftlicher Gruppen in Russland. Menschenrechtsorganisationen im Vergleich | ISBN 978-3-8382-0673-8

138 *David R. Marples, Frederick V. Mills (Eds.)* | Ukraine's Euromaidan. Analyses of a Civil Revolution | ISBN 978-3-8382-0660-8

139 *Bernd Kappenberg* | Setting Signs for Europe. Why Diacritics Matter for European Integration | With a foreword by Peter Schlobinski | ISBN 978-3-8382-0663-9

140 *René Lenz* | Internationalisierung, Kooperation und Transfer. Externe bildungspolitische Akteure in der Russischen Föderation | Mit einem Vorwort von Frank Ettrich | ISBN 978-3-8382-0751-3

141 *Juri Plusnin, Yana Zausaeva, Natalia Zhidkevich, Artemy Pozanenko* | Wandering Workers. Mores, Behavior, Way of Life, and Political Status of Domestic Russian Labor Migrants | Translated by Julia Kazantseva | ISBN 978-3-8382-0653-0

142 *David J. Smith (Eds.)* | Latvia – A Work in Progress? 100 Years of State- and Nation-Building | ISBN 978-3-8382-0648-6

143 *Инна Чувычкина (ред.)* | Экспортные нефте- и газопроводы на постсоветском пространстве. Анализ трубопроводной политики в свете теории международных отношений | ISBN 978-3-8382-0822-0

144 *Johann Zajaczkowski* | Russland – eine pragmatische Großmacht? Eine rollentheoretische Untersuchung russischer Außenpolitik am Beispiel der Zusammenarbeit mit den USA nach 9/11 und des Georgienkrieges von 2008 | Mit einem Vorwort von Siegfried Schieder | ISBN 978-3-8382-0837-4

145 *Boris Popivanov* | Changing Images of the Left in Bulgaria. The Challenge of Post-Communism in the Early 21st Century | ISBN 978-3-8382-0667-7

146 *Lenka Krátká* | A History of the Czechoslovak Ocean Shipping Company 1948-1989. How a Small, Landlocked Country Ran Maritime Business During the Cold War | ISBN 978-3-8382-0666-0

147 *Alexander Sergunin* | Explaining Russian Foreign Policy Behavior. Theory and Practice | ISBN 978-3-8382-0752-0

148 *Darya Malyutina* | Migrant Friendships in a Super-Diverse City. Russian-Speakers and their Social Relationships in London in the 21st Century | With a foreword by Claire Dwyer | ISBN 978-3-8382-0652-3

149 *Alexander Sergunin, Valery Konyshev* | Russia in the Arctic. Hard or Soft Power? | ISBN 978-3-8382-0753-7

150 *John J. Maresca* | Helsinki Revisited. A Key U.S. Negotiator's Memoirs on the Development of the CSCE into the OSCE | With a foreword by Hafiz Pashayev | ISBN 978-3-8382-0852-7

151 *Jardar Østbø* | The New Third Rome. Readings of a Russian Nationalist Myth | With a foreword by Pål Kolstø | ISBN 978-3-8382-0870-1

152 *Simon Kordonsky* | Socio-Economic Foundations of the Russian Post-Soviet Regime. The Resource-Based Economy and Estate-Based Social Structure of Contemporary Russia | With a foreword by Svetlana Barsukova | ISBN 978-3-8382-0775-9

153 *Duncan Leitch* | Assisting Reform in Post-Communist Ukraine 2000–2012. The Illusions of Donors and the Disillusion of Beneficiaries | With a foreword by Kataryna Wolczuk | ISBN 978-3-8382-0844-2

154 *Abel Polese* | Limits of a Post-Soviet State. How Informality Replaces, Renegotiates, and Reshapes Governance in Contemporary Ukraine | With a foreword by Colin Williams | ISBN 978-3-8382-0845-9

155 *Mikhail Suslov (Ed.)* | Digital Orthodoxy in the Post-Soviet World. The Russian Orthodox Church and Web 2.0 | With a foreword by Father Cyril Hovorun | ISBN 978-3-8382-0871-8

156 *Leonid Luks* | Zwei „Sonderwege"? Russisch-deutsche Parallelen und Kontraste (1917-2014). Vergleichende Essays | ISBN 978-3-8382-0823-7

157 *Vladimir V. Karacharovskiy, Ovsey I. Shkaratan, Gordey A. Yastrebov* | Towards a New Russian Work Culture. Can Western Companies and Expatriates Change Russian Society? | With a foreword by Elena N. Danilova | Translated by Julia Kazantseva | ISBN 978-3-8382-0902-9

158 *Edmund Griffiths* | Aleksandr Prokhanov and Post-Soviet Esotericism | ISBN 978-3-8382-0963-0

159 *Timm Beichelt, Susann Worschech (Eds.)* | Transnational Ukraine? Networks and Ties that Influence(d) Contemporary Ukraine | ISBN 978-3-8382-0944-9

160 *Mieste Hotopp-Riecke* | Die Tataren der Krim zwischen Assimilation und Selbstbehauptung. Der Aufbau des krimtatarischen Bildungswesens nach Deportation und Heimkehr (1990-2005) | Mit einem Vorwort von Swetlana Czerwonnaja | ISBN 978-3-89821-940-2

161 *Olga Bertelsen (Ed.)* | Revolution and War in Contemporary Ukraine. The Challenge of Change | ISBN 978-3-8382-1016-2

162 *Natalya Ryabinska* | Ukraine's Post-Communist Mass Media. Between Capture and Commercialization | With a foreword by Marta Dyczok | ISBN 978-3-8382-1011-7

163 *Alexandra Cotofana, James M. Nyce (Eds.)* | Religion and Magic in Socialist and Post-Socialist Contexts. Historic and Ethnographic Case Studies of Orthodoxy, Heterodoxy, and Alternative Spirituality | With a foreword by Patrick L. Michelson | ISBN 978-3-8382-0989-0

164 *Nozima Akhrarkhodjaeva* | The Instrumentalisation of Mass Media in Electoral Authoritarian Regimes. Evidence from Russia's Presidential Election Campaigns of 2000 and 2008 | ISBN 978-3-8382-1013-1

165 *Yulia Krasheninnikova* | Informal Healthcare in Contemporary Russia. Sociographic Essays on the Post-Soviet Infrastructure for Alternative Healing Practices | ISBN 978-3-8382-0970-8

166 *Peter Kaiser* | Das Schachbrett der Macht. Die Handlungsspielräume eines sowjetischen Funktionärs unter Stalin am Beispiel des Generalsekretärs des Komsomol Aleksandr Kosarev (1929-1938) | Mit einem Vorwort von Dietmar Neutatz | ISBN 978-3-8382-1052-0

167 *Oksana Kim* | The Effects and Implications of Kazakhstan's Adoption of International Financial Reporting Standards. A Resource Dependence Perspective | With a foreword by Svetlana Vlady | ISBN 978-3-8382-0987-6

168 *Anna Sanina* | Patriotic Education in Contemporary Russia. Sociological Studies in the Making of the Post-Soviet Citizen | With a foreword by Anna Oldfield | ISBN 978-3-8382-0993-7

169 *Rudolf Wolters* | Spezialist in Sibirien Faksimile der 1933 erschienenen ersten Ausgabe | Mit einem Vorwort von Dmitrij Chmelnizki | ISBN 978-3-8382-0515-1

170 *Michal Vít, Magdalena M. Baran (Eds.)* | Transregional versus National Perspectives on Contemporary Central European History. Studies on the Building of Nation-States and Their Cooperation in the 20th and 21st Century | With a foreword by Petr Vágner | ISBN 978-3-8382-1015-5

171 *Philip Gamaghelyan* | Conflict Resolution Beyond the International Relations Paradigm. Evolving Designs as a Transformative Practice in Nagorno-Karabakh and Syria | With a foreword by Susan Allen | ISBN 978-3-8382-1057-5

172 *Maria Shagina* | Joining a Prestigious Club. Cooperation with Europarties and Its Impact on Party Development in Georgia, Moldova, and Ukraine 2004–2015 | With a foreword by Kataryna Wolczuk | ISBN 978-3-8382-1084-1

173 *Alexandra Cotofana, James M. Nyce (Eds.)* | Religion and Magic in Socialist and Post-Socialist Contexts II. Baltic, Eastern European, and Post-USSR Case Studies | With a foreword by Anita Stasulane | ISBN 978-3-8382-0990-6

174 *Barbara Kunz* | Kind Words, Cruise Missiles, and Everything in Between. The Use of Power Resources in U.S. Policies towards Poland, Ukraine, and Belarus 1989–2008 | With a foreword by William Hill | ISBN 978-3-8382-1065-0

175 *Eduard Klein* | Bildungskorruption in Russland und der Ukraine. Eine komparative Analyse der Performanz staatlicher Antikorruptionsmaßnahmen im Hochschulsektor am Beispiel universitärer Aufnahmeprüfungen | Mit einem Vorwort von Heiko Pleines | ISBN 978-3-8382-0995-1

176 *Markus Soldner* | Politischer Kapitalismus im postsowjetischen Russland. Die politische, wirtschaftliche und mediale Transformation in den 1990er Jahren | Mit einem Vorwort von Wolfgang Ismayr | ISBN 978-3-8382-1222-7

177 *Anton Oleinik* | Building Ukraine from Within. A Sociological, Institutional, and Economic Analysis of a Nation-State in the Making | ISBN 978-3-8382-1150-3

178 *Peter Rollberg, Marlene Laruelle (Eds.)* | Mass Media in the Post-Soviet World. Market Forces, State Actors, and Political Manipulation in the Informational Environment after Communism | ISBN 978-3-8382-1116-9

179 *Mikhail Minakov* | Development and Dystopia. Studies in Post-Soviet Ukraine and Eastern Europe | With a foreword by Alexander Etkind | ISBN 978-3-8382-1112-1

180 *Aijan Sharshenova* | The European Union's Democracy Promotion in Central Asia. A Study of Political Interests, Influence, and Development in Kazakhstan and Kyrgyzstan in 2007–2013 | With a foreword by Gordon Crawford | ISBN 978-3-8382-1151-0

181 *Andrey Makarychev, Alexandra Yatsyk (Eds.)* | Boris Nemtsov and Russian Politics. Power and Resistance | With a foreword by Zhanna Nemtsova | ISBN 978-3-8382-1122-0

182 *Sophie Falsini* | The Euromaidan's Effect on Civil Society. Why and How Ukrainian Social Capital Increased after the Revolution of Dignity | With a foreword by Susann Worschech | ISBN 978-3-8382-1131-2

183 *Valentyna Romanova, Andreas Umland (Eds.)* | Ukraine's Decentralization. Challenges and Implications of the Local Governance Reform after the Euromaidan Revolution | ISBN 978-3-8382-1162-6

184 *Leonid Luks* | A Fateful Triangle. Essays on Contemporary Russian, German and Polish History | ISBN 978-3-8382-1143-5

185 *John B. Dunlop* | The February 2015 Assassination of Boris Nemtsov and the Flawed Trial of his Alleged Killers. An Exploration of Russia's "Crime of the 21st Century" | ISBN 978-3-8382-1188-6

186 *Vasile Rotaru* | Russia, the EU, and the Eastern Partnership. Building Bridges or Digging Trenches? | ISBN 978-3-8382-1134-3

187 *Marina Lebedeva* | Russian Studies of International Relations. From the Soviet Past to the Post-Cold-War Present | With a foreword by Andrei P. Tsygankov | ISBN 978-3-8382-0851-0

188 *Tomasz Stępniewski, George Soroka (Eds.)* | Ukraine after Maidan. Revisiting Domestic and Regional Security | ISBN 978-3-8382-1075-9

189 *Petar Cholakov* | Ethnic Entrepreneurs Unmasked. Political Institutions and Ethnic Conflicts in Contemporary Bulgaria | ISBN 978-3-8382-1189-3

190 *A. Salem, G. Hazeldine, D. Morgan (Eds.)* | Higher Education in Post-Communist States. Comparative and Sociological Perspectives | ISBN 978-3-8382-1183-1

191 *Igor Torbakov* | After Empire. Nationalist Imagination and Symbolic Politics in Russia and Eurasia in the Twentieth and Twenty-First Century | With a foreword by Serhii Plokhy | ISBN 978-3-8382-1217-3

192 *Aleksandr Burakovskiy* | Jewish-Ukrainian Relations in Late and Post-Soviet Ukraine. Articles, Lectures and Essays from 1986 to 2016 | ISBN 978-3-8382-1210-4

193 *Natalia Shapovalova, Olga Burlyuk (Eds.)* | Civil Society in Post-Euromaidan Ukraine. From Revolution to Consolidation | With a foreword by Richard Youngs | ISBN 978-3-8382-1216-6

194 *Franz Preissler* | Positionsverteidigung, Imperialismus oder Irredentismus? Russland und die „Russischsprachigen", 1991–2015 | ISBN 978-3-8382-1262-3

195 *Marian Madeła* | Der Reformprozess in der Ukraine 2014-2017. Eine Fallstudie zur Reform der öffentlichen Verwaltung | Mit einem Vorwort von Martin Malek | ISBN 978-3-8382-1266-1

196 *Anke Giesen* | „Wie kann denn der Sieger ein Verbrecher sein?" Eine diskursanalytische Untersuchung der russlandweiten Debatte über Konzept und Verstaatlichungsprozess der Lagergedenkstätte „Perm'-36" im Ural | ISBN 978-3-8382-1284-5

197 *Alla Leukavets* | The Integration Policies of Belarus and Ukraine vis-à-vis the EU and Russia. A Comparative Case Study Through the Prism of a Two-Level Game Approach | ISBN 978-3-8382-1247-0

198 *Oksana Kim* | The Development and Challenges of Russian Corporate Governance I. The Roles and Functions of Boards of Directors | With a foreword by Sheila M. Puffer | ISBN 978-3-8382-1287-6

199 *Thomas D. Grant* | International Law and the Post-Soviet Space I. Essays on Chechnya and the Baltic States | With a foreword by Stephen M. Schwebel | ISBN 978-3-8382-1279-1

200 *Thomas D. Grant* | International Law and the Post-Soviet Space II. Essays on Ukraine, Intervention, and Non-Proliferation | ISBN 978-3-8382-1280-7

201 *Slavomír Michálek, Michal Štefansky* | The Age of Fear. The Cold War and Its Influence on Czechoslovakia 1945–1968 | ISBN 978-3-8382-1285-2

202 *Iulia-Sabina Joja* | Romania's Strategic Culture 1990–2014. Continuity and Change in a Post-Communist Country's Evolution of National Interests and Security Policies | With a foreword by Heiko Biehl | ISBN 978-3-8382-1286-9

203 *Andrei Rogatchevski, Yngvar B. Steinholt, Arve Hansen, David-Emil Wickström* | War of Songs. Popular Music and Recent Russia-Ukraine Relations | With a foreword by Artemy Troitsky | ISBN 978-3-8382-1173-2

204 *Maria Lipman (Ed.)* | Russian Voices on Post-Crimea Russia. An Almanac of Counterpoint Essays from 2015–2018 | ISBN 978-3-8382-1251-7

205 *Ksenia Maksimovtsova* | Language Conflicts in Contemporary Estonia, Latvia, and Ukraine. A Comparative Exploration of Discourses in Post-Soviet Russian-Language Digital Media | With a foreword by Ammon Cheskin | ISBN 978-3-8382-1282-1

206 *Michal Vít* | The EU's Impact on Identity Formation in East-Central Europe between 2004 and 2013. Perceptions of the Nation and Europe in Political Parties of the Czech Republic, Poland, and Slovakia | With a foreword by Andrea Pető | ISBN 978-3-8382-1275-3

207 *Per A. Rudling* | Tarnished Heroes. The Organization of Ukrainian Nationalists in the Memory Politics of Post-Soviet Ukraine | ISBN 978-3-8382-0999-9

208 *Kaja Gadowska, Peter Solomon (Eds.)* | Legal Change in Post-Communist States. Progress, Reversions, Explanations | ISBN 978-3-8382-1312-5

209 *Paweł Kowal, Georges Mink, Iwona Reichardt (Eds.)* | Three Revolutions: Mobilization and Change in Contemporary Ukraine I. Theoretical Aspects and Analyses on Religion, Memory, and Identity | ISBN 978-3-8382-1321-7

210 *Paweł Kowal, Georges Mink, Adam Reichardt, Iwona Reichardt (Eds.)* | Three Revolutions: Mobilization and Change in Contemporary Ukraine II. An Oral History of the Revolution on Granite, Orange Revolution, and Revolution of Dignity | ISBN 978-3-8382-1323-1

211 *Li Bennich-Björkman, Sergiy Kurbatov (Eds.)* | When the Future Came. The Collapse of the USSR and the Emergence of National Memory in Post-Soviet History Textbooks | ISBN 978-3-8382-1335-4

212 *Olga R. Gulina* | Migration as a (Geo-)Political Challenge in the Post-Soviet Space. Border Regimes, Policy Choices, Visa Agendas | With a foreword by Nils Muižnieks | ISBN 978-3-8382-1338-5

213 *Sanna Turoma, Kaarina Aitamurto, Slobodanka Vladiv-Glover (Eds.)* | Religion, Expression, and Patriotism in Russia. Essays on Post-Soviet Society and the State. ISBN 978-3-8382-1346-0

214 *Vasif Huseynov* | Geopolitical Rivalries in the "Common Neighborhood". Russia's Conflict with the West, Soft Power, and Neoclassical Realism | With a foreword by Nicholas Ross Smith | ISBN 978-3-8382-1277-7

215 *Mikhail Suslov* | Geopolitical Imagination. Ideology and Utopia in Post-Soviet Russia | With a foreword by Mark Bassin | ISBN 978-3-8382-1361-3

216 *Alexander Etkind, Mikhail Minakov (Eds.)* | Ideology after Union. Political Doctrines, Discourses, and Debates in Post-Soviet Societies | ISBN 978-3-8382-1388-0

217 *Jakob Mischke, Oleksandr Zabirko (Hgg.)* | Protestbewegungen im langen Schatten des Kreml. Aufbruch und Resignation in Russland und der Ukraine | ISBN 978-3-8382-0926-5

218 *Oksana Huss* | How Corruption and Anti-Corruption Policies Sustain Hybrid Regimes. Strategies of Political Domination under Ukraine's Presidents in 1994-2014 | With a foreword by Tobias Debiel and Andrea Gawrich | ISBN 978-3-8382-1430-6

219 *Dmitry Travin, Vladimir Gel'man, Otar Marganiya* | The Russian Path. Ideas, Interests, Institutions, Illusions | With a foreword by Vladimir Ryzhkov | ISBN 978-3-8382-1421-4

220 *Gergana Dimova* | Political Uncertainty. A Comparative Exploration | With a foreword by Todor Yalamov and Rumena Filipova | ISBN 978-3-8382-1385-9

221 *Torben Waschke* | Russland in Transition. Geopolitik zwischen Raum, Identität und Machtinteressen | Mit einem Vorwort von Andreas Dittmann | ISBN 978-3-8382-1480-1

222 *Steven Jobbitt, Zsolt Bottlik, Marton Berki (Eds.)* | Power and Identity in the Post-Soviet Realm. Geographies of Ethnicity and Nationality after 1991 | ISBN 978-3-8382-1399-6

223 *Daria Buteiko* | Erinnerungsort. Ort des Gedenkens, der Erholung oder der Einkehr? Kommunismus-Erinnerung am Beispiel der Gedenkstätte Berliner Mauer sowie des Soloveckij-Klosters und -Museumsparks | ISBN 978-3-8382-1367-5

224 *Olga Bertelsen (Ed.)* | Russian Active Measures. Yesterday, Today, Tomorrow | With a foreword by Jan Goldman | ISBN 978-3-8382-1529-7

225 *David Mandel* | "Optimizing" Higher Education in Russia. University Teachers and their Union "Universitetskaya solidarnost'" | ISBN 978-3-8382-1519-8

226 *Mikhail Minakov, Gwendolyn Sasse, Daria Isachenko (Eds.)* | Post-Soviet Secessionism. Nation-Building and State-Failure after Communism | ISBN 978-3-8382-1538-9

227 *Jakob Hauter (Ed.)* | Civil War? Interstate War? Hybrid War? Dimensions and Interpretations of the Donbas Conflict in 2014–2020 | With a foreword by Andrew Wilson | ISBN 978-3-8382-1383-5

228 *Tima T. Moldogaziev, Gene A. Brewer, J. Edward Kellough (Eds.)* | Public Policy and Politics in Georgia. Lessons from Post-Soviet Transition | With a foreword by Dan Durning | ISBN 978-3-8382-1535-8

229 *Oxana Schmies (Ed.)* | NATO's Enlargement and Russia. A Strategic Challenge in the Past and Future | With a foreword by Vladimir Kara-Murza | ISBN 978-3-8382-1478-8

230 *Christopher Ford* | Ukapisme – Une Gauche perdue. Le marxisme anti-colonial dans la révolution ukrainienne 1917-1925 | Avec une préface de Vincent Présumey | ISBN 978-3-8382-0899-2

231 *Anna Kutkina* | Between Lenin and Bandera. Decommunization and Multivocality in Post-Euromaidan Ukraine | With a foreword by Juri Mykkänen | ISBN 978-3-8382-1506-8

232 *Lincoln E. Flake* | Defending the Faith. The Russian Orthodox Church and the Demise of Religious Pluralism | With a foreword by Peter Martland | ISBN 978-3-8382-1378-1

233 *Nikoloz Samkharadze* | Russia's Recognition of the Independence of Abkhazia and South Ossetia. Analysis of a Deviant Case in Moscow's Foreign Policy | With a foreword by Neil MacFarlane | ISBN 978-3-8382-1414-6

234 *Arve Hansen* | Urban Protest. A Spatial Perspective on Kyiv, Minsk, and Moscow | With a foreword by Julie Wilhelmsen | ISBN 978-3-8382-1495-5

235 *Eleonora Narvselius, Julie Fedor (Eds.)* | Diversity in the East-Central European Borderlands. Memories, Cityscapes, People | ISBN 978-3-8382-1523-5

236 *Regina Elsner* | The Russian Orthodox Church and Modernity. A Historical and Theological Investigation into Eastern Christianity between Unity and Plurality | With a foreword by Mikhail Suslov | ISBN 978-3-8382-1568-6

237 *Bo Petersson* | The Putin Predicament. Problems of Legitimacy and Succession in Russia | With a foreword by J. Paul Goode | ISBN 978-3-8382-1050-6

238 *Jonathan Otto Pohl* | The Years of Great Silence. The Deportation, Special Settlement, and Mobilization into the Labor Army of Ethnic Germans in the USSR, 1941–1955 | ISBN 978-3-8382-1630-0

239 *Mikhail Minakov (Ed.)* | Inventing Majorities. Ideological Creativity in Post-Soviet Societies | ISBN 978-3-8382-1641-6

240 *Robert M. Cutler* | Soviet and Post-Soviet Foreign Policies I. East-South Relations and the Political Economy of the Communist Bloc, 1971–1991 | With a foreword by Roger E. Kanet | ISBN 978-3-8382-1654-6

241 *Izabella Agardi* | On the Verge of History. Life Stories of Rural Women from Serbia, Romania, and Hungary, 1920–2020 | With a foreword by Andrea Pető | ISBN 978-3-8382-1602-7

242 *Sebastian Schäffer (Ed.)* | Ukraine in Central and Eastern Europe. Kyiv's Foreign Affairs and the International Relations of the Post-Communist Region | With a foreword by Pavlo Klimkin | ISBN 978-3-8382-1615-7

243 *Volodymyr Dubrovskyi, Kalman Mizsei, Mychailo Wynnyckyj (Eds.)* | Eight Years after the Revolution of Dignity. What Has Changed in Ukraine during 2013–2021? | With a foreword by Yaroslav Hrytsak | ISBN 978-3-8382-1560-0

244 *Rumena Filipova* | Constructing the Limits of Europe Identity and Foreign Policy in Poland, Bulgaria, and Russia since 1989 | With forewords by Harald Wydra and Gergana Yankova-Dimova | ISBN 978-3-8382-1649-2

245 *Oleksandra Keudel* | How Patronal Networks Shape Opportunities for Local Citizen Participation in a Hybrid Regime A Comparative Analysis of Five Cities in Ukraine | With a foreword by Sabine Kropp | ISBN 978-3-8382-1671-3

246 *Jan Claas Behrends, Thomas Lindenberger, Pavel Kolar (Eds.)* | Violence after Stalin Institutions, Practices, and Everyday Life in the Soviet Bloc 1953–1989 | ISBN 978-3-8382-1637-9

247 *Leonid Luks* | Macht und Ohnmacht der Utopien Essays zur Geschichte Russlands im 20. und 21. Jahrhundert | ISBN 978-3-8382-1677-5

248 *Iuliia Barshadska* | Brüssel zwischen Kyjiw und Moskau Das auswärtige Handeln der Europäischen Union im ukrainisch-russischen Konflikt 2014-2019 | Mit einem Vorwort von Olaf Leiße | ISBN 978-3-8382-1667-6

249 *Valentyna Romanova* | Decentralisation and Multilevel Elections in Ukraine Reform Dynamics and Party Politics in 2010–2021 | With a foreword by Kimitaka Matsuzato | ISBN 978-3-8382-1700-0

250 *Alexander Motyl* | National Questions. Theoretical Reflections on Nations and Nationalism in Eastern Europe | ISBN 978-3-8382-1675-1

251 *Marc Dietrich* | A Cosmopolitan Model for Peacebuilding. The Ukrainian Cases of Crimea and the Donbas | ISBN 978-3-8382-1687-4

252 *Eduard Baidaus* | An Unsettled Nation. State-Building, Identity, and Separatism in Post-Soviet Moldova | With forewords by John-Paul Himka and David R. Marples | ISBN 978-3-8382-1582-2

253 *Igor Okunev, Petr Oskolkov (Eds.)* | Transforming the Administrative Matryoshka. The Reform of Autonomous Okrugs in the Russian Federation, 2003–2008 | With a foreword by Vladimir Zorin | ISBN 978-3-8382-1721-5

254 *Winfried Schneider-Deters* | Ukraine's Fateful Years 2013–2019. Vol. I: The Popular Uprising in Winter 2013/2014 | ISBN 978-3-8382-1725-3

255 *Winfried Schneider-Deters* | Ukraine's Fateful Years 2013–2019. Vol. II: The Annexation of Crimea and the War in Donbas | ISBN 978-3-8382-1726-0

256 *Robert M. Cutler* | Soviet and Post-Soviet Russian Foreign Policies II. East-West Relations in Europe and the Political Economy of the Communist Bloc, 1971–1991 | With a foreword by Roger E. Kanet | ISBN 978-3-8382-1727-7

257 *Robert M. Cutler* | Soviet and Post-Soviet Russian Foreign Policies III. East-West Relations in Europe and Eurasia in the Post-Cold War Transition, 1991–2001 | With a foreword by Roger E. Kanet | ISBN 978-3-8382-1728-4

258 *Paweł Kowal, Iwona Reichardt, Kateryna Pryshchepa (Eds.)* | Three Revolutions: Mobilization and Change in Contemporary Ukraine III. Archival Records and Historical Sources on the 1990 Revolution on Granite | ISBN 978-3-8382-1376-7

259 *Mikhail Minakov (Ed.)* | Philosophy Unchained. Developments in Post-Soviet Philosophical Thought. | With a foreword by Christopher Donohue | ISBN 978-3-8382-1768-0

Endorsements

Ukraine's 2014 law on local government was among the most ambitious reforms in the country's three decades of independence. Valentyna Romanova provides a detailed analysis of the political sources and consequences of the law. She shows how the increased power of local governments has altered electoral behavior and the party system across the country, as local party politics have become partly delinked from the national level. The consequences that Dr. Romanova demonstrates will have significant effects on politics and democratization in Ukraine. This is a valuable book for those interested in Ukrainian politics or in local government reform.

— Paul D'Anieri
Professor of Political Science and Public Policy
University of California, Riverside, USA

In contemporary politics, authority is divided not only among branches of power but also between central and local levels. This distribution of power is usually contested by different groups and organizations which leads to an important political dynamic in each state. Valentyna Romanova offers a brilliant and detailed analysis of such dynamic in contemporary Ukraine whose political system is still under construction. Based on deep and empirically sound research, this book is a must-read for all students of Ukraine and post-Soviet politics.

—Mikhail Minakov
Professor, Head of the Ukrainian Research Program
Kennan Institute/Wilson Center

Decentralization and Multilevel Elections is a timely account of the importance of elections in Ukrainian sub-national governance. Valentyna Romanova presents a rich study based on detailed understanding and years of research of local politics and elections in Ukraine. The book will be an invaluable resource for researchers of post-Soviet Ukrainian politics, and its analysis provides important lessons for Ukrainian policy-makers.

— Paul Chaisty
Professor of Russian and East European Politics
Department of Politics and International Relations
University of Oxford

Packed with insightful analysis and providing a longue durée outlook, Decentralization and Multilevel Elections in Ukraine *is an indispensable read to understand the complexity of uprooting the Soviet legacy in governance. This is a profoundly interesting read that highlights the drivers behind the decentralization and also outlines the unfinished business of boosting local electoral democracy. Ukraine's journey is instructive for many in the region still struggling to reinvent governance. This book offers a fascinating guidance for such an exploration!*

—Orysia Lutsevych
Head and Research Fellow
Ukraine Forum
Russia and Eurasia Programme, Chatham House

This is a very sophisticated study of decentralisation and multilevel elections in Ukraine. The study is very well grounded in theory and provides a wealth of new empirical data to back up its novel conclusions. In six beautifully crafted chapters it succeeds admirably in answering the two key puzzles addressed in the book, 1) why reformers consolidated and empowered local governance, but failed to strengthen the directly elected regional authorities, and 2) the implications of decentralisation policy on multilevel elections. The book makes an important contribution to the field of territorial politics and democratisation in Ukraine, and also to the wider field of comparative studies and local politics.

—Cameron Ross
Professor, Head of Discipline
Research and Scholarship
Convenor in Politics and International Relations
University of Dundee

This book provides students of Ukrainian politics with amazing and surprising insights into the peculiarities of local power and a rather contradictory decentralisation process consolidating centre-periphery relations in Ukraine. Moreover, it shows also that decentralisation had considerable impact on multilevel elections in Ukraine.

—Nicolas Hayoz
Professor at the Departement
European Studies and Slavistik
University of Fribourg, Switzerland

Discussions of decentralization are universal, but it is not least through detailed studies of single countries that we learn about some of the more indirect and somewhat unintended consequences of changing the balances between the central, regional, and local levels. Romanova's book on the most recent reforms in Ukraine is exemplary in that respect, since she unfolds the party systems at the lower political levels in times of changes in the multi-level governance structures. The very careful and detailed study of current affairs in local and regional Ukraine makes this a must-read for students of Ukrainian politics.

—Ulrik Kjær
Professor, Department of Political Science
and Public Management
University of Southern Denmark

Decentralization policy in Ukraine is one of the most significant reforms implemented in any post-Soviet state. Ukraine's regional policy is not just a matter of domestic politics and scholarly analysis but has also major international ramifications. The study by Valentyna Romanova provides a meticulous analysis of the decentralization process and outcomes. The book uncovers the complex dynamics that are re-shaping of centre-periphery relations in Ukraine. It is strongly recommended for everybody interested in Ukrainian politics and those interested in understanding and/or promoting reforms in the post-Soviet space.

—Prof Kataryna Wolczuk
Professor of Politics at the Centre for Russian
European and Eurasian Studies
University of Birmingham, UK

ibidem.eu